I Was a White Knight…Once

An Uncommon Memoir

by nathan timmel

DEDICATION

To Lydia, who believes in me.

CONTENTS

BLOCK I

BIRTH TO AGE 6

NATHAN TIMMEL

1 - A MOMENT IN MY MOTHER'S SHOES

I was born in November, 1969. Madison, Wisconsin, is still a very progressive city, but back then it was defined by outright revolution. Psychologists will argue until blue in the face over what influence atmosphere has on an infant, so I will simply note that for the first two years of my life I was surrounded by a turmoil I do not remember. Whether or not it affected who I am today I cannot determine, but the possibility exists that my personality was in part shaped by the chaos that existed around me at that time.

The Vietnam War had college students protesting as loudly as possible, and the University of Wisconsin was a hotbed for revolutionaries. With every demonstration came the hint of violence, and on the occasion police became involved a riot would ensue. My mother recalls a time when I was nine months old; it was early August and she was searching for an apartment. She and my father were students, her twenty-two and he six years above that. They had been doing well enough in their one-bedroom dwelling when an

3

accident came along in the form of a very time demanding creature, me. Both my mother and father tell the same story of their nuptials: Mom was very young, and being from a small town thought being married was a woman's life ambition. She pushed, he relented, and before either could see the error of their ways I arrived and solidified the mistake of it all, a bright red cherry sitting atop their sundae of failure.

My entrance signified the time to shuffle into a two-bedroom residence. While Dad spent every waking hour studying for his PhD or working at the University Bookstore, Mom carried me around with her, including during one memorable trip to University Housing. After searching the student listings and filling out applications, we left the building and stepped into a full-blown melee. It had popped up out of nowhere, as happened often in Madison at that time. Our car was two blocks away, so she had to carry me past riot police shooting tear gas, anarchists lighting fires, and through a mob she feared would knock her over and trample me. Though I have never experienced such a fear, I can imagine holding your infant child to your chest in a moment of uncertainty ranks up there with the deepest of them. That Mom could have turned around and gone back inside the building until all had ended is a thought, but back then there was no way of measuring how long an upheaval would last. Students were continually being beaten, and Madison was constantly making the national news for incidents of police on student brutality. Over time, you learned to accept it as a facet of life you didn't enjoy, but dealt with. Instead of hiding, you put your head down and waded forward the best you could.

Like everything tolerated, though, a breaking point was eventually reached. For my mother, that day was August 24th, 1970. At 3:42 a.m., radicals set off a bomb designed to destroy an Army Mathematics Research Center inside Sterling Hall, part of the University of Wisconsin. A van with 2,000 pounds of ammonium nitrate was parked next to the building and detonated; to give perspective, Timothy McVeigh used 5,000 pounds of ammonium nitrate in his attack in Oklahoma City. The bombers failed their intended task—the Research Center was only mildly damaged—but managed to destroy huge portions of the building and many surrounding it. They also killed an innocent researcher working in a lab, a man unrelated to the military or anything being targeted. Until

4

the first World Trade Center bombing in 1993, the attack stood as the largest act of terrorism ever to take place on American soil.

How this relates to my mother is simple: having finally found a new apartment for us a few weeks prior, on that August day at 6:00 a.m., she began the process of moving the family belongings from home to home. Whether my father was sleeping or already studying is not remembered by either of them, but it is a testament to the strength that is woman that she began to load and unload boxes all on her own, and all the while watching me fuss. We were moving to the lower half of a duplex by Camp Randall, the football stadium. Mom filled our VW Bug with boxes of belongings, and me, her little poop machine. The city was a ghost town in the dawn light as she drove down University Avenue past Sterling Hall. Today, both rapid-response teams and the media would have been on the scene at 3:43 a.m., one minute after the initial explosion; twenty-four hour news channels would be broadcasting live, using local remotes to speculate as much as possible and drive up their ratings. In 1970, however, with no internet and only three television stations and little awareness of what a terrorist attack was, my mom drove by a building blocked off by nothing more than yellow police ribbon. There were no crowds, no police, no reporters, just rubble and blown out windows. The Big Three networks were showing their nightly test patterns, having ended all broadcasting somewhere around the midnight hour. Though a newspaper reporter might have been busy researching and writing up a story, such information wouldn't hit the streets for hours and hours; unable to hit "enter" and post an immediate story to the Internet, they had to wait for the presses to be fired up.

So back and forth my mother went, from old to new home, filling and emptying the Bug with me always in tow, each time noticing a little more of the devastation as she drove by Sterling Hall. While her initial thought was that a gas leak or the like was responsible, soon more negative images entered her mind. Every time my mother passed the building, the rubble looked more ominous. It was several hours later a news report finally confirmed a bombing directly related to war protesters had caused the damage, not an innocuous gas main.

That, as said, was the final straw. The event set the wheels in her mind moving; it was time to leave Madison and the unstable nature the city existed in. Before I was born, staying might have been acceptable. My mother was open minded and forward thinking, and in 1967 lingered at a gathering to listen to speakers protesting Dow

Chemical. She only remained a little while, and upon returning home discovered the police stepped in after she left. Everything had turned violent, and students were beaten and tear gassed. Seventy-four people were injured, and the incident is still noted today as one of the most violent clashes of the era. Sadly, Kent State would take that title in the most tragic of ways in 1970.

The moments that lend themselves to the thought, "That could have been me" always give one pause, and doubly so in times of tragedy. When you're alone in the world, you can brush almost anything off; you get into a car accident and laugh, or hear a mortar round land 200 yards from where you were sleeping and sort of give a confused-dog head cock in wonder more than fear. My mother existed inside a city torn between authoritarian rule and angry youth for years before I came along, and did so without much concern. After she fell in love and then had a child, though, she tended to notice the darker sides of life. Now that she had someone she was responsible for, many things in Madison looked a little murky and a lot more unsafe. Not that every day held the promise of protest, and not that the violence was city-wide or invading every neighborhood, but as the possibility always existed and the campus held a tension ready to pop was enough for my young mother to re-evaluate her living situation.

It would take her one more year to get me out—she and my father both needed to finish school, that they might be employable after escaping—but when she did, Mom took the family as far away from the age of protest she could and into the middle of Wisconsin farmland.

2 - THE SHADOW THAT SHOULDN'T BE

Wanting to escape Madison, but without a job or anywhere focused to go, my family landed in Waupaca, Wisconsin. We only remained there for several short months when I was three, but that was long enough for one event to enter my mind and stick there with dangerous force. A memory is a curious thing. It can be vivid, vague, or transformed from the actual event into a feeling of what you think occurred. For years I was aware of the sensation of what happened, but had no clue it was an actual incident from my childhood.

Needing a healthy diversion from the day-to-day drudgery of full-time motherhood, my mom enrolled me in swimming lessons. She and the other parents would bring us to the pool, which was indoors, though I cannot recall if it was a YMCA or school, and take their place in an enclosed viewing area. To hear my mother tell the story, she was sitting in the room, half visiting with other parents, half watching me splash about in my attempts to float, when a woman near her stood and walked to the glass.

The woman looked concerned, and began pounding, open palm, against the glass. Parents' heads turned, but in the pool area, the noise and confusion of children playing was too great to notice her or the pounding.

This is what I recall:

I am standing at the edge of the pool, at the shallow end.

No one is paying attention to me; I am looking into the right-hand corner of the pool, and something is wrong.

There is a dark spot at the bottom of the pool, an outline.

I begin to point.

Inside the booth, my mother noticed the woman pounding on the glass, who began to scream and was growing hysterical.

All the parents became panicked; my mother looked to the pool area to find me, and she saw me staring intently into the water, arm outreached, index finger out, but curved as if hesitant or scared, not confident.

I hear a whistle sound.

The adults begin to shout.

A hand takes me firmly by the shoulder, turns me away from the water.

Someone jumps feet first into the pool.

My mother watched as the lifeguards and instructors grabbed children and shuffled them together to count heads.

The mother beating the glass began sobbing, hyperventilating.

The children were escorted out of the pool.

I glance back and see someone kneeling in front of and kissing a small child.

My mother wants to leave quickly.

We do not talk about what happened.

I do not attend swim class again.

During a discussion with my mom many, many years later, I brought up the sensation of standing at the edge of a pool and pointing at a figure. I had no idea why, but every so often the image would return to me, causing the hair on my arms to rise.

My mother filled in the blanks.

I was there.

The child drowned.

That is the only image I retained from that period of my life.

3 – THE DISAPPEARED PHOTOGRAPH

When I was five years old, my family went on welfare.

I have no real memory of this, and at five probably couldn't have told you what welfare was, but children have an innate ability to absorb their surroundings and internalize what they don't exactly understand. If you've ever volunteered at a soup kitchen or within the walls of some other place of need, there hangs in the air a feeling of nervous desperation. People are generally proud by nature, and being reduced to a state of charity weighs heavy on the ego. There becomes a shame in simple existence, with protective body posturing and lowered eyes worn by many of those using such services. When my mother bundled up my newborn baby sister and ushered the two of us off with her to sign up for food stamps, though I wasn't acutely aware of what was occurring, the sense of anxiety surrounding my mother probably became ingrained in my psyche and shaped my adult life in ways I'm only now understanding. I've always been cautious with money, perhaps visiting the welfare office is why.

Reaching this level of need took some time. During our time in Madison, my father had been earning his PhD. In the 1960s and early 70s men within a certain age range had two options: stay in school, or sign up for the draft and cross your fingers.[1] Dad chose college, but wasn't alone in doing so; if you want to flood a field with qualified applicants, give the incentive of war to explode academic achievement. When he eventually graduated, he was part of a tsunami of other men who had followed the same path. It was an employer's market, with corporations having their pick of the litter.

Most people exiting college have a small adjustment into reality to make, but my father was doing so with the bonus of an uncertain marriage and accidental son. His life in confused flux, Dad took one of the few jobs offered, overseeing a new teen "rehabilitation" center smack dab in the center of Wisconsin. Only a few months after arriving in Waupaca, the family bundled up, and we moved to Amherst.

The facility was Tomorrow's Youth and is both long gone and difficult to research; I couldn't find any real record of it among the wonders of the Internet. I do know, however, its name was a misnomer. Teenage detention is not a pretty thing. Those too young to go to prison, yet too much a detriment to society to remain in public, end up in such places. The title, "Tomorrow's Youth," was designed to be both positive and upbeat. Hopeful, if you will, to mislead surrounding neighbors and avoid protests. After all, which would you rather live next to, a facility named "Fresher Futures" or "Secure Confinement Teen Rehab Facility"?

Our living quarters were within the walls of the main structure. A small apartment was allocated for the director, so we had a couple bedrooms and a common area/living room. Having no kitchen meant our three-squares a day were eaten in the mess hall, among what would be known as "general population," had any of the inhabitants been older than eighteen.

This was not the life my young mother fantasized about; doubtful it would be any mother's idea of excitement. Already her plan to get married and live the American Dream was being challenged; living among agitated teens only fueled the fire. My father was having

---

[1] Fake joining the Alabama National Guard wasn't an option for everyone, after all.

somewhat similar thoughts, and in essence says he chose the job of working with troubled teens to prevent them from making the same mistakes he made in life, possibly saving them where he had failed himself.

Like any new detention facility, every other overcrowded center in the state used it as a dumping ground for the worst of their worst. My dad received the boy whose father burned his ear off by holding his head down on a hot stove, the violent offenders who were interested in things like breaking and entering, and those who had already graduated to assaulting others.

One teen in particular remains a snapshot in my mind.

I cannot recall who exactly the person was, but the image of him is ingrained in me due to a Polaroid that once resided in the family photo album. I remember a young man with an emotionless face. He wore a thin, brown leather jacket, and was of dark complexion, either Native American or Hispanic. His hair was jet black and eerily akin in style to that worn by Javier Bardem in *No Country For Old Men*, which is appropriate as the dead stare emitted from his eyes was just as cold as that of Javier's murderous character. That the picture was taken in our living room and subsequently placed in our photo album means he grew closer to us than most residents of the detention center.

I do not know if he was friendly with my father or the entire family; however friendships are created between people is unknown to me. There is the possibility we represented what he lacked and therefore wanted: a mom, dad, and child representing a family. As seen from the outside, a normal life. My father, then, may have taken him under his wing as a pupil, someone to steer in the right direction, that he too not end up trapped in marriage with child. Irony is always hilarious in its sick ways.

As I grew older, the picture represented that period of my life. Looking over photos, I would see it and think, "That's when I lived in Amherst." Then, one day the picture was gone. Erased as if never in existence in the first place, save for the continuity gap left on the page. I don't know if I ever asked what happened or justified its departure like the misplacement of an item used in everyday life; I lost my car keys the other day, and oh, a picture went missing from the photo album. It would be years before a random synapse fire in my mind had me ask my mother if she remembered the picture and/or boy, and what happened to it/him. Mom admitted to knowledge of both the boy and picture, and explained that indeed he had kept in touch with the family for a while after we moved on from Amherst.

Sadly, sometime in his mid-twenties, whatever childhood damage done to him resurfaced. One day he up and broke into an elderly woman's house and assaulted her.

Physically.

Sexually.

The young, confused teenager from our photo album had become an angry, violent rapist. I don't know if he wrote from jail looking for help, forgiveness, or understanding, but after that action reached my mother's ears, his picture was quietly removed from within the pages of our photo album, never to be seen again.

Tomorrow's Youth eventually went bankrupt, but my father was long gone by then. Questionable motives by the founders then surfaced, when it was discovered landowners created the facility in order to devalue the area so they could buy surrounding plots and develop everything later at huge profit.

Having made friends in the community and without work elsewhere, my family remained in Amherst instead of moving on. We lived on a rented farm, and I would scurry among the chickens until it was mealtime, when one of my feathered playmates would be beheaded and join us at the dinner table. Chickens weren't the only animals we had; larger, more dangerous beasts lived close at hand and I "played" with them, also. I would put on my red Superman cape and run the length of the bull's field, taunting and getting him to chase me, the exhilaration of being chased by an animal that could kill me outweighing consequences I didn't fully understand. Every time I eeked my way through the fence and out of his territory as he stampeded towards me was an adrenaline rush unparalleled.

Though my Superman cape came from a Halloween costume, was professionally crafted and carried the "S" emblem on it, I only wore it when taunting the bull. I knew Matadors used red when in the ring, and I figured it was best to emulate them when playing with my own four-legged steak factory. My favorite superhero was Batman, and I lived almost 24-7 in my "Batman cape." Though it was nothing more than a blue-green towel cut at one end and attached around my throat by an enormous safety pin, it was still my prized possession. According to my mother, I have attended church once in my entire life. On the Sunday morning she took me, I refused to go without my Batman cape. My poor mother put up a small fight, but eventually figured a relationship with Jesus was more important to my childhood development than the embarrassment she would suffer by my attire. She relented and allowed me to wear the towel, much to her chagrin. As the sermon began, I started singing the theme from the 1960s Batman show. My mom says she tried to quiet me and even attempted reasoning with my underdeveloped mind, explaining, "You're not supposed to sing the Batman song in church," but it was all for naught. "Why not?" I asked in innocent response and launched right back into an extended refrain of, "Na-na-na-na-na-na-na, Batman!" After that, it was determined Jesus could wait for my adolescence to pass before saving me.

Like Samson with his hair, I believed wearing the cape gave me Batman-like abilities. I would jump around the house while wearing it, eventually leaping from the dresser to the bed one day and missing, tearing open my mouth at the cheek on the bedpost. I still have a stitches scar on the inside of my mouth, my tongue unconsciously rubbing it just now as I type.

I played all day, dawn to dusk, built my first tree house, and had no idea what television was until my sister arrived in October of 1974. After she showed up, I was allowed to discover PBS and Sesame Street, but not network television. That would wait one more year, when Saturday Night Live came along and my dad kept me awake late in order to see the silly people in their bee outfits.

Money grew scarce, and my grandfather eventually arrived with his mobile home. He parked it in the yard and lived there in order to help take care of my sister and I while my parents did their best to scrape by. While raising one child may have been difficult enough, now that there were two young mouths, my mother put provision before pride and took state's assistance.

I may not have known what white trash was, but damn if I didn't live it when I was five.

4 – THE FOCAL POINT OF FALLING APART

When examining someone with an addiction, there is usually a moment in the person's past that can be traced to where their tumble started. It can be as tragic as rape, or as innocent as divorce. Regardless the event, from that point on the person assumes a stride of downward spiral that ties them too tightly to drugs, alcohol, religion, or some other crutch.

My drug of choice is the stage, and I believe I can trace my need for attention, acceptance, and understanding to a tipping point that occurred when I was six years old.

After leaving Tomorrow's Youth, my father encountered enormous obstacles finding work. When the institution started gasping its dying breaths, he did something both honorable and unwise. Payroll was not being met, and as he was the director of the facility, my father forwent his salary so the employees could be paid.[1] Revisiting the event thirty-odd years later, my father believes he made

---

[1] Imagine the CEO of a company doing that today.

the decision while in the grip of a deep depression; his life was not working out in the manner he had hoped, so he began championing righteous causes. If the working man was being screwed over by the powers that be, my father would issue protest and challenge said power. Regarding Tomorrow's Youth, my father deluded himself into believing the board of directors would reimburse him when they got everything sorted out from the top down. Unfortunately, the governing body had little interest in keeping the center afloat, meaning my father was dead wrong.

In an attempt to restore our decimated bank account, my dad sued to retrieve his money, but all attempts failed. Naturally, when you sue your former boss it is difficult to obtain a proper recommendation from them, even if your lawsuit had merit. So as he hunted for gainful employment, anyone who decided to contact the listing atop my dad's résumé got an earful, and my father received no work.

With nothing left to lose, he applied for a job advertised by the Nigerian government. They were looking for American educators to train teachers inside their West African nation, so dad scrounged up what money he could and flew to the embassy in Washington, D.C. After an interview, he signed a two-year contract. This would not be a solo run for my father; as soon as the family could get passports and shots, away we'd all go.

Within the years of my life already lived, I've had the opportunity to meet people who spent time living abroad, and I have to admit to a smidgeon of jealousy. They often seem more adaptable and open to new ideas than adults in America, many of whom spend an entire life living within a fifty-mile radius of their birthplace. I say I am jealous, because while plans were made to move, the actual event never occurred.

My mom put together a garage sale and proceeded to sell all our winter clothes, much of our furniture, and many other belongings. After that, we began the waiting game.[1] Visas were due any day, but as happens all too often in Africa, a military coup played "Swap this Government" with our plans. The ruling body that had been looking to educate its people was replaced by a military dictator who began buying arms from the Soviet Union and issuing anti-American sound

---

[1] The waiting game sucks. Let's play Hungry-Hungry Hippos.

bites. In the 1970s, fresh off the Vietnam War and the phrase "the domino effect" still looming large in the public lexicon, visiting such a country was a very poor idea. Suffice to say, our visas never arrived, and my father's signed contract was not honored. Thankfully.

Now my parents were scrambling. They were broke, and living inside an uncertain moment projecting a bleak future. We were still renting a farm outside Amherst, so my mother drove into town to register me for kindergarten. While at the school, she inquired about substitute teaching and was offered a part-time position as a math instructor. She accepted on the spot.

Shortly thereafter, my father fought through the blot on his résumé and signed a one-year teaching contract with the Hammond Indiana School District. Now a decision needed to be made: move the family, or split it apart?

By whatever process they used, it was determined my dad would live in Indiana during the week and return home on weekends. His father Rudy extended his stay at the farm, continuing to live in his mobile home parked in the yard. While my mother worked, Rudy would look after my sister Amanda and me. As Amanda was but a baby, this must have been quite an undertaking. That Rudy decided to help his daughter-in-law raise her children could be an example of his "do what needs to be done" generation, but in this particular case the psychology of support could delve a little deeper.

Patterns repeat themselves; it is an inevitability in life. I was witness to my parent's disaster of a marriage and thus threw six years of my twenties down the toilet chasing a relationship that was never meant to be. Likewise, my grandparents were unhappy and divorced before I was born. My grandfather, when married, traveled as often as he could for work. He felt trapped, was unsure how to be a father and avoided his family the best he could. With my father now spending the workweek away from my mother, sister and I, a familial pattern began to emerge. While Rudy may have been rolling up his sleeves to help my mother because his generation didn't shy away from hard work, absolution of his own history may have played into my grandfather's assistance.

For one school year we lived this way. In the fall of 1975, my father was offered a one-year extension to his contract, and he accepted. According to my mother, he enjoyed the living arrangement the way it was and wanted to continue commuting between Indiana and Wisconsin. My father has always been a fan of nature, and whether he enjoyed the weekend getaway of the farm or preferred the weekday time away from family, I do not know. But as happened often back then, my mother pushed and my father relented. She was fed up with living isolated in the country and raising two kids with a grandparent; she got married to have a husband, not a ghost. The living situation shifted against my dad's will, and our nuclear family of four moved to Long Beach, Indiana.

I attended first grade and hung out with my cousins; one of my mother's many sisters lived close by. We rented the home of a well-to-do dentist, one who "wintered elsewhere," and when spring arrived, so did he. My father's contract was not extended a second time, the dentist wanted us out of his house, and work wasn't readily available. Though my parents wanted to stay in the area, the resources did not exist with which to do so. Neither had a job, nor any clue what to do next. They loaded our belongings into a U-Haul, drove to my maternal grandparents' house in Kaukauna, Wisconsin, and used their garage to store everything while they looked for a city to settle in.

As he had done at the farm, Rudy assisted the best he could. He was teaching at the Interlochen Center for the Arts in Michigan, and sent my mother an application for a job as the cafeteria supervisor. She was easily qualified and hired immediately. As if by established legal precedent, my father was then hired to teach summer school in South Bend, Indiana. Like the year before, my mother found work in one region and shortly afterward my father discovered employment elsewhere. So like the year before, he would work away for the week, and return home on the weekends.

For the summer months of 1976, my mother, sister, and I lived at a campground in my grandfather's mobile home, while my grandfather rented a camper and lived one lot over. Every morning at five, Rudy would come over and fix Amanda and me breakfast as my mother biked to the cafeteria. She would return between 9:00 and 9:30 a.m., and the three of us would have until four in the afternoon to attend art, craft, and music classes, or inner tube in a local creek. At four, my mother would bike away again and my grandfather would arrive to baby-sit until after dinner, when Mom would be finished working for the day.

One weekend, my father didn't make the trek north, so my mom gathered up her children and we took a ferry across Lake Michigan to Manitowoc, Wisconsin. A teaching position was available, and my mother's application garnered enough interest to warrant an interview. My father did not have anything lined up once his summer position ended, so when my mother was offered the job, she accepted. As if written in a shitty sitcom or by fate, not long after, my father found work at the University of Wisconsin-Milwaukee. Once and again, decisions needed to be made.

The two of them looked for a house in Milwaukee, but my mother was no longer within the bonds of starry-eyed youth; two children and a half-decade of struggle had put an end to that. While she admits to pushing for the marriage, my mother was no longer certain it was what she wanted. Instead of forgoing her obligation to the teaching position in Manitowoc, my mother decided to hold fast and move to the tiny city with my sister and me. My father offered up the continuance of the separate-but-together living situation they had been using; he wanted to buy a house in Manitowoc and commute there from Milwaukee every weekend, but my mother desired solitude of a different kind. Even though they had barely lived with one another for several years, or maybe because of it, my mother wanted to make a firm decision in her life.

This would be her first step on a twenty-year walk toward divorce.

My mother's pronouncement did not sit well with my father, and what exactly happened next is unknown. If ten people are witness to one event, in interviewing everyone you will likely gather ten different accounts of what happened. In talking to my parents, I have two diametrically opposed points of view, and neither is very pretty.

Before she was able to secure an apartment in Manitowoc, my mom lived with Amanda and me at her parents' house in Kaukauna; my father moved to Milwaukee for his job at the University. In her memory, my father showed up one day, saying that if she wanted to move on, that was fine, but he was taking the kids. A shouting match ensued, and at some point Amanda and I were grabbed and put in his car. My father started to drive off, my sister and I screaming and crying—confused, as any child would be in such a situation—when my mother threw herself across the hood of his car. She says she remained there, crying hysterically as my father backed out of the driveway, drove uphill to the end of the block, and turned left. My mother remembers him finally stopping at the nearby cemetery, which would have been a good half block away. Not a huge distance, but probably an eternity for both a mother watching her children being taken from her and said children crying inside the car.

That's not where it ends.

My mother rented an apartment and moved to Manitowoc with Amanda and I in tow. As the unplanned abduction didn't work, my father made sure to do it right the second time. A month into our new residency he showed up at my school, excused me from class, and took me back to Milwaukee while she was at work. My mom remembers the principal of the school telling her I was gone and little else. She was in shock. One moment she was teaching wee little minds the wonders of the world around them, the next she was being told her son was no longer in her life.

To complicate matters, my dad tells an altered version of the tale of how I ended up with him. He recalls arriving in Kaukauna to spend the day with his children. When he pulled into my grandparents' driveway, the first thing he saw was my mother with her "new boyfriend," a person my mother says, if he existed, was a friend at worst and in no way a lover. My dad was not happy. There was a fight, with shouting and accusations thrown all around. Amanda was outside and began to cry, so he put her in the car in an attempt to dampen the effects of what was happening around her. The shouting continued, and at some point he looked up and was witness to me standing in the living room, looking out the window, crying. Realizing the situation was both out of control and detrimental to childhood development, he left. A few weeks later, my mom called him out of the blue; two children were too much for her to handle, and I was quite unruly. A Sophie's Choice was made and she had called him to come retrieve me.

So my past has either a father who took, or a mother who didn't want, neither an exciting truth to stomach. Over time I've been able to dissect other events, and sometimes truth just has a certain ring to it. When listening to each parent volunteer their version of what happened, one voice sounds wide and sympathetic, the other tense and inventive. It is what it is, and even if I was a pawn for a failing marriage back then, today I steadfastly refuse to be a part of the divorced dance the two still tango.

However it happened, I ended up in Milwaukee, living in the lower half of a duplex on Sherman Boulevard. My mother says she visited a lawyer to inquire about getting me back, but his response was that legally the courts would issue a lovely 1970s shrug and there was nothing she could do. He did point out, however, that child psychologists believed that separated siblings was the worst way for them to grow up, and she never should have let me be taken in the first place. There are many reasons lawyers are despised, and I would guess guidance like that is but one of them.

For six or so weeks, I alternated weekends between them. One weekend I would visit my mom and sister, the next Amanda and I would spend in Milwaukee. The exchange between parents took place at a McDonald's halfway between the two cities.

Eventually, this wore on me. I didn't like Manitowoc and didn't have any friends there. One day I balked during a transfer, and my mother realized the situation wasn't going to work as it stood.

Mom was depressed. She was earning $6,700 a year teaching at a small Catholic school and could in no way fight a losing battle in court. She went to see a therapist and instead of helping, he hit on her. At home, she had the pleasure of listening to her downstairs neighbors fight, with one or two such melees ending in violence as the man physically assaulted his wife. My mother was too terrified to call the police, because if the woman didn't press charges, the man would be free to exact revenge on the only person who could have tattled. She was heartbroken when on the worst occasion the couple's two children escaped up to her place to call their grandmother to come get them.

With all this stress raging in her life, my mother decided to do what she thought best for her children. The weekend after I refused to spend time in Manitowoc, she brought my sister to Milwaukee and we sounded out a formula for becoming a family again. Amanda and I seemed happy to have everyone together, so instead of shuffling us back and forth, every weekend after that she and my mother visited my father and I.

At the end of the school year, my mother gave up her lease, a house was purchased in Milwaukee, and an attempt at reconciliation was made.

It would not last.

INTERLUDE

IRAQ, 2004

5 – TEN DAYS IN THE DESERT

"Was that real?" Drake deadpanned. Drake carried himself with the stoicism of a comedic William Shatner, but I could tell he was alarmed even though his face didn't show it. While on stage at Camp Cooke, north of Baghdad in central Iraq, an extremely loud BOOM! interrupted his act.

"If the walls move, we're fine," our base contact, Joni, informed us. "When the ground moves, take cover."

"I think my bowels just moved," another entertainer, Curtis, muttered.

In the end, everyone was safe; the blast was a controlled munitions dump being destroyed by American troops. To the soldiers, a random explosion was no cause for alarm; a near-daily occurrence, those in uniform barely flinched when it sounded. The four other comedians and I, however, had never heard anything like it before, but we would again. By the tour's end we had experienced armed escorts whizzing us between checkpoints, Black Hawk helicopter rides, a prisoner transfer (albeit accidentally; it was not meant for our eyes), incoming mortars, a gunfight (though only auditory), and perhaps the most pure aspect of military life, "hurry up and wait."

Morale, Welfare, and Recreation is the division of the military assigned to provide support for American troops, and we flew under their banner. The comedians on the run were the aforementioned stone-cold Drake, Curtis (our male "Gidget"), ex-army Danny, Jim (described best by Danny as a "Goodfella with A.D.H.D."), and me, Nathan Timmel, idiot. The blast at Cooke came several days into our ten-day tour, but we received our first scare before ever entering into country.

* * *

You don't just fly into Iraq; it's not open to commercial flights. At least, it wasn't in 2004. Our group was on a public plane inbound to Kuwait, ready to spend a day visiting and performing, when the pilot made an announcement.

I wasn't paying attention, but Curtis frowned.

"Well, that's just great," he said angrily.

"What?" I asked.

"The announcement: There is a small, black pouch in the restroom; would the passenger who left it there please claim it?"

I was confused, "And?"

Curtis stared at me as if I was a dimwit, a look I have received often in my life. On a full plane, I was most likely the only person thinking "shaving kit." After several seconds, I caught on.

"Oh..." I said reassuringly. "Well, if it is a bomb, we'll most likely feel nothing before we die."

Curtis wasn't happy with this, but Jim took my lead and soon the two of us were spitting out jokes and irritating everyone within our vicinity. As we began our descent and heard the captain announce, "We are arriving at Kuwait International Airport," we added—in Arabic-accented English—"This wasn't supposed to happen and I am very disappointed in one of you! I finish this myself!" and imagined him throwing us into a sudden nosedive. We cracked wise about the "Fasten Seatbelt" and "No Smoking" icons, wondering where the "No Lighting the Fuse on Your Shoe" outline was. When it came to dark humor, Hawkeye Pierce had nothing on us. Of course, we weren't limited by "Standards and Practices."

Kuwaiti customs, however, we did dance with, and they were unfamiliar with kindness, courtesy, and soap. Over a decade ago Americans may have been liberators, but by the time I got there we were guests who just wouldn't leave the party. Where many nations are interested in building a tourist industry, Kuwait is oil-rich and not overly excited about foreigners poking around. What should have been a quick, five-minute process of checking our passports took well over an hour, as customs repeatedly bounced us between two desks staffed by bored workers.

They eventually allowed us to enter the country, and it was in the airport I saw my first burka-clad woman. As I walked, there she was, displayed for all the world to see as if not an oddity. Then another appeared, and another until they littered the landscape like little black ghosts, covered head-to-toe, only their eyes visible. While the image is almost ubiquitous on television and in print, actually experiencing it first-hand was startling. We were told not to stare or take pictures, which is frustrating; the only way to change a negative behavior is to acknowledge and expose it. Our posse was under instruction to accept the blatant sexism and passive abuse as normalcy, and all I could do was seethe internally.

Shallow though it may be, I was distracted from my anger upon exiting the air-conditioned safety of the airport; the heat hit like an oppressive presence. Our military contact, Donovan, joked about it being a dry heat, so I responded, "Yeah, because dry is such a great qualifying agent for better, since dry humping is much more fun than actual sex."

As we meandered around Kuwait City, the people we interacted with were kind and gracious. It was a peculiar sensation, mingling among people who could be warm with one hand, yet disrespect an entire gender with the other. I found it difficult to reconcile inside my mind that the people greeting me with such gentle smiles also believed in complete subjugation to their religious beliefs.

Donovan escorted us to our first show at Camp Patriot, Kuwait, and as we readied ourselves to perform, we realized much was unknown about one another. Would our acts gel? What order should we perform in? How would the soldiers react?

Jim grabbed the hosting reigns like a pro. A veteran of stage and television, he was animated and had everyone rolling with laughter at his tales of growing up Italian. The fact he was a motor mouth served him well. "Jim wakes up talking," Drake observed, and on stage it was a lifesaver. We never performed under optimal conditions, and though microphones failed and lights flicked off, Jim powered along the whole tour, talking until the problem was fixed and he could bring up the next comic.

Drake, a master of minimalism, became the second performer. We had been given a promotional flier with our pictures on it, and for ease of flow decided to follow the running order given, which worked quite well. Drake's jokes sold themselves in a manner similar to Steven Wright, with punch lines mattering more than the silly faces or wacky voices a less talented writer relies on.

I took the third slot, and when I opened my dog-and-pony show with comments on the dry heat, I related to the soldiers experiencing it day in and out and they followed me down my sarcastic little trail.

Curtis followed me, and the man was energetic. Self-deprecation regarding his size (or lack of it) combined with a likeability factor off the charts endeared him to the female soldiers, many of whom wanted to "mother" him at every base we visited.

Danny closed the show, and it couldn't have been any other way. Ex-army himself, he said what the troops could not. He'd been there, knew the ins and outs of military life and exposed the absurdities and hypocrisies with a laser-like focus. Danny fit the description of saving the best for last to a "T." In fact, everything worked so well, we kept that running order for the rest of the tour.

Show number one under our belt, we were invited to explore the camp, the centerpiece of which was a piece of artillery left by retreating Iraqis after the Gulf War. We knew it was Iraqi because "Made in the U.S.A." was proudly stamped on its side. Donald Rumsfeld had opened up the channels for many weapons to reach Saddam back in the 80s, then acted surprised when Saddam actually used them.[1]

The next day we transferred to Iraq. All were issued flak jackets and helmets, and I have to admit to minor embarrassment when putting mine on. I felt I was playing "dress up" and being disrespectful to soldiers wearing the gear authentically. It made me uncomfortable every time I donned them. We boarded a C-130 cargo plane, which was exactly like flying as luggage. Unlike conventional

---

[1] Irony runs as thick as oil in the Middle East.

planes, where all seats face forward, these seats lined the edge of the hold so the center could be left open for storage.

With no soundproofing lining the plane, the engines roar was louder than a rock concert, and having minimal insulation meant it got cold, cold, cold. Heaters existed, but they were tiny and seemingly random in location; to attempt to warm the entire space enough to be tolerable, they were turned "to eleven." Pockets of extreme heat and cold filled the plane, meaning the left side of your body could be sweating while the right side grew icicles.

Landing in Baghdad was surreal to my civilian eyes; tanks, helicopter patrols, Bradley fighting units, and guns surrounded us. Everyone carried an M-16, and they carried them everywhere. To the mess hall, on bathroom breaks, and to our comedy shows, which gave a whole new twist to the vaudevillian concept of throwing tomatoes at a performer.

We headed to Camp Victory, a converted palace of Saddam Hussein, and it was easy to see why the United States chose Saddam's compounds for military bases: they all had protection built right in. It was widely reported the Iraqi people hated Saddam, and such reports rang true when visiting his secure homes. High walls and limited access checkpoints surrounded every one of his mansions and the actual dwellings were situated deep within the acreage. Saddam had no interest in seeing or being seen by his own citizenry, so our military didn't have to add many security measures when they arrived.

The compound we housed at was a study in contrast, like a movie set or home built by the Bluth family. Saddam's homes may have played well on the screen, but up close you found all the flaws. Ornate chandeliers were actually plastic, and fancy marble railings weren't secure and unable to bear weight. We were witness to the vanity of a man surrounded by illusion and had to wonder about the extent of his insanity. As he lived a hollow life, he must have been genuinely surprised when he went from ally to enemy in 1990.

The next eight days became a blur. We completed two to three shows daily, usually at different camps or forward operating bases. Our schedule was: fly in, perform, fly out. We moved mainly on Black Hawk helicopters, which is about the most fun anyone should be allowed to have in life. Sleek, fast, and precise, the pilots used the controls like second nature. We were taken on high-speed flights at treetop level; after the debacle in Somalia, where they flew high and hovered and made easy targets, low and fast became the call of the day. Our pilots shot straight towards power lines, veered up sharply to miss them, then dive-bombed the ground immediately as they passed under us. My stomach usually ended up somewhere around my ears with the drop, and I loved it; the ride was a roller coaster on steroids. A few months after my trip ended, a Black Hawk running the maneuver accidentally ended up in the very power lines he was playing chicken with, and the practice was halted. Reading about it in the news startled me; knowing you were one of the last few people to participate in a dangerous operating procedure is a unique feeling indeed.

Later in the tour, the switch was made to twin-propeller "46s"—smaller versions of Chinooks—and it was a shock to the system. They were slow, hot, and uncomfortable. Imagine dating the hottest cheerleader you can, then switching to a pre-surgery transvestite. It was kinda like that. Engine exhaust flowed right into the body of the chopper and I became nauseous on every one we rode; I barely managed not vomiting.

All along the way, every morning and at every stop, four of us were usually waiting for a fifth: Jim. While a kind and talented fellow, he was also a very tardy person. If we had a 7:00 a.m. pick-up, at 6:59 he'd be sitting at the edge of his bed, belly out and boxers scrunched up, asking, "I gots time for breakfast and a shower, right?"

After several embarrassing waits, revenge was decided. On our first Blackhawk ride, we were warned the right rear seat is called "The Flapper." For an unknown-to-me aerodynamic reason, it catches all the wind generated in flight and is to be avoided by passengers at all costs. With Jim bringing up the rear by a mile, we asked the gunner (our official loader) to place our overdue compadre in the dreaded seat. Though a little confused, the gunner shrugged and went along with it. As Jim has the attention span of a caffeinated gerbil, he had long forgotten all warnings when it came to loading and was excited we saved him a window seat.

Mischievous glances were exchanged as we lifted off, and a mere thirty seconds into flight, something hit my leg. I glanced down to see Jim's sunglasses flying out the door. Turning, I looked over to see him being tossed around like a sock puppet on an epileptic hand. Jim struggled to keep his helmet on, his face butter in a wind tunnel and filled with confusion and fear. The entire fifteen-minute ride was a bumpy mess for him while we all howled the howl of friends watching a drunken friend puke himself. As the flight ended, and we thought we were finished laughing, a stunned Jim declared, "I didn't like that ride at all!" Once more we howled.

Base to base, camp to camp, every "stage" was a last minute invention by the camp. We performed standing on tables, chairs, the floor, anything available. Sometimes we had a microphone hooked to a small speaker; on other occasions we had to muster up our best theater voice and project as best we could to the back of a deep room without any amplified help. We performed in palaces, chapels, outdoors in the heat, chow halls, one movie theater, and even on the back of a flatbed trailer at night. The only way to describe performing comedy under desert stars on a pitch black night in a war zone is to say you did it. Imagination has to fill in the rest; words are only an imperfect medium of expression here. Performing in a Mess Hall, however, is easy to summarize: it's an excellent ego boost. Nothing fills you with pride like reading the sign, "10:00, Comedy Show. 12:00, Hamburgers."

Surroundings changed, people did not. The soldiers were beyond appreciative of the visit, to the point where once again I was embarrassed. As my hand was shaken repeatedly and thanks given over and over, my repeated refrain became, "It's the least I can do." Because if they're in for a year (or more), and I tell jokes for a living, that ten-day tour literally was the least I could do.

(Aside from nothing)

It is only when I had a private conversation with one soldier, Leah B., that I grasped the enormity of what our little tour meant. Leah told me, "Sitting in the theater, in the darkness, just laughing... I actually forgot where I was for a second. I was just laughing, and then I looked down and saw my uniform. I looked around and actually wondered why everyone was in military garb for a moment, and then remembered how far from home I was. But for a second, I forgot." I had no clue how to respond, and stood there accepting the compliment with as much humility as possible.

So it went, each day blended together like a waking dream. We arrived at Cooke and had our scare with the munitions dump, which I treated as a photo opportunity. With the first BOOM!, I was up and out the door, video camera in hand, excitement in my eyes. I filmed the night sky in anticipation of incoming, when a soldier approached.

"You know," he cautioned, "that red light on your camera makes a great target for snipers."

I sheepishly put the camera down and returned to the show to find I was wasting my time anyway; it was a controlled blast from our own forces.

Our departure from Cooke provided another once-in-a-lifetime moment as our bus pulled alongside a truck on the airfield. We civilians didn't think anything of it, but confusion spread among our guides.

"What're they doing out here?" the driver asked.

There is a moment of silence, then with quiet authority Joni ordered, "Move the bus."

Without question, our driver re-positioned us thirty yards away. The truck contained prisoners waiting for transfer, and we watched as they unloaded and were made to kneel on the ground, their hands atop their heads. Any one of the men could have been responsible for car bombings or kidnappings; some were picked up on intelligence reports, others were trying to sneak into the camp. We were told of two insurgents killed trying to crawl under the concertina wire several days previous.

Naturally, Kodak best defines a time like this, so all five comedians reached for cameras like tourists in a fantasy war camp. Chastisement came quickly from Joni; if the men were innocent, photos would humiliate and endanger them. If the men were guilty, well, let's just say Abu Ghraib made the military very sensitive where cameras and prisoners are concerned. We watched in silence until our flight arrived. We had seen the enemy firsthand, and it wore a surprisingly human face.

Outside Fallujah, our next contact, Maverick, casually informed us that by standing on the roof of headquarters, you could see whatever fighting happened to be taking place in town. He also had frightening information for us as we stood inside our new kerosene-soaked tent being briefed.

"In case you're interested," Maverick began, "you're staying about fifty yards from where a rocket hit two weeks ago. Took out the tent behind you. They usually launch mortars, but this time they had a bigger gun."

It was good information, but no cause for fear. A shrug, maybe, but not fear. Mortars and rockets hit randomly; to spend time worrying about them would be a 24-7 job, so we took our cue from those who serve and let it go. While bases weren't under constant attack, it happened daily. Nowhere in Iraq was truly safe; rockets could be launched from up to 25 miles away, and mortars set to fire off timers. They struck with little or no warning, and tales of loss were recalled everywhere we visited.

Regardless, Maverick wasn't finished with us and continued his welcome.

"You want to keep food out of your tent," Maverick told us. "It attracts the camel spiders."

"Spiders?" we collectively asked.

"Yeah, they have an anesthetic in their venom, so you don't feel them biting you. You just wake up and your arm or leg is swollen. Kinda sucks. Anyway, about the shows…"

"Hold on," Danny began. "I didn't sign up for spiders."

Maverick was taken back. "Didn't I just tell you about the rocket?"

"Yes."

"And you're worried about spiders?"

But that's the trick of the mind. Signing up, insurgents and violence were expected. It's in the contract, so you prepared mentally for them. But camel spiders were a new development. Not only are they spiders (almost enough for anyone), but gigantic spiders to boot.

Danny wasn't the only one alarmed by the new development; we were all fairly unhappy by the announcement. Having a *Stand By Me* rotating night watch was discussed, but in the end we finally decided we weren't entirely pussies and went to bed. In, as said, our kerosene-soaked tents. Apparently it keeps them, no lie, water repellent. In a desert situation with little rain and incoming explosives, it seems extreme flammability is a must. Ah, Great White… did you teach us nothing?

Going in to any show, we were told a little about the audience in front of us, and one of my favorite moments occurred at Maverick's base. He informed the group he was bringing us to a small quadrant of the camp where the Oklahoma National Guard was stationed. Now, at every performance Jim would take the stage, pick out a couple soldiers, ask their name, where they're from, and crack wise about the city or state. Knowing this, I figured he would pay attention to this little nugget of geographic information. I was wrong.

Despite being informed who we were in front of, and regardless of the fact the walls around us were littered with Oklahoma references, Jim either forgot or didn't notice; the butter-face incident in the Blackhawk taught him nothing about paying attention to detail.

Jim walked on stage and started right in.

"Hey fella, where you from?" he asked an innocent in the front row.

"Oklahoma," came the expected (to everyone but Jim) response.

"Oklahoma? What, you sing musicals? Ha!"

Our host turned to another. "Where you from?"

"Oklahoma," the second soldier answered.

Jim was surprised, and looked back and forth between the two men. "What is this, a family reunion? Meet your long lost cousin!"

Best to move on; Jim turned to someone new, "Hey, where you from?"

Again, the answer arrived, "Oklahoma."

Jim paused, and a moment of genuine confusion crossed his face. "You guys putting me on?" he stammered.

Silence filled the room, as he looked from soldier to soldier, unsure how to continue. Finally, a barrel-chested sergeant from the back of the room bellowed: "We're the Oklahoma National Guard, dumbass!"

Everyone burst into laughter, and though a great comedian, Jim never really recovered that afternoon.

* * *

At our final stop, outside of Balad, the camp went on Red Alert twice in one day. The posted definition of Red Alert is "Attack is Imminent or IN PROCESS." Each time that day, it was "in process," specifically warning against incoming mortars. Thankfully, there were no casualties, but touring the base we were shown new construction on the PX.[1] Several weeks previous, a round hit and killed Major Paul R.S. III as he stood outside the store. I have to admit, I did not remember that name when writing this. In one of those small coincidences life brings us, years later I made a friend on MySpace, an Iraqi war veteran named Stu. As we talked of where he was and what he experienced, the event came up. Stu provided the name of the fallen soldier in Balad; the man had been in his unit. Stu had been there. They were friends. It is sometimes a very small world we live upon.

---

[1] The Base Exchange is like a convenience store; soldiers can buy snacks, sundries, or any slew of needed items.

It was in Balad I felt the largest sense of unfairness in the current system of Iraqi operations. We were given two escorts while on the base: one M-16 toting soldier acted as our bodyguard, one un-armed Halliburton contractor was our chauffeur. The soldier, when not with us, left the base on missions. He risked gunfights, capture and torture, or worse. Our driver never left the base and drove a double-armored Ford Explorer at the same time many Humvees were unarmored. The soldier earned roughly $25K a year; the driver over $110K, with the first $80K being tax-free. While in no way do I begrudge a man landing a great paying job in a dangerous country, the discrepancies speak for themselves. Whether or not you draw a line between former vice-president Cheney and his buddies at Halliburton—a company that got no-bid contracts for war efforts—when you examine the two salaries and comparative duties, it's enough to disgust anyone. The thing to remember is: the money used to pay both the soldier and Halliburton employee was governmental, and therefore from collected taxes. I felt so awful about the situation, to assuage my own guilt I ended up walking everywhere I could and forwent the four-mpg ride offered.

I heard my first bout of actual combat in Balad. I woke up early one morning and made my way to the Internet Tent to check my email. While typing away casually, I heard gunfire. At first I thought I was hearing a firing range, but then quickly realized the shot pattern did not lend itself to such a controlled event. When I bumped into our camp liaison later, I asked him about it and he laughed.

"We don't have a firing range," he explained. "We don't want to confuse anyone, so if you hear gunfire, it's game on."

By tour's end, each member of our unit made connections of sorts. I experienced a sixth degree of separation; I wore my Wisconsin T-shirt on stage and found myself talking to the cousin of a friend after the show. Danny received a take-home message; he was given a care package and asked to deliver it back in the states. Drake kept eye contact and listened intently to anyone interested in conversation, while Jim talked to anyone who would listen. And Curtis, our little Gidget? Curtis went home with the email addresses of many, many female enlisted. Solace exists in many forms.

Do I miss it all, typing it up after the fact? Absolutely. I wasn't ready to leave; there were still more bases to attend, more Americans to amuse. They're still there, waking up every day in an uncertain life, and every day I long to return. My first night back, my sleep was restless. Jetlag woke me at 3:00 a.m., where I saw I had a message on my phone. I stared at it dumbly, wondering where in the fuck I was I had service.

Oh yeah, home.

Would that our soldiers could say the like.

BLOCK II

AGES 7 – 10

6 – EVERYTHING CHANGES BUT BLACK

There are days when I miss vinyl records.

I understand change, and I enjoy it. Progress transformed the rotary phone I used in my childhood—an expensive device rented from the phone company since they were too pricey to own—to the relatively inexpensive, portable, cellular phone. Likewise, the VHS tape of poor quality and deterioration with each use has been replaced by Blu Ray discs: high quality, amazing sound.

When it comes to music, however, I am quite happily a curmudgeon. I was raised on records, and I believe they will hold a special place in my heart until the day I die. There is something about the physicality of a vinyl recording; placing the needle on the edge and listening to the pre-song pops and whistles as it settles into the groove is a much more appealing ritual than double-clicking a mouse and streaming a song to your computer. The artwork on a cardboard sleeve was part of a record's overall charm—The Beatles crossing the street on *Abbey Road*, the montage representing The Police on

Synchronicity—cover art meant something back then; it was big, and difficult to dismiss.

The rise of Compact Discs in the 1980s was an important leap forward for music; digital recording capabilities created a seemingly limitless sonic canvas to paint upon. Listen to *Achtung Baby* with headphones; the layers of sound are delicately nuanced and amazingly interesting. Unfortunately, the smaller size of a CD meant the cover image became a little less important; instead of a big picture that could contain subtleties, the picture now had to be entirely to the point immediately. Even worse, people could buy carrying cases and discard everything but the disc itself. One step forward for the recording process meant three steps back for the physical representation of a musician's art.

Napster was another important leap for music. Anyone old enough to buy records can tell you many a story of having been burned by someone who put out a twelve-track record when only the single was worth listening to. You wasted your hard earned money for one song and got pissed; beyond the radio hit, the album would be so awful it was unlistenable. Napster was great payback for a consumer burned by bad purchases. iTunes then advanced the idea the song was more powerful than the album. Instead of dropping $13.99 for one good song and eleven mediocre tracks, you could quickly grab what you liked in an individualistic manner. Marketing individual singles, however, hurt musicians who put effort into their art; bands who created records that had a shape and flow to them, themed releases with an emotional arc throughout the album, making the narrative as a whole more important than the singularity of any one song, went the way of the dodo.

The CD revolution occurred in the mid-1980s; in 1985 *Brother In Arms*, by the Dire Straits, was one of the first releases pushed in a CD-heavy format, leaving the cassette and 33-rpm record to waste away with the 8-Track. Though CDs are easier to care for, lighter and smaller, and though digital recording creates endless sonic opportunities, there is a warmth to vinyl that has yet to be replicated. For the life of me, I cannot listen to Pink Floyd's *The Wall* on CD; the hisses and pops that accompany my turntable copy of the song "Mother" add as much to the listening experience as does an understanding of the lyrics and overall theme of the album.

The first record I bought was *Double Platinum*, by KISS. I already owned several KISS albums, but *Double Platinum* was the first one I actually purchased with my own money. I picked it up when I was eight, but getting to that point would be a two-year adventure.

At six years old, I lived in Milwaukee with my father. We lived in the lower flat of a duplex, one rented to us by its upstairs owners, an ex-nun married to an ex-priest. They had three children and were kind in nature.

I was an original latchkey kid, and every morning would wake and eat breakfast while watching *Fury* and *The Little Rascals*, then hike my mile to school. Every evening I would walk home, let myself in, and watch either *Voltron* or some other Japanamation; UHF channels 18 and 24 were my best friends back then. Occasionally I would spend time with the family that lived upstairs, but overall I was already learning to become an isolationist.

Dad and I lived across the street from Sherman Park, third house from the corner of Burleigh Avenue, and hiking across the park was the easiest way both to and from school. Instead of walking all the way to the corner of a block and turning, I shortcutted it across the open space twice daily. Shrubbery surrounded Sherman Park back then, but it's gone now. Around the time we left Milwaukee a few years later, a rise in crime created the need for a clean line of sight, as robbers and rapists and junkies[1] began hanging out in the hidden areas. Those hidden areas, then, were thusly removed.

But while I lived there, the bushes were to me a godsend on several levels. Though my morning walk was an easy one, the trip home was trying, as I usually had a full little colon from lunch. Sadly, in no way could I bring myself to do the deuce in a public bathroom. I shall explain why.

I attended the 38th Street School. A foreboding 2.5-story brick building—the levels split as you entered and you could go up a half-flight to the first floor, or down a half-flight to the basement—the public school's façade suggested more a prison than a place of learning. Perhaps that was done with architect intent, a sort of "spare the rod" intimidation for those entering, that they may not rise up against any figure of authority.

I should have been in second grade but instead was placed in a third grade class. Someone, somewhere along the way had received the impression I was "smart," and my dad absolutely wanted me to

---

[1] Oh my!

live up to my full potential in life. I wasn't too disturbed by the upgrade; unrest would come the following year, when growth spurts would hit those older than I and leave me a midget among men.

One day, I went to the bathroom to relieve my bowels. I'm not sure anyone likes using public toilets, but I had to, *had* to, *had to* go. I cautiously entered a stall, lowered my pants and sat down, embarrassed to be doing something so awful in public. While sitting there, I heard the bathroom door open and listened to the footsteps of an entering arrival. I then grew nervous as the person paused in stride and all grew silent in the little tile room. I am by no means psychic, but there exist moments when we are all clairvoyant. I knew that whoever walked in had seen my little legs dangling below the stall door, and had frozen in response. I froze, too, tightening my small sphincter in fear.

"He knows I'm in here" raced through my mind, and I felt shamed.

The footsteps started sounding again, only this time more slowly, cautiously. The person was shuffling and in no way headed toward the urinals. Perhaps he was looking to use a toilet himself? Indeed he did enter into the stall next to me, but I heard no belt buckle unfasten or zipper lower. What I did hear was a scuffling against the stall wall next to me.

A panic infused me, and I fixed a cold, dead stare straight ahead.

There is a feeling one gets when they know they are being observed—a sixth sense that springs into action when needed. Personal reactions differ, whether raised gooseflesh of the skin or a tension felt in the muscles, but at that moment I knew someone was staring at me.

Slowly, I raised my head and looked directly up.

Leaning over the wall, gazing down at me was a little black head shaped oblongly, not unlike a football. Though I now know he was just a kid being a kid, playing "So, what's going on in here," at the time it traumatized the hell out of me.

I became prudish, a boy only able to use the urinal in a men's room and nothing else save for the sink. Back then, it created the problem of what to do mid-day when my young little bowels wanted to release the combination of breakfast and lunch. I could make it most of the afternoon, but every single day, or close to it, I would hold what I could as long as I could, then on my walk home after school, had to shit. So every single day, or close to it, I would stop in the shrubbery of Sherman Park and relieve myself. I learned to bring napkins with me, that I not walk home squishy.

Of course it was more than unusual, a boy who could not crap in public if enclosed by a locked stall able to do so hidden away in bushes in the wide-open air of the city, but kids always do what feels right to them. Sometimes we carry this instinct through to adulthood, which has both its advantages and disadvantages—it's all in the difference of maturity: are you childlike, or childish? One is fun, the other petty.

So it came to pass that one day, tucked away in those very bushes, I saw a little red change purse while pooping. The sparkle of a stale sequin is what caught my eye, so I picked it up, looked inside and found a delight: $50.

An honest child, on a weekend visit, I informed my mom of the find and she reported it to the police. Milwaukee's Finest asked us to bring it in, so they could return it to its rightful owner, but my mom was more savvy than to fall for that old ruse. A small change purse with no identification inside, turned over to the MPD, would most likely become an afternoon of beer and pizza for them. Mom instead gave our phone number, that anyone who might report the item missing be directed our way to claim their two lost twenties and one misplaced ten.

At the end of that school year, in the spring of 1977, my mother and sister moved to Milwaukee to reunite the family. We purchased a home three houses south of Hadley on 41st Street. While only a stone's throw from where my father and I had lived, it was still two blocks deeper into what was being kindly called a "transitioning neighborhood." The inner city was expanding, and the "white flight" to the suburbs was in full swing. With our move, my family was actually pulling a Phil Donahue and moving in opposition to the general consensus.

With my mother and I under the same roof again, and after several months of impatient waiting, the time to claim ownership had passed. I was told the purse and all its green-papered belongings were mine, and I knew exactly what I wanted to buy: a record. I loved records; I loved my little turntable and the cheap speakers that went with it. My bedroom was a home inside my home, where I could escape the world outside and immerse myself in music. I also, when necessary, used my room to escape the turmoil of my parents' unstable marriage.

I already had a fine little collection building; I owned the *Star Wars* soundtrack, and played both the opening track and "Cantina Band" to death. As an adult looking back on "Cantina Band," I realize that in some ways I was connecting to the very music I was rebelling against at the time. My father was a Big Band Jazz nut and would play Woody Herman and Glenn Miller loudly enough that he could hear it reverberate throughout the house no matter what room he was in. Naturally I did everything I could to avoid hearing such noise, claimed to hate big band music into my teens, and missed the parallels between "Cantina Band" and swing bands until years later. Strangely enough, I now love swing bands and enjoy how Woody Herman and Glenn Miller serve as a mini-arc for my own life, as one was a Milwaukee native and the other a son of Iowa.

The *Wizard of Oz* soundtrack, another bit of vinyl within my possession, played a special role in my childhood. I'm not ashamed to say that as a seven-year-old boy I loved the music, but as an adult being a "friend of Dorothy" would have a whole new meaning. Something I loved about my copy of The *Wizard of Oz* was the skip on my record. The album had bits of dialogue before each song— snippets of each scene from the movie—and my copy had the most perfect chip in its grooves. As the intro to "If I Only Had A Heart" played, the needle would up, jump, and scoot back to the start of the line, "Go ahead, bang on it." Like a Little Engine That Couldn't, my needle would not pass that phrase. To the irritation of my parents, I didn't always help it along its intended path. Not that I could listen for hours, but for a good goddamn minute or two, I could sit, enthralled by the perfection of repetition, "Go ahead, bang on it. Go ahead, bang on it. Go ahead..."[1]

With $50 in hand, my mother, sister, and I went to a record store just across from the Capitol Court Shopping Mall and I purchased my very first record, the aforementioned *Double Platinum.* Many hours of air-guitar and air drumming followed.

After the acquisition, my mom decided to treat us to McDonald's. The closest location was but a few blocks away fringing the Capitol Court parking lot. Though I cannot recall what day of the week or what time of day we were there, I do know it was busy. Not overly so, but neither was the restaurant empty. Three registers were open,

---

[1] Remember, I was being advanced in school due to my intelligence.

and we waited in line until our turn to order arrived, when a shouting match erupted next to us. Like the parting of the Red Sea, customers, my mom included, suddenly shunned the front counter for the back of the store. An angry man had pulled a switchblade out and was screaming at his clerk. My mother, from her (hopefully) now-safe vantage point, gripped her daughter in fear, only to realize she was only holding one young hand. Looking up, my mom discovered that while everyone with half a brain had rushed away from the irate, knife-wielding man, I was standing right next to him, staring up with what my mom describes as a, "Wow... cooooool..." look on my face.[1]

The man jumped up onto the counter and thrust the blade toward the clerk. Not exactly in a stabbing manner, more a threatening one, like, "Look, I've got a knife so pay attention to me!" To my immature eyes the gesture didn't seem at all to say "I'm gonna cut you," and that's what makes all the difference. I don't remember exactly what happened, I just remember feeling oddly safe. I had the sense everything was occurring outside of my realm of existence, and that I was casually watching an event that didn't pertain to me. Neither do I remember exactly how it all ended, but I'm pretty sure I didn't get my McDonald's that day. No matter, I had always preferred the now-disappeared Burger Chef anyway.

We lived on 41st Street for several years, and in the fall of 1979, I turned ten. I was still attending advanced classes, but in the 38th Street School back then, they had a "progressive" way of teaching, using mixed grades. After third grade, I entered a fourth/fifth split class, and all was well. The following summer, however, no one informed me I should probably do my best to hit puberty and grow a little. Entering the new, fifth/sixth mix, I became nervous. Though the difference between ages twenty-one and twenty-three or seventy-five and seventy-seven may not seem like much, the twelve-year-old classmates who surrounded me seemed enormous.

Though I initially feared merciless beatings or being ostracized by turned backs, I was looked out for by two kindly peers, Loy and James. I've no idea how exactly I ended up under their protective wings, but luck had me slide inside the slipstream of their safety, and I was thankful. I remember them quite clearly. James was black, like the majority of the school population, with a decent 1970s afro and

---

[1] Again, advanced class.

always wore a smile on his face. In school or while out playing, James was the most vivacious, upbeat and happy kid around. As night drew near and curfew arrived, however, his demeanor would stiffen and grow somber. Where his "hello" was always bouncy and upbeat, his "goodbye" would be hesitant and halting. James's father was a Vietnam vet and either insane, angry, or both. James visited my home often, but I have no memory of ever playing at his. I never knew what happened under his father's roof, but you could read in James's face and eyes that it was nothing he enjoyed returning to.

My other protector, Loy, arrived some time after the school year started. In the white minority like me, as if the color of his skin didn't cause him to stand out enough already, Loy had the most platinum blond hair I'd ever seen. It was blinding, almost albino in nature. We bonded over comic books, and would skateboard together to Polaris, a comic book store on 50th and Center. West on Center to Polaris gave us the advantage of a slight decline, and the trip to was fast and painless. Pushing uphill the nine blocks back exhausted our little legs, but considering the X-Men rewards we were carrying, it was worth it. Little did we know back then we were joining the series during its peak years; the Chris Claremont/John Byrne paring is still considered to be the pinnacle of the comic's entire run.

As said, James and Loy looked out for me. I was smaller and weaker than any of my classmates and could have been bullied, but wasn't when they were around. Some kids tried, but they were quickly put in their place. One evening on Grant Boulevard, one street over from my house, Loy and I stumbled across a nemesis of mine, someone who had given me flack on the playground or threatened bodily harm in a hallway. Somehow, Loy shrewdly invested the boy in a game of "Who can hit the softest." Though hesitant at first, the boy eventually relented and decided all was legit and that he would play. Loy held up his palms so the boy could go first, seeing if he could lightly tap one and "win." The boy completed his round quickly, and it became Loy's turn. The boy raised his palms, and when his defenses were down and the moment ripe, Loy clocked him unconscious with one punch. I remember seeing blood spurt, though from broken nose or split lip I do not know. A concerned citizen was witness to the blow and came rushing out of the house screaming, so Loy and I ran. The boy never bothered me again.

I cannot say I was entirely safe because of their protection, though. Violence, especially that of the random variety, was a common event in our neighborhood. At the outset of the school year, every student, classroom by classroom, was taken outside to a waiting cube truck. It was a mobile police station, and one by one we were fingerprinted and given a file. Ostensibly, this was done in case we should ever go missing—the Atlanta child abductions were just getting under way and would scare the unholy hell out of the nation for two years—but in retrospect, I'm certain the police loved having fingerprints on hand for all the future little miscreants in its district.

Many bikes were stolen back then; it was a nice cottage industry for burgeoning criminals. One sunny summer day, my neighbor Mike and I were riding west on Center Street. A busy thoroughfare, Center was lined with shops and stores more than homes, and their flat business fronts pushed right up to the sidewalk on which we rode. The street was by far too busy with cars for our limited reflexes, so we played it safe with multiple games of chicken involving pedestrians trying to use the sidewalk for its intended purpose. As Mike and I rode in tandem between 40th and 41st, mere moments from the safety of home, a slender figure jumped from a tiny alcove. Moving with a dexterity I could barely comprehend, the figure swung a hard fist across Mike's jaw with one hand, while grabbing the handlebars with his other. Mike tumbled from the bike a dead weight and the thief was on it and riding off seamlessly, almost as if no pause had taken place. Like a rider mounting a horse in full gallop, the bike's stride was never broken.

My own two-wheeled trauma came not with bodily harm, but the intimidating threat of it. One day as I rode my bike around the corner on Hadley south onto 40th Street, I saw a group of teens standing across the sidewalk. They were spread out before me, a little way down the block and hindering my two-wheeled adventures. All were eyeing me, seemingly lying in wait, and I panicked slightly and had no clue what to do. I was too young and uncoordinated to turn and flee, nor did I have the necessary muscles to pedal off at a furious enough rate to escape, so I silently resigned myself to what was about to happen. I slowed the bike, stopped, possibly said, "Excuse me," and prayed they would allow my trespass. Instead, we began a verbal little dance.

"That's a sweet ride you got. You should let me try it," one started.

Even at ten I knew that translated to me never seeing my bike again.

"I have to get home, my mom is waiting for me," I responded.

By invoking mom, the protector of all, I was hoping they would allow me on my merry little way.

"Come on, man. I'll bring it right back," the boy intoned, leaning in to show serious intent.

My two options seemed to be: lose the bike easily, or with injury. I chose easily. I climbed off and held the handlebars out to the little clique's leader, who then got on and started riding back north on 40th, back towards Hadley and presumably his home. In the most incredible case of instant karma I've ever been witness to, as the new owner of my bike slowed by the corner, looking his left, right, and left again for traffic, a figure jumped out from behind a hedge I had passed mere moments earlier, hammer-punched the rider square across the jaw and deftly performed the same bike control maneuver I'd seen done on Mike just a few days earlier. The rest of the posse, who had been meandering off in the same direction, dismissedly tossing a "later" my way as they did so, now broke out in a sprint. Whether they meant to aid their fallen leader or grab the new bike thief I do not know, but with the rising of their ire, I took off for home before I could become the catchable target. I never got my bike back, but I did feel at peace with what I had just witnessed.

Of course, I couldn't always escape attack and was jumped once. It happened right on the school grounds during recess. Our playground, like the building it surrounded, was of hard exterior, with one small patch of green grass tucked neatly away in the northeast corner of the cement sea. In winter our biggest recess activity was trying to find a way to sneak back inside and stay warm. One day, my friends and I were discovered and shuffled back into the open air. As chance would have it, on this crisply chilly day, a teenager wandered into the schoolyard and began attacking kids farthest from the teachers. When he reached me, he put my head between his knees and pummeled away without reason or warning. Fortunately, in pinning me, he protected my face and ended up punching my thick little noggin with his soft knuckles, doing little in the way of damage. There was no reason behind the action, he was merely lashing out and assaulted several random students before being chased off and into a house across the street. The police were called, but they arrived to find the teen did not live in the home; he merely ran in the front door, through the living room and kitchen and out the back, into the alley and away scot-free. I was taken to the local constabulary and had to go over mug shots, but the array of angry black faces were all too similar yet unfamiliar. I never identified the attacker.

Many events involving intimidation and brutality happened in broad daylight. Few residents were willing to get involved with outside occurrences and thus have their houses targeted for vandalism. That someone had chased Loy and I the day he punched the boy on Grant Boulevard was an oddity, and something I can only suspect involved reverse "racism." As Loy and I were white, we were probably deemed less threatening than the local African-American youth.

With violent culture comes criminal action, and though we were not angry, James, Loy, and I were not innocent. I learned to steal by and with my two friends. When bored, Loy and I would hop on a bus and head to Capitol Court. Today, two very young kids riding a public bus in the near inner city would most likely be an invitation for disaster. Maybe it was then, too, but we were too immature to see it. For our existence, it felt natural to be independent of our parents, and youth is generally more accepting of surroundings than adults ever are. Regardless, we probably never should have been roaming so far from home while unattended, but maybe it was Zen in a way, where acting on instinct and trust over thought and worry got us optimal results.

We weren't thugs, we were thieves, and we put thought behind our targets; Loy showed me how to shove a book under my shirt and into the front of my waistband, so I showed him how to pick up two books, read one over while pilfering the other, then return the first innocently to its home on the shelf. Yes, we were the worst kind of robbers out there: nerds. We. Stole. Books. We stole science fiction, and I personally stumbled my way into adult erotica science fiction, where the lead hero would not only save the day, but also make descriptive, graphic love to a female extraterrestrial in reward.[1] After a heist, we'd make our way to the same McDonald's my mother vowed never to set foot in again, where I'd disgust everyone by dipping french fries in my hot fudge sundae.[2]

We would also steal donuts, and James came with us more often on these little excursions. There existed a bakery on Burleigh, off the

---

[1] "How do you tell if it's a female?" "'Cause it's got tits."

[2] Still a delicious treat, by the way.

northeast corner of Sherman Park, across the street. The bakery was like every bakery in the world, with boxed items out front and freshly created goods tucked behind the counter displayed for all the world to see and savor. Two of us would enter into the store first, full of nervous excitement over the impending snatch, to distract the shop-keep. We'd hem and haw and point at one or another of the fattening treats, while the third member of our party gingerly arrived and remained in the front of the store. Sooner or later, we'd get the storeowner to turn his back, and then whoever was closest to the door would grab a box of donuts and dart. Naturally, as we were full of giggles and nerves, the two distracting figures would also run. We were either too wise or too dim to stick around and play innocent know-nothings.

Around the corner we'd sprint, north on 41st for a quarter block, then east down an alleyway for another block or two. I only remember the baker giving chase once, and it was as if we were all in a sort of madcap comedy, where he ran only to the alleyway entrance, then stood there either shaking his fist or with arms akimbo in frustration. My memory would love to make him an Italian stereotype, with a big bushy mustache and broken English, yelling, "You kids! I get-ah you someday!" Sadly, I'm guessing that would just be fanciful recollection.

Our bounty was shared on the rooftop of a daycare center, one whose storefront was on Burleigh. We'd climb on their dumpster, then shimmy our way up a telephone pole until we were safely out of sight in the sky. Or so we thought; the reality of the situation is it was a one-story flattop roof and not too difficult to navigate for anyone with a modicum of coordination. But back then, in our minds we were risking great peril to get to our secret hideaway.

We would eat our fill in caked goods, then lament the fact we never thought to buy (or steal) any milk beforehand and make our way down to whatever corner store was closest. I would usually pick up a classic Reggie Bar, my favorite chocolaty treat until I discovered Bar None, both of which have long since disappeared. We always returned home happy, high on sugar, and not in the slightest hungry for dinner.

If being a decade into life is a true milestone, it would make sense then that 1979 is also the year I saw my first pornographic magazine. A not quite understood lower-hemisphere longing for both a cast member of ZOOM and Pamela Sue Martin of Nancy Drew fame had already informed me biologically I was heterosexual, even if I didn't know the term.[1] I just knew I liked women. If there is a way to discover the female form in all its naked glory and a way not to do so, my accidental initial wander was down the wrong path, with Hustler magazine. While I don't recall who brought it to my house, I do remember the focus of the issue was a fetishist's delight: pregnant women. I remember staring at the flawlessly round bellies, and more importantly the engorged breasts the babies inside were helping to create, and being fascinated. The women were as captivating as anything my feeble little mind could comprehend, and though I had little real idea what sex was, I knew there was a connection between the breasts in the magazine and the fact my little penis became quite hard. School ground whispering informed me that if I plopped a lob of Vaseline in my palm and rubbed myself, it was exactly what sex felt like. Sadly, little did the boys speaking of sex understand the difficulty of cleaning a viscous, water-resistant gel off one's Johnson. Oh well, live and learn.[2]

In the few months before my family moved for the umpteenth time in my childhood, gangs started making their presence known in the neighborhood. *The Warriors* was a teenage hit, and my friends and I loved the idea of having one another's back in a situation. We formed our own little version of a band of hooligans, "The 41st Street Gang." Never mind the 41st ran quite a distance and we only knew several blocks of it at best, we were laying claim to the entire run with our name. In all honesty, we had no clue what a gang really was, but the concept sounded cool and we went with it.

---

[1] When I originally wrote this, I did a little Internet search to see if I could find the girl from ZOOM who had captured my heart, but nothing turned up. Two years later, however, some kind soul loaded all the opening sequences to the show onto YouTube. Seasons 1–3 proved fruitless, but the instant, and I do mean instant, I cued up season 4, I recognized her hairstyle from the wide-angle shot. The year would have been 1974, making me 5 years old, and she looked to be somewhere a little above 10. So it appears I was into Cougars before they even had a label. Go me.

[2] And for the record, I would have much rather been introduced to naked women via the 1978 Pamela Sue Martin issue of Playboy. Again, oh well.

I've no idea how, but another gang in the neighborhood, one situated one block north and closer to Sherman Park, caught wind of us and sent an emissary down with word that we would have to rumble for turf. To us, "rumble," meant "rock fight," because we were young boys and well versed in the ways of damaging one another under the guise of fun. We bundled together, there were probably only four or five of us at most, and went to the scheduled rumble point at the scheduled rumble time. Once there, we found genuine high school gang members waiting for us. I remember being confused more than scared, and fortunately for us they must have been taken aback, too. Instead of beating us to a pulp, they realized there had been a severe misunderstanding and that our "gang" was in no way a threat to them. We were dismissed with an eye roll and nothing more. In 1979, such was the way things were. Today, sadly, we probably would have been beaten and incorporated into the real gang to be used as runners and lookouts. While real estate is all about location, violence is in the timing. Luckily, we accidentally had excellent timing in both our age and that of societal disintegration.

The rest of the year is wrapped up in vignettes, little synapse fires of memory that find no real home among the narrative; sometimes I remember images more than specifics. I know there was a fourth boy that spent time with James, Loy, and I, and though I can picture him quite clearly, I cannot find the candle of thought to light his name.[1] Though James, Loy, and I all had our share of less than stellar experiences at home, the nameless image I remember as friend had it worse than all of us, because his pain was public.

He wasn't a troublemaker, but neither was he studious. He was failing several courses, and his father (or step-father) arrived at the school to have a conference with my friend and our teacher. They stepped into the side, walk-in closet where we hung our coats and placed our moon boots with their bread bag linings, and though I remember hearing no noise, when all three returned several minutes later, my friend was crying. My eyes moved to his stoic father, and all I could do was stare at the belt he was wearing wrapped around a calloused fist. There are moments in life when you are at a genuine loss for words, such as hearing the diagnosis of cancer, the loss of a loved one, or an alike tragedy. Moments that hit you in the gut and

---

[1] This is too obvious an homage for me to claim it as my own, duh.

remove all speech. At that moment I had no words with which to comfort my friend. Chances are, I could barely even reconcile the fact I had just witnessed the immediate aftermath of his beating.

Another random image in my mind is of learning how to protect myself from a nuclear attack, with *Duck and Cover* being the national standard for safety in case World War III broke out. The Cold War was in full swing back then, and those goddamn commies[1] were an ever-present threat. When the sirens went off, you were to climb under your desk, tuck your head down, and cover it up with your hands. While making sure every body part is covered by blanket in bed is surprisingly effective when avoiding nighttime monsters, I'm not sure this defense related well to the atom bomb. I would stare out the grated windows—fire safety was of little importance to the school system—and imagine a mushroom cloud in the distance. All the rooftops in my eye line would be evaporated away clean, yet I would remain safe thanks to government grade furniture? Even a child is not so naïve. A thought as to why teenagers turn surly is possibly because we spend so much time lying to them as children.

I also saw my first live concert at age ten, KISS. They were on their Dynasty tour and came to the Mecca Arena, where the Milwaukee Bucks used to play. My mom didn't want an unescorted ten-year-old or even a pair of ten-year-olds attending, so she took me herself. I'm sure I was embarrassed by the idea of it all, until we got to the show and saw what I assume is a familiar sight to fans of any tween sensation: the entire audience was comprised of parents escorting their children. Unfortunately for KISS, the best way to lose your cool is to capture the elementary school market, because the rebellious youth that loved you up to that point will walk away faster than they ever embraced you. In 1980 KISS released *Unmasked*, and it was their first true failure. Significance lost, several years later they would have to take their trademark makeup off to shock the world into paying attention to them once again. Even after doing so, they remained on the periphery of cool instead of being the defining aspect of it. Once you become irrelevant, it's near impossible to become a trendsetter again.

That was it; one year together was all Loy, James, and I got. After sixth grade, we went our separate ways. My family moved to

---

[1] Reagan's catchphrase for election.

Appleton, Loy's family went somewhere else in Milwaukee, and I've no idea what happened to James. I wish I did.

Loy made it out, and we reconnected 29 years later as adults headed into middle age. His photogenic memory and the wonders of the Internet had him stumble across me and shoot off an email. It is only in adulthood we begin to understand how strongly environment can shape who we become, and Loy and I spoke of the dangerous "what ifs," a memory game involving different events and life outcomes. What if our families had stayed in the neighborhood? Would we have either joined gangs, or became excluded from them as race became more important a factor in friendship and clique creation the older you got? Stealing books could have turned into stealing cars; robbing the bakery could have become robbing houses. A perpetuation of violence and failed future existed a mere cunt-hair away from our future, but we were lucky enough to escape. Thank God for that.

In 2008, I visited Milwaukee for the first time in years. I didn't go looking at all the old haunts, but I did take a slight detour into childhood. Around the time I moved, in 1980, an attempted revitalization was taking place in the neighborhood. For years and years, a huge swath of city blocks running east to west between North Avenue and Meinecke had been empty, plain fields. The rumor was a highway was to be placed there, a new four-lane easy access to Lake Michigan. When this goal never materialized, a developer (or the city) made an attempt to gentrify the area a little, return some money to it, and hopefully ease the rate of devastation. A middle-class "paradise" was created, with nice two-story houses, picket fences and cobblestones being placed into the city streets for atmosphere. The hope was to slow the white flight so popular in the 60s and 70s, return a tax-base to the area, and shore up funding for local schools, police, and the like.

The experiment did not succeed.

In 1980, Sherman Boulevard, a four-lane large street with a nice median between the north and south lanes, created a sort of unspoken buffer between the "still good" and "going bad" neighborhoods. What I witnessed in 2008 was a poverty line that spread west well beyond Sherman, up into the sixty-block range of houses. I used to go to a library on North and Sherman to read *Doonesbury* collections; the library was boarded up and gang-tagged.

I attended The University of Milwaukee in my twenties, but hadn't seen Milwaukee since the year 2000. In the eight years since leaving, many areas of the downtown and east side of Milwaukee had seen development, growth, and change. Stagnation and even regression, however, were still ever-present in my childhood neighborhood. The same closed shops of old were still shuttered, and businesses once thriving had long since failed. As I drove around, two young men who spent more money on the rims of their car than they did their education eyed me at a red light. It was the first time in my life I actually felt uncomfortable being in the area.

The 38th Street School was abandoned, an empty brick monster sitting in the middle of an impoverished neighborhood. What's funny—or sad, depending on your point of view—is when I called the Milwaukee Public School System just to quiet an inner curiosity regarding why it was no longer in use, I was transferred four times and given three different phone numbers to call. One woman informed me that it shut down in 2007, while another said she still had it listed as an active place of education on her computer. It was somewhat depressing, knowing these people were in charge of opening children's eyes to information and they didn't even know which institutions were still functional.

After twenty minutes of confused turnaround, I finally found a gentle woman who told me lack of enrollment was the institution's death knell. From what I saw of the teens and young adults in their twenties roaming the streets, it didn't look like they'd been interested in school for years. Poverty may be a bitch to overcome, but it has to start from within, first. Willful ignorance will kill a person faster than anything else.

It is near impossible to choose the right words for reflection. While memories and feelings pound away at me profoundly, to anyone else they are mere tales. Maybe I am romanticizing my past and adding too much value to friends I only knew for such a short period of life. But if so, fuck it.

Better to remember the past fondly than be haunted by it.

NATHAN TIMMEL

7 – I REMEMBER HARRY HOUDINI

When I was ten, my parents let me make my first real life decision.

We were moving again, leaving Milwaukee and heading north to Appleton, Wisconsin. Gainful employment awaited my father at a local hospital, where he was going to work in the field of administrative training. My mother, tired of having lived hand-to-mouth for so long, had responded to an advertisement back in Milwaukee; the department store J.C. Penney was training and hiring systems analysts. My mother always had a strong analytical mind, and in 1978 could sense that computers were the wave of the future. She took the course and was quickly hired. Thus when the family arrived in Appleton, she had a unique skill set and was able to find well-paying work quite quickly.

The decision to be made was what grade to place me in at school. When I was in kindergarten, my mother stopped by the classroom one day and discovered me sitting inside my flip-top desk. I was playing with Hot Wheels cars, while the rest of the students were doing reading assignments. Asking the teacher why I was allowed to fuck around and not pay attention, she was told I was already above and beyond the rest of the class in the language arts department, and thus was given extra free time. That I may live up to my full potential, my mother arranged for me to travel from kindergarten into second grade during the reading portion of class.

Switching classrooms was unnerving for my wee sensibilities. On my first day, when everyone was ushered onto the floor and into a sitting-circle to read, I was so nervous I eventually peed myself. I didn't know anyone in the room, the kids were all bigger than me, and for some reason the combination of these two factors intimidated me into thinking I should hold my bladder rather than ask for a bathroom pass. I remember lying on my stomach, my book in front of me, and pressing my little hips down as hard as possible to create a pressure that would hold the urine in. Naturally, this did not work. Several drops became a trickle, the trickle became a torrent, and soon I was soaking in a puddle of my own piddle, with my clothes absorbing it like Bounty and creating a nice wet spot from nipples to knees across my front.

My memory has blanked out whatever reaction the rest of the class had; they may have laughed, they may have been disgusted. I was ushered into the office and my mother was called to bring me fresh dressings. Sadly, I had to return to the classroom again the next day and finished out the year among those I had embarrassed myself in front of.

Though that auspicious beginning should have been the end of my days of advancement, instead I was soon bumped up entire grades. When the time came to move to Appleton I was technically ready to enter junior high. I would have been ten and entering seventh grade.

My parents were split on the issue. I was very young and would easily be the smallest child, and therefore the largest target. Even the weakest of nerds would be able to vent their hormonal frustrations onto me. But, as I had already completed the grades my peers were in, why would I mingle among them a second time? After discussing it heatedly amongst themselves and coming to no conclusion, I was asked what I wanted to do: enter fifth grade and be around kids my own age, enter sixth grade and be slightly younger but mostly compatible with those around me, or venture onward into a Doogie Howser future of academics and angst. I've no idea why I chose the way I did, but I opted to start all over and meander into the fifth grade at Franklin Elementary. Maybe I was shooting myself in the academic foot, but I really didn't care. Losing all my Milwaukee friends was upsetting enough; to be the smallest kid in class again wasn't appealing to me in the slightest.

Arriving in Appleton, the biggest shock to my system was the small-town societal psyche. In Milwaukee, I had been a minority in my next-door-to-inner city neighborhood; in Appleton, all was white. With the city's relative seclusion from the outer world, then, came fear and judgment. Even among those at my young age were racial epithets tossed about with a surprisingly casual nature. I was confused; everyone was complaining about "niggers," when there weren't even any black people in town. As a child, I had no idea what impact media portrayal played on people's beliefs. If you have no interaction with a race, religion, or sexual orientation, yet are exposed through your television set to either gross stereotypes or only the most negative of events, you will form a perception based not in truth, but limited exposure. Thus you will consider yourself aware while remaining utterly ignorant—an interesting irony.

Donna White had been my first schoolyard crush, back at the 38th Street School in Milwaukee. A cute little blonde, she taught me the importance of athleticism and alpha male attitude by favoring David Sutphen over me. David was going to be the next Pelé, while I was, well, not. Learning from this rejection, upon discovering Melanie Marceau, who became my second classroom crush, I quickly signed up to play soccer that I might impress her. Unfortunately, soccer wasn't exactly as popular in Appleton as it had been in Milwaukee, and I was reaching for the low rung on the jock-oriented totem pole. Even worse, upon first meeting Melanie I believe I said in the worst French accent possible, "Ah, Marceau, eh?" and pantomimed a bit, probably the "I'm in a box" routine. At the time, I took her look to suggest she heard the bit all too often, but I'd go on record today and guess she had no idea who Marcel Marceau was and thought me an idiot.[1]

Despite my idiosyncrasies, over the course of the school year I wore Melanie down, and in summer actually got her to go on one

---

[1] I would not learn from this experience and subsequently shot myself in the foot often around women I was attracted to.

date with me. I cannot remember if she went begrudgingly or willingly, but it was my first date, and it was every bit as lovely and embarrassing as first dates are supposed to be. My mom drove me to Melanie's house, where I got in the back of the car and Melanie sat up front. While I did my best not to die of mortification, the two females proceeded to bond in a way utterly confusing to me. They chatted away happily, and I sat in back thinking, "Melanie, don't you understand? That's my mom! She's old and not cool!" Having Mom there was bad enough. Having my date enjoying her company was a fate worse than karaoke with your co-workers.

In my mind, I wanted to be driving. It would have been phenomenal had I, at my young age, been able to roll up all on my own. Melanie would have been so impressed, she probably would have let me get all the way to second base, which for an eleven-year-old boy like me meant rubbing a girl whose chest had the same curvature as my own.

To make matters worse, my mom had to buy the tickets for our mid-day matinee; the theater wouldn't sell seats to such young kids. No idiot I, I wanted to take Melanie to a scary movie, one I had just seen and knew would startle her right into my waiting arms. I had already seen said scary movie thanks to my mother being delightfully out of touch with the world around her. The previous weekend, she took the family to the theater, but had done so without researching exactly what it was she wanted everyone to see. There was a blockbuster of epic proportions currently running riot across the country, a family friendly crowd-pleaser that was getting great reviews and selling out theaters everywhere. Approaching the ticket booth with her husband, son, and six-year-old daughter, my mom told the teenage ticket clerk "Two adults and two children for the new Spielberg film she'd heard about." Well, this was enough for anyone, especially a teenager with a sense of humor, to send us into the horror movie Mr. Steven had just produced. The woman buying the tickets hadn't, after all, said, "The movie Spielberg *directed*."

It wasn't until the paranormal researcher began tearing his own face off in a bathroom did my mother ultimately understand we were seeing the wrong movie. As quickly and quietly as she could, she escorted my terrified and crying sister out of *Poltergeist* and into the lobby. My dad and I refused to budge, however, and remained and had a dandy of a time.

The next day, three of us returned; my dad had enough of the movies for one weekend and stayed home. This time, tickets to *E.T.* were purchased. It was near sold out by the time we arrived, and we could only find two seats together. Amanda and my mom took them, leaving me to my own devices. Now, the funny thing about embarrassment is that it's something we generally do to ourselves. As I was sitting all alone, there was no way for anyone in the packed theater to know I was my mother's son; any actions of mine would in no way reflect on her, sitting rows away with her daughter. Yet at the movie's climax, as E.T. withered away and several hundred people started crying, a high-pitched laugh rose above the sniffled din, and my mother began to grow beet red. She recognized the sound, and worried people would somehow connect it to her.

Had I known what emotional manipulation was, I would have yelled, "It's a goddamn puppet and a contrived scene!"

Though I didn't know exactly how, I still understood I was being toyed with, and I wanted nothing to do with it. As the puppet passed away and hordes of people blew their runny noses and wiped teary eyes, I laughed harder and harder, to the point I almost peed myself like second grade reading period.

So the allure of *E.T.* was lost on me, as was the fun of *Poltergeist* on my mom. Sadly, when it came to my first date, Melanie enjoyed neither the scary movie nor my company. She didn't jump into my arms at the most terrifying of times, nor did she deem to dine with me a second time; that one moment with her was also my last and if I said it didn't bother me, I'd be lying. After all, I still remember her name thirty years later.

Nichole Bouvery was my second Appleton crush, but I was too obnoxious for her to ever consider being seen with a single time. As strange as it sounds, I cannot recall the name of the one who did become my first girlfriend, which happened in Appleton in sixth grade. I can remember her brown hair, blue eyes, and spotted freckles, but no name rushes to the forefront of my memory. It's funny how failure and rejection remain ingrained, while success fades with time.

Soccer having been a poor choice of "cool" sports, as the days grew short and winter entered into the northern Wisconsin town, basketball became my next attempt to attract women. I remember playing one game, for about one minute, and shooting one basket for two points. Whether or not I put it in the correct basket or for the opposing team I do not know. That minute aside, I was a benchwarmer. Being new to the sport meant I wasn't all that good at it, so I practiced, and practiced often. Even in the cold outdoors of lunch and recess I'd be on the playground performing shooting drills in my jacket and boots, snow be damned.

This obsession ultimately led to my demise. One winter day, I launched the ball into the air, and like most of my shots, it was well off the mark. The basketball lodged itself between the rim and the backboard, leaving me to climb up and knock it free. Unable to retain a grip while wearing gloves, I barehanded it up the cold metal post and reached for the stuck sphere. Dislodging the ball was easy enough; getting down was not. While my original plan had been to simply let go and fall to the ground, I had not anticipated my bare skin freezing lightly to the pole, making my dismount ungraceful to even the most forgiving judge. Instead of descending feet forward, I managed to somehow pull my hand back in alarm, and then twist and drop to the concrete elbows first.

What happened next comes in snippets to my memory.

I landed hard and heard a crunch emanate from my left elbow. Springing to my feet, though no doctor, I could tell something was wrong given the new geometric angles my jacketed arm was sporting. I started to scream, and made a crying dash for the school. Only one teacher was my nemesis back then, she who thought I was a brat and a troublemaker, and while she was probably right, she was also a bitter, uncaring woman. As I ran screaming and crying past her, one arm holding the malformed mess of the other, she actually grabbed my collar and said something about not being allowed inside until the bell had sounded. I pulled free and bellowed "FUCK YOU," something she later tried getting me suspended for, and darted into the office where I passed out.

According to my mother, the school, acting in its infinite wisdom and compassion, didn't call an ambulance, nor did they dial her with worry in their voice. The direct quote was, "You need to come pick Nathan up, he hurt himself at recess." That's all they would say; no sense of urgency was given. In a panic, my mother rushed out of work immediately and made her way to the school.

According to her best estimates, I sat in the office with a shattered elbow for anywhere between an hour and ninety minutes before she arrived. Apparently the school didn't exactly call my mom immediately, but had discussions as to how to appropriately proceed when they saw me enter the office screaming for help. By the time my mother walked through the door, I was sheet-white, deliriously fading in and out of consciousness, and couldn't walk. Though my mother should have demanded an ambulance on the spot, she was too panicked and enraged and had the principal help her carry the chair I was haphazardly balancing on to her car. She hurried me to the emergency room—something only a half mile away—where the doctors looked me over, then quickly re-set my elbow, saying it was merely dislocated.[1]

Fortunately for my future, I was an inquisitive little bugger. As they were rolling me out the door in a wheelchair, releasing me back into the wild, I innocently asked, "So it's okay that I can't feel or move my hand?" Whoever was pushing me paused in his stride, did a one-eighty and then and only then, decided to order some X-rays.

What they discovered was the bone had not just dislocated, it had broken, and several pieces were pinching a nerve in my arm. A few more hours of remaining in such condition would have rendered my left arm a paperweight. Had I not opened my mouth and asked while still in the hospital, had I become inquisitive only after arriving home, any small little accident of fate and the nerve would have died and today I'd be typing these words one handed.

They prepped me for immediate surgery. I was nervous, but all I remember was lying on a gurney, staring at the ceiling, and a man telling me to count backwards from ten. I made it to nine. After that I awoke to a lovely plaster cast outside my arm and two metal pins inside it. My injury allowed me to quit basketball, which was fine by me, as sitting on the bench hadn't done much for my self-esteem (or my love life) anyway.

While I wouldn't actually go back and change a single day of my life, I do sometimes smile and wish the elbow event had occurred later on, say in the 1990s. By then my family and I would have known all about lawsuits. In the early 1980s, however, suing the shit out of someone wasn't yet the fashion trend it later became. So the school system that should have been bankrupted by a settlement, the hospital that could have made my family millionaires due to negligence? Well, they both existed to be continually incompetent to others who needed help.

---

[1] "Tis but a scratch!"

When I finally returned to school several days (or weeks, my memory fails) later, my broken arm covered in a cast and held together by pins, I again encountered the one teacher I was at constant odds with. As she had actually tried to prevent me from seeking help the day of my injury, when I came across her in the hallway on my first day back, frustration, snotty arrogance, and a feeling of self-righteousness overtook me. I held up my barely-mended arm and shouted, "I told you I was hurt!"

Without flinching, she shot back angrily, "Do you want detention tonight after school?"

How some people are allowed to work around kids is beyond me.

* * *

Living in Appleton gave me my first glimpses into what would become my living, though there would be no way of knowing that at the time. Stand up comedy first reached my eyes and ears in those young years through the ignorance of the elderly and the excitement of youth. My maternal grandmother still lived fifteen minutes away in Kaukauna, and we visited her often. I would find out much later in life that grandmother's house was used as an escape both from and for infidelity, as well as arguments at home, but as a child it was an opportunity to be doted upon. Kaukauna, for the record, is a town whose major industry is a paper mill. If you've never smelled one, it is not unlike the scent of a freshly filled diaper. Thus every time we visited my grandmother, I thought she had had an "accident," something that I feared came with advanced age. But, she made me Oscar Meyer cheese-filled hot dogs whenever I wanted, something my mother frowned upon, so I always forgave the smell for the reward of my taste buds.

My grandmother, like most spoiling grandparents, would usually take me shopping for little nothings. We generally went to the dime store downtown, but on occasion sojourned at the mall where the biggest and best presents lay. It was on one of these jaunts I made one of the most important discoveries of my life. My favorite present was always music, and on one occasion when perusing through records I browsed my way past an album with an attention-grabbing cover. The picture was of a denim-clad man. He was bearded, had long hair, and was faking one finger up his nose. The man was sitting on a dunce's chair in front of a chalkboard that had the words "Class

Clown" inscribed on it. I had no idea what it was, but I knew I wanted it. I was a class clown, and picking your nose was hilarious to me. Seeing as there were no "Parental Advisory" stickers back then, I pointed, my grandmother shrugged, and I took home a copy of one of George Carlin's most infamous records. To say it was beyond my eleven-year-old sensibilities would be saying too little; the first time I listened to it, I don't think I even knew what to think. I was, however, utterly transfixed by the words. Words about war, America, and racism. Words about life, living, and growing up different. Dirty words. Very dirty words. Seven, dirty words.

I listened to the album obsessively, memorizing every syllable and nuance. I absolutely absorbed the seven dirty words contained within the oil-based grooves and proudly repeated "shit-piss-fuck-cunt-cocksucker, motherfucker, and tits" to all my peers. I started trying to figure out exactly what stand up comedy was, and in 1982 in a wonderful little bit of manipulation, convinced my mother that seeing the R-rated *Richard Pryor Live on the Sunset Strip* would be a great "mother/son" moment to share. It was playing at a single location, the Viking Movie Theater in downtown Appleton, and I reveled in the big screen experience. Hearing George Carlin had been one thing; seeing Richard Pryor's full body interpretation of ideas and words was sensory overload. I loved it all and wanted more.

I enveloped myself in the world of stand up comedy. I'd been watching Saturday Night Live since its inception and had recently discovered SCTV, being enthralled with its opening credits showing people throwing televisions out their windows. I was a Steve Martin fan, and though I could sing *King Tut* by heart and would often walk around with a shuck and jive, proclaiming to be a "Wild and crazy guy," in my mind Steve Martin was a TV/movie star. I knew little of his actual touring comedy, but I got the bug up my butt to learn. I wanted to learn about his early career and what other comics were out there. Though I never remember entertaining the thought, "Hey, I could do this, too!" my interest in comedy would last until high school. Once there, music and the bass guitar would surpass comedy in the foot race for my spare time.

There is only one other memory of note from my two years in Appleton, and it wobbles forth from my mind randomly. It is a wistful-to-me tale that only gained relevance in my adult years, when an unexpected source gave me powerful insight to my childhood. During our time in Appleton, my father was able to bring a small, suitcase-sized movie projector home from work. As chance would have it, the local library had old, silent movies on film you could check out as easily as books. So it was in the eleventh year of my life I discovered Buster Keaton, specifically his classic *The General.* I'd thread the film between the two spinning reels and project it onto my bedroom wall. After the climax of the bridge collapse, I'd stop the movie, scan-rewind it to watch the structure rise from its ashes, then watch the trestles tumble earthward again. I tried inviting friends over for movie adventures, but they always seemed bored by the silence and confused by having to read a movie like a novel, so the magic of silent movies remained an event flown solo.

How this relates to my adult years comes from an accidental occurrence. One day, somewhere in my late twenties or early thirties, I visited my father at the same time one of his oldest friends was in town. As the man shook my hand and clapped me on the back, he jokingly said, "Well it's damn fine to meet you! I honestly didn't think you actually existed. When you were a kid, all I saw when I stopped by your house was a closed bedroom door. Your mom and dad would say they had a son, but you could have fooled me."

Though he was laughing, there is always truth in humor. Every time I moved, I grew less and less inclined to make new friends. I don't think I made a conscious decision in this action, I believe it is something I started feeling internally: friends were made for losing. There was no point in meeting people, as sooner or later I'd move and have to start all over. Naturally, I then began spending more and more time holed up in my bedroom. I don't think I was in training to be an outcast like some may prepare for a marathon, but I do remember spending an awful lot of time in my bedroom watching movies, reading comics, or listening to music. As an adult, then, I have always been at ease in circumstances many people find uncomfortable, such as dining or seeing a movie alone. Though I didn't know it at the time, I was actually preparing myself for the life of a stand up comic, he who travels alone from town to town, from hotel room to hotel room, isolated.

And alone.

INTERLUDE

MILWAUKEE, WISCONSIN

1996

8 – AN ATTRACTION TO THE IDEA OF ME

On December 26, 2008, I spent the day in Madison, Wisconsin, with my mom and fake dad. Fake dad had been doing some winter cleaning and came across an old floppy disk of mine, God knows from where. He said it contained a single Word document, titled "Psycho." My jaw dropped, and I became exceedingly excited. In the days before blogging, I would write several long letters each year about my life, then copy and mail them (at a decent expense) to friends around the country who may or may not have been interested in receiving such nonsense. "Psycho" was the tale of a woman who had a unique obsession with me in 1996, and I thought any physical copy of the tale had been as long lost as the mental version in my muddled mind. To have it back made me giddy.

I have had two stalkers in my life: one was an Asian exchange student, someone I met while tending bar at a restaurant called Nancy's; the other was a woman from South Dakota. Someday I'll sit down and do my best to recall what happened with the Asian sensation; "Psycho" was the story of the Midwestern woman.

For those unfamiliar with the year, in 1996 the Internet was in its infancy and email was foreign to most people. When I described what is known today as forwarding, it was something done with amusement and interest; today, most sane people delete forwards without even opening them. Texting hadn't yet been created, and public phones were still prevalent, as cell phones were not. The Fox network was considered a rebellious challenge to the big three networks, and when I mention taping The Tick, I was using one of those now wonderfully antiquated objects, a VCR. Computers used floppy disks to store files, and they couldn't hold even a quarter of what a flash drive could today. That my mom and fake dad had a computer in 2008 that still accepted floppies tells you how often they update their technology.

That background given, here is the story as it was written fresh off the experience.

* * *

It started innocently enough. Then again, I suppose it always does, doesn't it? A friend of mine in Boston, Peite, has a mailing list on his computer. Not a standard mailing list of addresses, but one of those Internet email deals you've probably heard so much about. I am on this list, so is she. "She," is Jean, a thirty-year-old graduate student in South Dakota. This is our story.

Peite's list has a theme to it: humor. If you happen across something amusing, such as a joke or story, you electronically send it in, and he zaps it to the people on file. One day I decided to offer a story I had written about Peite and I and our contributions to a sperm bank in Boston. The story was quite well received; I got many compliments from strangers. Jean was one of the complimenters. Trying to be considerate, I sent "Thank You" notes to anyone who wrote kind words my way. Jean replied to the thank you, and a dialog was started.

Common interest came by way of "The Tick," a Saturday morning cartoon show. Living in South Dakota prevented her from watching the program regularly, as no Fox affiliate existed there; South Dakota ranks somewhere behind most third world countries in this case. I was taping the show on a regular basis and offered to send her a copy. She was ecstatic. I was amused. We began emailing one another daily, and my eyebrow raised itself in curiosity; could this be one of those "internet romances" the media said was popping up across the country? I sent the tape, and with that she got my physical address.

Two weeks later I received a female condom in the mail. I thought it an odd thank you, as our interactions had never been anything more than friendly to this point. Though we got along easily, we never discussed any sort of sexual attraction and had never even exchanged photos. Regardless, a note was attached to the condom: "Save this, I'm coming to visit." In my imagination, should this woman happen to look like, say, Jennifer Aniston, I would be in heaven. No dummy I, I did not believe fortune would smile upon me so and became cautious. I asked Peite if I should be afraid. His single word reply was, "Yes."

Jean manned up first and asked for a picture. Playing off Peite's chillingly brief warning, I sent a photo of me skydiving. My head was bowed and the protective, centimeter-thin helmet—obviously designed to protect my noggin should my chute fail to open, sending me 10,000 feet to the ground—covered my face. It gave no indication of my looks and was half joke, half identity protection. Jean emailed me that she loved the picture and hung it in the middle of the living room she shared with four other roommates. They told her I was "something special," which alarmed me more than Peite's warning. Not only had I no idea how I was being described to warrant such a compliment, but I hadn't really told anyone about her, because there was nothing to tell. I was exchanging emails with a random woman, big whoop. To me, she was a neat correspondence with a hint of "could-be" fantasy and nothing more. Meanwhile, I was common knowledge to her friends? Creepy.

The condom was followed by a string of erotic messages left in my email account, each more graphic than the one before. They began to detail what she wanted to do to me and how her visit was going to be "the best night of my life." Though several weeks had passed since I sent my picture, the favor had not yet been returned, a definite cause for alarm.

I immediately cut the number of messages I responded to in half. Where to this point I had always dropped a decent reply to each message, I now began sending short notes to roughly every third one. A detailed account of actions she was going to perform on my body would receive, "Just got home from work, got your letter, am too tired to write" from me. She used my shying away as a sign to double her efforts, and began sending two or three emails a day. Some would be violently angry, decrying her life and position in it, then mid-paragraph would make the most bizarre switch into how I would rescue her from her mundane existence. "I hate my job! Everyone I work with is stupid! I need a vacation. Can you perform oral sex for hours on end?" is a direct quote.

I was told my picture was masturbation material and received a second package in my physical mailbox. Nothing sexual this time, thankfully, but instead several small, peculiar, gifts. According to the accompanying note, she thought of me when she saw each item and decided to buy and send them. One trinket was a bizarre looking plastic mug shaped like a cartoon vampire, another was a Frankenstein refrigerator magnet. As I didn't have a particular affection for old horror movies and had never hinted to her I might, why these reminded her of me I do not know.

I decided I needed to stop being a pussy and just get everything out on the table. Where was she going with all of this, what did she look like, and what did she think we had going on? Her reply was hesitatingly honest, and I felt somewhat ashamed.

"I am a little self-conscious because I am surrounded by women who eat red meat all the time and never exercise," she wrote. "It wears off on me and makes me lazy."

At the end of the note, she dropped a mini-bomb; "By the way, I'll be visiting friends in Wisconsin in two weeks, and on December 28th we're going to road-trip to Milwaukee to meet you. You better be home, or else..."

The "or else" was probably meant playfully, but my reaction was immediately opposite: I told her I was going to be out of town. At the time, it was a true statement. There was a photography exhibit at the Chicago Museum of Contemporary Art by Andres Serrano I wanted to see, and several friends and I had plans to spend several days visiting the Windy City.

She was furious. "ASSHOLE MOTHERFUCKER BASTARD SHITBAG ASSHOLE MOTHERFUCKER" was left in my inbox the very next day. "I AM COMING TO MEET YOU WHETHER OR NOT YOU WANT ME TO, SO YOU BETTER FIND TIME FOR ME TO DO SO BEFORE SUNDAY!"

Her "How to Win Friends and Influence People" response sealed the near-contracted deal for me. I told her my schedule was full and that there was nothing I could do about it. I received another thrashing. I also received an oddly timed surprise. On the same day her second email of vitriol and spite found its way into my inbox, my actual mailbox received an envelope from her, something obviously mailed before I told her I wouldn't be around for her arrival. Gathering up great courage, Jean had finally sent her picture, along with the note, "Just wanted to send something so you'd know who was knocking at your door when I get there."

The picture was only her face, which was enough. As cruel as it sounds, it was a face that created the phrase, "...only a mother could love"; I probably gave Homer Simpson's fear bleat upon gazing upon it. As much as I knew I was dealing with an easily wounded ego, I was also concerned with the tone of her emails and entirely sure I didn't want to end up in a room alone with her.

Two weeks passed quickly, with Jean continuing to insist she was going to meet me no matter what. My plans to visit Chicago fell apart, and I couldn't think of a thing to do for the weekend. I picked up a couple shifts at work and figured that in the least I just wouldn't answer my door if at home on the 28th.

As if on cue, at one o'clock that very afternoon, I was home alone, sitting in my room reading when the door buzzer went off. Someone was in the lobby looking to get in. I closed the book and frowned; no one ever visited my apartment. The door buzzed again—I got up cautiously—and the door buzzed once more. I decided against answering, and instead walked into the living room and sat down behind a plant next to the window. From this vantage point I could see the front porch; my apartment was on the first floor, and when the person left I would know who it was. If friend, I would knock on the window, bid them back and explain my childish behavior. If foe...

The door buzzed. Two minutes had passed since the first sounding; this person was persistent. I remained seated. Two more minutes passed filled with intermittent buzzing. I was now irritated. When phoning someone, how many rings do you wait before deciding no one is home? Twenty? Fifty? This was absurd. What was running through this person's mind? "Maybe someone's home, but in the shower. If I keep ringing, they'll get out and come to the door!" I have no idea.

After six minutes, the front door to the building opened. My mystery woman from South Dakota stepped out, shook her head, and walked away. As cruel as it is to say, her description of being "lazy" told only half the story. She was roughly 5'4" and topped 250 pounds easily. I could see where the self-esteem problem came from, but the aggression that went with it is what had me on edge. I went back to my room and resumed reading. Moments later the door buzzer went off and was held for ten seconds. While not a long time in most cases, when listening to a door buzzer it is an eternity. I closed the book and wondered; had she somehow seen me step away from the window? Three short bursts filled the air, followed by silence. I began reading again and after several hours took a peek out the window, didn't see her waiting for me, and went to work undisturbed.

This action repeated itself several times a day over the next few days, all the way until December 31st. On that evening, I was at work, and it being New Year's Eve, my first call of order was to get as much stock ready as possible. The reservation book was full, and we expected to go through liquor like mad. I was in back of the restaurant grabbing bottles when the word came, "Nate, there's someone here to see you." My mind went on red alert. Never before had words spoken so innocently filled me with dread. Had I ever told Jean where I worked? Sometime in the beginning of our correspondence? She often referred to my early mailings, so I suspected she saved them. This was not good.

"Who is it?" I asked.

The hostess didn't know.

"I'm busy," I said flatly and resumed pulling stock for later.

The hostess shrugged and walked off.

Five minutes later my partner bartender came back, "Nate, your sister stopped by and dropped off some things for you."

I thumped my head against the wall. I was now officially paranoid.

After my shift, I went out with co-workers, and finally returned home and got to bed around 6:00 a.m. At 9:00 a.m. my alarm went off; I was driving to Oshkosh for the day to visit a friend. I got up from my three-hour nap and called him, checking to make sure he was awake and such. The door buzzer went off in the middle of our brief conversation. I excused myself from the phone and hung up. Something didn't feel right.

I took my seat by the window and waited. The door buzzer sounded repeatedly over three minutes, then paused. Moments later, I heard my neighbor's door open; the lobby security door soon followed suit. Two seconds later the other apartment door closed and a knock came upon mine. This was not a knock used to wake a person on New Year's morning, but a cautious one, almost too quiet to be effective. A tapping, if you will.

It was repeated several times over the minute it took me to gently tiptoe across my creaky living room floor in order to reach the door. Once there, I looked through the peephole. As sunlight was pouring into the inner lobby behind the figure, all I could see was a dark silhouette. It was very large. I couldn't be 100% positive, but who else could it be? I stood bent over, watching every move, listening to every knock resound a mere inch from my head.

My breathing was light. The figure leaned over. It looked into the peephole from the outside. We were now watching each other separated only by two inches of wood. I had to fight back laughter over the absurdity of the situation, but held my position tight, so no movement could be seen as she peered inside.

Then the doorknob turned.

Slowly.

Quietly.

Methodically.

This wasn't a person casually entering a room. Someone was testing waters here, easing their big toe in to check for warmth. The knob reached its crescent and paused. Gentle pressure was applied; the door creaked in my ear. Someone wanted in. The door moved a millimeter, was halted by the lock, held in place a moment, then relaxed. I returned to the peephole.

The figure stood with slumped shoulders, a defeated pose. Its head looked up and to the side, as if in thought. It retreated into the light and was exposed; Jean looked out the lobby door, back at the apartment, and left. I got dressed in twenty seconds and left out the back, un-showered and unconcerned by that stinky fact.

At 10:32 p.m. I returned to my apartment; it had been a good day. At 10:35, the door buzzer fired. Fortunately, I never lighted the entire apartment when entering. I had walked in, gone to my room, and flipped only that switch on. My bedroom could not be seen from the front of the building, which meant there was no sign of life in the apartment. I stole to my window seat in the darkness. The buzzer rang again. A minute later, my now nemesis left; her waits were growing dramatically shorter. I sat wondering how many times she had repeated this action throughout the day.

The next morning I woke around 8:00 a.m. and lay in bed for about thirty minutes alternately cursing my alarm clock and swatting the snooze bar. I heard the phone ring in the living room, and laughed as my roommate Jack rushed for it in a panic. Something about a ringing phone made Jack trip over himself to answer it, as if one day he would receive the winning lottery call from a beautiful nymphomaniac waiting to give him great sex along with his million dollars. I heard Jack's "Hello?," and a moment later he was knocking on my door.

"Hey," he said, opening my door with a look of caution across his face. "The phone's for you. Some woman I don't recognize. Should I say you aren't home?" Jack knew the situation. How could he not? My South Dakota stalker had been buzzing our door for five days now.

I half-thought it over. It was Tuesday. Jean had mentioned she needed to be back in South Dakota this very morning. She left so quickly last night it looked like a last ditch effort.

"Nah," I replied. I had never sent Jean my number anyway, and I wasn't listed in the phone book. "Probably work calling me in to cover for someone."

"You sure? I'll run interference for you."

I waved him off, which I'll call an early morning not-yet-awake mistake.

I took the phone from Jack.

"Hello," I stated.

"Is this Nate?"

I didn't recognize the voice, and therefore knew exactly who it belonged to. Was I fucking retarded for taking the call? Jesus.

"Yup."

"Do you know who this is?"

There was giddiness in her tone.

"I've got a pretty good idea." I said flatly, suggesting this was not interesting to me.

"Okay, well, I'm coming over now."

"Don't bother."

"I'm right around the corner on a pay phone, so don't even try to get away. I'll only stay for a minute, there's something I want to give you."

I paused. This would be difficult to get out of. Even if I hung up, she knew I was home. I decided she was *not* getting into my apartment. I'd meet her in the lobby.

"Whatever."

"Okay, great, see you in a minute."

She hung up. I shook my head. This would all be over soon. Why hadn't I let Jack tell the person I wasn't home?

Within minutes, the sound of knuckles rap-tap-tapping our front door reached my ears. My first thought was, "Great, the lobby must have been unlocked." My second thought was, "Little pig, little pig, let me come in."

I walked into the next room and placed my hand on the knob; one more thought flashed through my mind, a manic Jack Nicholson shouting, "Here's Johnny!"

I shook my head to clear all thoughts and opened my door only as wide as my body; inviting her in was not on the menu.

Jean stood in the hallway; she was smiling, almost beaming.

I frowned and gave a squint of irritation in greeting.

"DON'T SAY ANYTHING!!" She shouted, raising one hand in alarm. "DON'T SAY ANYTHING!! I don't want to ruin the moment!"

Ruin the moment?

She put forth her hand; in it was a small Tick figurine.

"DON'T SAY ANYTHING! Just take it... NO! DON'T SAY ANYTHING! Don't ruin the moment... just stand there with my gift. My gift to you..."

I held out my hand, now more confused than irritated, accepted the action figure and watched as she clasped her hands together as if showing the joy of a child.

"DON'T SAY ANYTHING!"

This seemed to be all she could get out.

"I'm going now... I just wanted to meet you and give you that."

She waved and moved away from the door.

I stood there dumbfounded; I would have been unable to say anything had I even wanted to.

She left.

I closed the door.

What the hell had just happened?

That's where it ends. Jean never emailed me again, and I never reached out to her. I asked Peite about her once and he had little to say, so I let it go. The only thing that remained to be explained was her phone call, which Jack had a theory about. I cannot prove or disprove it, and I can't say that I disagree with his thoughts. Jack said she called two minutes after he walked in the front door that morning. This is the amount of time it would take a person to get to the pay phone around the corner if standing in front of our building. Was she watching? Standing in the cold or sitting in her car, waiting for someone to enter the apartment? Jack was roughly my height and we both had dark hair, so from a distance...

Either way, the phone was in Jack's name. She must have looked him up after not finding my lovely moniker in the white pages and grabbing his off the mailbox in the lobby. I didn't need Magnum P.I. to figure that out for me.

So, as Vonnegut wrote, it goes.

BLOCK III

AGES 11 – 22

NATHAN TIMMEL

9 – PERSPECTIVE

In seventh grade, I stopped smiling.

I know this not from memory, but from interviewing my parents. Right before I turned twenty-nine, five days before my birthday, in fact, I went through a very painful breakup. Actually, I was cheated on, then dumped. It was the worst period of my life, and the experience shattered my psyche like glass; my thoughts scattered into a thousand unfocused tangents I could not maintain a grasp on. To regain clarity, I began seeing a therapist who suggested I talk to my family about the childhood I lived, yet did not remember. She rightly realized that my pain was centered deeper than a breakup, and wanted to find its source.

The incident was like an out-of-body experience; talking to my parents about my life was like having a movie described to me, the only problem being *I had actually seen the movie*. I lived my childhood. I just had no recollection of it.

My parents had been divorced for several years at the time I was in therapy and were at the height of their verbal assaults on one another. "Your father..." my mother would begin a sentence. "Let me tell you something about your mother," my dad would randomly insert into a conversation. They agreed on nothing, so when in separate moments both wistfully turned their head, looked into the distance, and said, "In the seventh grade, you stopped smiling," I took notice.

* * *

At the start of that school year, I moved to Oconomowoc, Wisconsin. My father had accepted a job outside of Milwaukee, and instead of living there, he wanted to commute from the town of his own youth. Unresolved issues from childhood traumas had him choose the city, though it would be years before he could look back on this decision and see that.

I also say I moved, because that's what happened. Due to the start date on my father's job and the closing on the house in Appleton, a decision needed to be made: I could either head to Oconomowoc ahead of the family, live with my paternal grandmother Evelyn for three weeks and start the school year with all the other kids, or I could attend school in Appleton for three weeks and then transfer.

My parents believed if I showed up on day one, it would make the transition easier, and I would make friends more quickly. They thought I could avoid being shut out of school cliques and decided I would move ahead of the family.

While this is sound reasoning on paper, Oconomowoc was a very small town. It was the kind of town that feared the outside world. Citizens supported God, guns, and the Republican Party, and though they had little interest in facts or world news, people knew what felt morally right, which is all that mattered. In that environment, all social circles had been determined long before junior high. Though I started seventh grade on day one, I was already an outsider. I hadn't come up in grade school with everyone else, and was therefore unknown. Add to that fact Oconomowoc was a town founded on wealth, and the school was divided by the elites with money, and those without or "not enough"; middle class in Oconomowoc was considered peasant status by some. The fact I was a lone child living with an octogenarian woman did not help my standing, even though it was a temporary situation.

I was already accustomed to spending time at my grandmother Evelyn's house. Several years earlier, when my parents had separated and I lived with my father in Milwaukee, he would put me on a bus and send me to her on weekends I didn't visit my mother. As an adult, I once talked to Dad about this. I had no real memory of my rides, yet sometimes had flashes in my mind of sitting alone, looking out a window and nervously counting stops so I wouldn't get off early. I asked him if I had ever been on a bus, and he said he had no recollection of it. I then brought the same question to my mom, who immediately grew somber. She told me that as Oconomowoc is only forty-five miles from Milwaukee, when my father had to work weekends and couldn't find anyone to tend to me, he would put me on a Greyhound and send me off to his mother's house for care. I would sit behind the driver, a child of six, and ride for several hours and through numerous stops from city to city. Like Linus, I carried a protective blanket and hugged it tightly to my chest the whole ride. Evelyn told my mother it broke her heart every time she met me at the station. I'd get off the bus and look frightened and lost, clutching the blanket tightly. A child among a sea of adults, much less the cross section of society that uses Greyhound, is a grooming ground for anxiety to a small child.

After the three-week layover at my grandmother's, my family arrived and I was able to join them in our new home. As embarrassed as I was living with a grandparent, I quickly saw that arriving in town early was indeed the better option; my sister Amanda started her school year three weeks late and was ostracized from the outset. While "small town values" may play every election cycle, in reality, small town generally means small mind and the community was unwelcoming to the outside world. Amanda never found a crowd to run with and eventually had to transfer to a private school in an attempt to leave the stress of spending her days friendless and surrounded by judgmental, ostracizing eyes.

I fared better, if only because I was older and in a larger school. Though there were several elementary schools in the district, they all flowed into one junior and senior high. While my sister was secluded, I swam in a larger pond. Fortunately, there are always more average kids in any school than there are popular kids, and they are usually more welcoming to people joining their ranks than the in crowd.

If I had thought Appleton was overrun with racist attitudes, I hadn't seen anything yet. Some students spoke openly of the Ku Klux Klan and their parents supposed involvement with it. Whether this was youthful ignorance or real boasting I do not know, but whispers of secret meetings in cornfields were often within earshot. I do remember a moment in 1988, my senior year, when I attended the homecoming football game with several classmates. By then I'd lived in the town six years and had made a few friends. Several were among the crowd I was walking with, while others in the clique were those I knew by reputation, but not friendship; I would soon learn more than I ever wanted to know about them.

The rival team that night drew a healthy following, a handful of which were African American. This seemed to set off a lynch-mob mentality among some of those I was with, and heated threats to go over and "get" or "teach them niggers a lesson" were spewed out like venom. At some point, alternately disgusted and irritated, I tossed out the comment, "Jesus Christ, this isn't fucking Howard Beach, let it go."[1]

Dumbfounded stares faced me, though to this day I'm not sure if it is because I didn't join in on the little hate-fest, or because I referenced an event that had made national news for several months the previous year, yet had obviously never made it anywhere near their radar. For whatever reason, whether I confused them into inaction or they were all bluster from the start, no rumble (or lynching) occurred that night.

The neighborhood I lived in was on the far reaches of the city limits. We technically had an Oconomowoc address, but were far out in the country, surrounded by farms. When I lived there, it was peacefully under-developed, with vacant lots both next to and across from our house.

One of the first things I noticed was a family down the road. They had a boy a year or two younger than me, and more importantly, a pool in their backyard. Lacking such an amenity at my

---

[1] Howard Beach was famous at the time for having had a group of angry white teens attack several African American men whose car stalled in the neighborhood. One man was killed.

own residence, I wanted to befriend the boy for two selfish reasons: one, I had no friends. Two, he had a pool.

Whether he suspected being used by me or whether I just didn't fit in with the family I do not know, but I remember being very unwelcome at both the house and in the cooling waters of their aquatic playground. Today my memories suggest it was a little of each; the mother of the household was an overbearing tank of a woman, and she seemed to think her mission in life was to protect her son at all costs. Thinking back, I don't remember him having many friends, either.

Spurned and angered by the rejection, I revenged my honor the only way a seventh grader could. For several weeks, I urinated into several two-liter soda bottles until I had filled them all. One night, under cover of darkness, I stole away to the forbidden pool and emptied my waste into it. The next day, watching the family splash about, I smiled a wide smile. I knew that chlorine and chemicals probably killed any personal germs I happened to pour in, but I still felt I had done my karmic duty in a way. "What goes around, comes around" is a popular phrase, and that day I was my own come around.

* * *

At some point during our time in Oconomowoc, my parents began sleeping in separate bedrooms. By this point in their marriage, each had colored a bit outside the lines of their wedding vows. Who did what first doesn't interest me much, but the events led to a coldness between them, and that was a presence known in the house even without their acknowledging any problems. The guise they erected to sell the sleeping scenario to Amanda and I was that they kept separate hours: mom had to get up early, dad had to stay up late, so it made nothing but sense to sleep apart.

I began disassociating myself from my family, and my bedroom became an isolationist's paradise. I arranged the furniture so that even within the walls of my bedroom, there was a separate layer of protection. I placed my bed very close to the door, creating a narrow space for entry. At the foot of the bed, I placed my dresser not with its back to the wall, as is custom, but perpendicular to it. The back of the dresser faced the door, so as you entered my room you were then blocked. Using those two items, I created in essence a wall that divided the room in two; behind it, I placed my desk. To get to my desk you would have to either crawl over my bed or shove the dresser aside. I know few parents interested in such gymnastics, and was thus left to my own devices whenever I needed to escape while still at home.

As an adult, I can look back on my home life and draw the definite parallel between unhappiness there and my actions at school; I was young, confused, and angry. So if I arrived in Oconomowoc surly, it only got worse as my first year in town progressed. At school, I battled daily with the band teacher, George W. I cannot recall what started it all, but there was friction between us, and I refused to back down when confronted. Eventually, my behavior landed me an entire semester's detention. An administrator named Charlotte grew so tired of dealing with me she put an end to my lunch period. Every day I brown-bagged it to the school office, where I sat in a side room and ate in silence. Char may have thought she was punishing me, but in reality I couldn't have cared in the least; I had no friends and therefore no one to eat with. Sitting in the office may have looked like torture, but to me it was escape. Better to eat away from everyone than to do so alone while in a cafeteria full of happy children.

My first friend in Oconomowoc was Alan M. His stereotype of living on the wrong side of the tracks cut so close to home he actually lived on the tracks; they ran right past the border of his backyard. Though not a teen interested in real estate, even then I surmised having locomotives disrupt your days and nights did not a decent property value create.

Alan welcomed me in friendship, and was in fact the person who introduced me to alcohol. As luck would have it, my first experience left me with little desire to drink again for several years. Alan somehow procured a bottle of Peppermint Schnapps, and we proceeded to down it as fast as possible. Disgusting, yes, but quite remarkable when the eventual sickness overcame our tiny bodies; rarely have I ever thrown up so much while the thought, "But my breath is so minty fresh!" ran through my head.

Alan and I drifted apart within a year; where I didn't enjoy the effect alcohol and other drugs had on my system, Alan did, and charted a course of experimentation I didn't want to follow. Economic status attaches itself to social stigma, and Alan was looked at as a "dirtball," as they were called back then. Whether or not this led to his troubles with liquor and the law I do not know, but the path he stumbled down was one filled with blackouts and bloodshot eyes.

We finally reconnected in our senior year of high school. Alan was starting to screw his head on straight, sober up, and wanted nothing more than to graduate with everyone else come spring. We ended up in chemistry class together, and every day had exchanges where I'd bust his determined balls.

"I'm gonna do it," Alan would state. "I'm gonna graduate."

"Not gonna happen," I'd say with a laugh. "You'll never make it."[1]

One night, as happens in rural areas, Alan was driving down a long country road after work when another vehicle crossed the yellow line and smashed into Alan's car.

He was killed instantly.

The next day, my chemistry class had an empty desk, and the air was uneasy. The desk was like a magnet. All eyes were drawn to it, all thoughts on the boy who had been sitting in it just yesterday.

In the middle of our session, the P.A. system sparked to life and called for a moment of silence to honor Alan. Many around me squirmed uncomfortably, as if in the presence of a ghost. Before I knew what was happening, I opened my mouth.

"Well," I offered, causing several people to jump. "I told him he wouldn't graduate."

I have been called a very dark comic, which I am fine with. I believe it is in our bleakest moments we need a little levity.

* * *

Eighth and ninth grades were a blur to me; I made a few friends, but again, ate alone if we ended up on separate lunch hours. My maternal grandmother, Elaine, lost her husband—a man I don't remember at all—and moved to Oconomowoc to be closer to her daughter. She rented an apartment directly across the street from the junior high and on the same side of the street as the senior high, so every day until my senior year (when school policy finally allowed students to escape to McDonald's or Burger King) I made my way to

---

[1] Male bonding often involves the best in negative reinforcement.

her house for lunch. Somehow, going to a grandmother's house for lunch was much less embarrassing than having to live with one.

The most important year of my youth would probably be 1984. That summer two bands entered my consciousness in ways that would forever alter me. Metallica released the album *Ride The Lightning*, while Slayer offered up *Haunting The Chapel*. My friend (and future Best Man) Brian Jones brought Metallica to my attention, and of all people, my father introduced me to Slayer.

College radio is an eclectic creation, where students create their own programming and offer it to the public. It's the only place on any radio dial you can hear Miles Davis one hour, and then German Industrial Techno-Polka the next. My dad has always had an obsessive-compulsive relationship with swing bands, and would record a weekly jazz program played on a somewhat-local college radio station; though we lived sixty miles from the transmitter, our receiver was able to pick up a decent signal. My dad happened to tune in early once and heard a compelling noise emitting from the stereo speakers. He called me into the room, and I was transfixed. I'd never heard anything like it before, and the best way to describe the sound would be to say I was experiencing raw power in the form of music.

I called the college and asked what the hell I was listening to, and the bright-voiced and bubbly girl told me the wonders of the band Slayer; the song *Chemical Warfare* was currently filling my ears.

The discovery of Heavy Metal was probably both my salvation and undoing regarding my teen years. Like a gang, the metal community offered me a place to fit in and surround myself with like-minded miscreants; confused youth who felt like outsiders joined the metal movement to feel the sense of family they didn't get at home. Attending a concert was a wonderful form of cathartic release; body slamming in a mosh pit released all aggression in a safe and controlled manner, and you went home cleansed. Though a pit might look violent from the outside, in the 1980s all was organized inside one. If you fell, hands immediately lifted you back up. No one was interested in damaging anyone else, which all unfortunately changed in the 1990s. As I was leaving metal behind, what had started as a movement for confused youth transformed into a violent culture, with skinheads showing up at concerts and setting out to inflict pain using balled fists and steel-toed shoes. Everything in life is cyclical, though, and soon enough Nirvana would arrive to give teen angst another safe outlet for its youthful confusion.

Only now do I understand the stereotypical nature of my existence from back then, that of a typical teenager. I craved attention and acceptance, yet only wanted it on my own terms. I did not want to dress like everyone else, vote like everyone else, or think like everyone else. In response or reactionary mode, I began wearing black T-shirts, torn jeans, and long hair. In classic silly psychosis, I began pushing people away, yet at the same time angrily wondered why they weren't embracing me. In my unwelcoming small town, instead of working to break the social barrier, I lashed out at it. When everyone else was listening to the bubble gum rock of Bon Jovi, I was supporting the hardcore likes of Exodus. My favorite bands sang about dark topics, like Satanism. While I had no interest in the occult or devil worship, the fact I wore the shirt of a band who sang songs about it was enough to scare the conservative segments of society that thrived in Oconomowoc. The more I altered my appearance from the norm, the more I was an outcast. The more I was an outcast, the angrier I got, and the further I became isolated. It was a vicious cycle very normal to that of the average teen, and I unfortunately carried the anger into my twenties.

I do, for the record, have happy memories of Oconomowoc; it wasn't all "woe is me" bitching and feelings of persecution. Though I remained a virgin until college, I was at least an aural witness to a friend's deflowering.

One thing no adult should ever do is entrust a teenager with the keys to their house. It doesn't matter how straight-laced the child is, it's all an act. When given William Wallace's freedom, teens act as irresponsibly as possible.

A neighbor of a friend of mine went out of town often. When this happened, my friend was told to bring the mail in, water the plants, and turn the lights on and off at night, so the house would not be an attractive target for thieves. Naturally, we used the adult-free zone as a party house. People would be called, beers would be marked,[1] and merriment had.

---

[1] As beer was difficult to come by, everyone marked beer cans with their initials. If you ran out early, you had to barter or buy more from your friends. Once, returning to the scene of the crime several months after our previous mixer, my friend Mark looked in the fridge

For one such gathering, we were lucky enough to attract some of the fairer gender. Most of our parties were sadly all male, making the attendance of women quite the treat. At some point of intoxication, the possibility of strip poker was tossed out, and the girls accepted the proposal. To a point, that is. There's no honorable way to put this, so I'll just out and say: we boys cheated. Everyone was drunk, so it was fairly easy to distract whoever needed distracting in order to win a hand. Well, the women weren't stupid, but they were shy, and when each came to the point a key article of clothing needed to be shed, they demurred and departed the game.

We booed, but what could we do?

Only one brave lass remained playing, and she did so only because she had a crush on another member within the circle. She also entered the game with a plan: when it was her turn to start exposing flesh, she said she would do so, but only alone with her object of desire. Again, we booed in protest, but we weren't about to cock-block a buddy. Everyone slumped their shoulders and accepted the loss. But, being young, drunk, and stupid, several of us gathered together our own idea.

We made our way to the master bedroom before the burgeoning couple could, and someone stole into the closet while I whisked myself under the bed. Once there, I wondered how I thought I was going to get a glimpse of bare breasts from such a stupid vantage point, but a mind drenched in alcohol rarely makes sound decisions.

The chosen one and his girl entered the bedroom, talked, kissed, and climbed onto the mattress. I lay underneath it all, cursing my stupidity.

Mr. Closet couldn't contain himself, and after several minutes of stifled giggles burst both into laughter and the room. The girl shrieked, Casanova laughed, and the drunken intruder stumbled away the best he could.

Now I was alone among the happenings.

---

and pulled a beer can from the back. On top were two letters, DP, for "Dan P." No Marine he, Dan left one behind, and it sat in the back of the family's refrigerator for months waiting to be claimed. Had they found it, I'm sure it would have been the end of our partying ways: "Honey, why does one of our beers have initials written on it in permanent marker?"

The couple resumed kissing, and after a few minutes, as clothes started hitting the floor next to the bed (and quite near my head), I realized something big was about to occur. Naturally, I started giggling, but silently so. Mustering up the best short-range power punch I could, I began messing with the enraptured couple. As their rhythm started, I shoved up on the mattress with as much force as possible, bouncing it off its frame and allowing it to slam down again.

The girl, using all her deductive reasoning skills, finally exclaimed: "I think someone's in here with us!"

No shit?

Somehow, using drunken reasoning like, "I'm kind of inside you right now," my friend convinced her they were as alone as Tiffany and they continued their trip into adulthood.

Meanwhile, I continued being an ass. I pushed on the bed, I pulled on the sides of the sheets, I did everything I could to be a jerk. But even I have limits. My friend was having sex, the oft dreamed of event of life for a teen, and I was ruining it for him. To allow him to finish in peace, I shimmied out from under the bed, stood, and left. To my credit, I didn't look back, either; I didn't want to see his lilywhite ass doing any gyrating. I did toss out one final giggle, though, saying in a high-pitched, mocking voice, "I think someone's in here with us!"

Oh, and for the record, no, no one washed any sheets when all was said and done. I believe the bed was re-made, but that was the closest they came to cleaning. The happy homeowners upon returning after their nice vacation? They got to sleep in the dried remnants of sweaty teen sex. How very crustilicious.

* * *

Another happy memory from back then is the Burger King parking lot on Friday nights. With nothing to do but cruise the short strip the town had, kids would end up in several parking lots to sit, smoke, and try to look tough while only succeeding in looking bored. A typical evening involved a combination of me with two friends—Ed and Mark—plus any extra person we might be hanging out with. One night we had an extra companion by the name of Tom, a man I will not identify any further due to the nature of this story. I was crammed into the back seat with Tom, when a knock came to the window. Outside was an attractive girl from another town. Ed was in the front, so he greeted the most polite, petite thing you'd ever seen who had come a knocking.

She leaned in and said to Ed, "Could you please pull your seat forward?" which he did. She then leaned in across me and said, "Hi, could you lean back a little please? Thanks." I gave her access, and what came next was quite unexpected. The polite, kind girl let loose a series of sailor-like swear words and started beating the unholy hell out of Tom. Added to the hilarity of the juxtaposition, she kept her civil nature going during the assault, alternately berating Tom, then asking Ed or I for more space quite courteously.

She dragged Tom out of the car by his hair and preceded to slap, punch, and kick him in the sac until he could take no more. I believe once he was lying on the ground, she actually spit on him before leaving. Maybe she threw food or a drink too, that I cannot recall. Naturally, the rest of us stood around both stunned and amused; there is little in life more funny than watching a friend of yours get his ass handed to him by a random woman.

Turns out, Tom had attempted his teenage best to perform on her orally, but was so disgusted by the yeast infection he found when he got to her holy hole he threw up right then and there. She had been laying back, eyes closed, and ready for the generated warmth an orgasm offers, and instead was painted upon by his half-digested dinner. As if that wasn't enough, Tom then spread word of the infection far and wide, giving her a reputation she didn't quite appreciate.

The beating was a just response, I suppose.

* * *

After graduation I spent very little time in Oconomowoc. I rarely visited and skipped my five, ten, and fifteen year reunions. Age, understanding, and distance, however, brought me to attend the twenty. A few months before that milestone, I stumbled across my senior yearbook. It was the only one I bought, and I almost forwent that purchase, too. I discovered the yearbook while in my mom's basement searching for other items, and looking it over is actually what kept me away from the previous gatherings. I would get an invite, pick up the yearbook, ancient resentments would bubble up to the surface, and I would take a pass on seeing my old classmates. Perusing the pages before the twenty gave slight hints it could do the same once more, but after so much time had passed, most of the names and faces meant very little to me.

In high school, I watched the rarified air the popular breathed in, and it all seemed so real and significant. After two decades, those who were deemed gods above mere mortals like me were disappeared from places of importance. Athletic heroes lionized by female eyes were never propelled into the elite arena of professional sports, and many weren't even able to cut it at the college level. They had been enormous fish in a very small pond, but once they left that realm of safety reality sent stars into their eyes with a quick jab to the nose; no halo of success encircled their head. It made me very happy my life didn't peak in high school, as happens to some.

I found it funny, though, that even looking over the snapshots after so many years I could still feel a twinge of the stings that once upset me. Little nothings, like having only two pictures in the whole yearbook. I have the standard class photo, and one candid shot. The candid was from something the administration called "Harmony Week." In a typical "We have no idea how to relate to kids" manner, the faculty dreamed up a melding week where students from all social rings and teachers were to express togetherness. On Monday, everyone received special T-shirts with the word "Harmony" on them. We were told to wear the shirt on Friday, when everyone would participate in an all-school picture to be taken on the football bleachers. Given I received the shirt several days in advance, I figured I had to alter mine slightly. I took it home, bought an iron on decal, and created the universal "anti" sign, a circle with a line through it. I placed it over the word "Harmony," creating an adverse effect to the administrations' idea. On Friday, students giggled and pointed, and teachers frowned and murmured. Someone took a shot of me wearing it in study hall, and somehow it was cleared to go the distance in the yearbook.

While two photos are the complete yearbook documentation of my high school existence, every other page is filled with the pledge kids for "Up With People." Today, the number of times I'm in my yearbook means nothing to me. Back then, it made me feel like a friendless failure. There are, however, two notable omissions the yearbook staff made, most likely because each did the most unspeakable of acts: showed the school up.

The first exclusion involved success. Discovering Slayer and Metallica got me interested in playing music, and while the six tiny strings on a guitar were too much for my limited dexterity, four fat bass strings suited me just fine. I joined a heavy metal cover band; our name was Euthanasia. I had researched the topic for speech class and the topic and name seemed cool. We covered songs by Judas Priest and Iron Maiden, and played them very well. Toward the end of my senior year, we got permission to perform with another band in the upper gym. I took flyers to every school within an hour radius of Oconomowoc and promoted the hell out of the concert. When all was said and done, around 700 people attended, and a decent chunk of that number came from outside our district. In my promotion, I capitalized on that ever-present plight of the small town teenager: there's nothing better to do, so come to Oconomowoc and rock out! The concert was better attended than a half-dozen school sponsored events, and it pulled in more cash than several of them combined. Naturally, neither Euthanasia nor the concert were mentioned in the end of year wrap up, while each failed school idea—Winter Carnival! Madrigal Dance!—received its own display page in honor and memory.

The concert, for the record, was also my first moment of clever, shrewd (or conniving) thought. In researching my future show, I attended a performance several months beforehand and learned something very important. Taking the information into my own production, I approached a member of the other band on the bill and schemed my way into success.

"Hey man," I said. "Just so there's no bullshit about anything, if you guys wanna headline, we'll be your opening act."

"Cool!" my mark said, falling for it.

The night of the show, everything happened exactly as I had seen several months earlier: Euthanasia went up to a full house. In the 20-minute intermission between acts, the audience left to go out and get drunk. Of course they did; it's what teenagers do. The second band went up to about 40 of their closest friends and I feigned ignorance. Golly! Who knew this would happen?

A quick side note involving the speech class mentioned earlier: when choosing a topic for persuasion, I discovered, as said, euthanasia. I was immediately interested in the pro side, believing those with terminal illness should be allowed to decide for themselves whether to live within the confines of a hospital bed or to die with some form of grace and dignity. I researched the topic diligently and presented my discoveries to my classmates. I think I scored well.

At the end of the year, everyone was allowed to choose both a style and topic for their final speech. A bright-eyed young classmate I won't name decided he had been so offended by my pro-human rights words, he gave an anti-euthanasia delivery as his closing counter.

To this day, I wish I had heckled him. Mocked his speech for what it was, emotionally trite nonsense. The lecture amounted to nothing more than him standing in front of the class, breaking down in tears, and openly weeping while saying, "I love my grandpa, and I don't want anyone to kill him."

I didn't have it entirely figured out then, but this was a shining example of the small-town attempt at understanding a complex problem. If you couldn't think rationally, you did so emotionally. Instead of listening to what I had said about personal choice, he countered with crazed murderers storming hospices and dragging the elderly out of their beds. The sad part is, people like that grow up to be not just voters, but usually single-issue ones. "Well, this person might have a better economic policy, but I don't like his stance on gay marriage, and my life is so pathetic I have to worry about what two people do in the privacy of their own bedroom."[1] His tears worked wonders that day, and probably convinced many his side was the chosen one. Emotion is understood and absorbed easily, while reasoning and logic require thought, and not everyone is up to the challenge. But I digress.

The other item unmentioned by the yearbook was one I expected to be neglected, as there was no way it was going to be promoted or even acknowledged. Bored with the traditional school newspaper, several students created an underground paper, *Banzai*, which was humor based. After the first issue, I was lucky enough to be approached by its creator, a quiet boy by the name of Sean. He asked if I wanted in, and did I ever.

Was what we put out genius? Of course not. It was lowbrow, teenage humor, and therefore exceedingly popular. We satirized the easy targets of any high school—the adulterous teacher, the administrator rumored to have had a facelift—as well as the student

---

[1] I'm paraphrasing here.

council and the student newspaper, the latter of which went on to honor us with an editorial on how funny we weren't. The more we wrote, the more people spoke out in anticipation of the next copy. To remain anonymous and not get into trouble, we would release copies by leaving them stacked in bathrooms between classes. They would then be discovered and passed around. The first couple issues had some people taking a copy, while others would naïvely ignore them. Before long, though, students making the initial discovery of a new issue would hoard the whole pile and give them to friends, leaving the unlucky in the lurch. As we had no budget, we weren't making very many of the Xeroxed little buggers, and the more popular *Banzai* became, the more valuable an issue became.

What's funny is, though only the people actually in on the production knew I was a part of it, I was a suspected ringleader from the start. Such was the reputation I had with the administration. Char, my wonder-love administrator from seventh grade, was promoted to high school supervision, and I immediately came under watch of her scrutiny. I was called in for questioning and was told "all eyes" were on me. Which, I hate to say, I was used to. I was lucky enough to be suspected any time anything out of the ordinary happened on school grounds. Only once was I was actually guilty of the offense they accused me of.

In tenth grade, the school sponsored "Flower Day." You could buy a rose and send it to anyone you wanted, including faculty. That year, I was not too large a fan of my English teacher, so I dictated a little "Holy-Christ-are-you-awful" note to my friend Mike, and he sent it to my teacher without signing any name. That evening, a town detective arrived at my front door to give me a stern little lecture. In his words, they had done a "handwriting analysis," and it was determined with conclusive proof I had written the awful note that had so traumatized the teacher. I wasn't in trouble, but I was being warned to straighten up.

I may have been young, but I've never been entirely clueless. I knew the reason I wasn't in trouble is because they had nothing on me. At the same time, I couldn't defend my innocence by saying, "You're full of shit. I know the handwriting doesn't match, because I had my friend Mike write the note." My evidence of innocence would have also been my confession, so to speak.

The funny thing is, aside from wearing torn jeans and black T-shirts, there was almost no reason for me to have the reputation I did. I didn't fight, do drugs, vandalize, or even skip much class until my senior year. The flower incident aside, I pretty much stayed out of everyone's way. It all traced back to my seventh grade battles with the band teacher: I was branded then, and in a small town, that was enough. I was so disliked by the administration that one assistant principal actually told me he saw jail time in my future. To repeat, I didn't fight, do drugs, vandalize school property, or do anything really outside the scope of normal teenage behavior, but was still looked at as someone who would probably go to jail.

What's sad is, in my senior year, I eventually started acting the way many people already saw me. I still didn't drink much, maybe four times the whole year, and I didn't do drugs other than trying pot once, but I began ditching class as often as possible. I was probably more a punk in my final year of high school than at any time previous, but by then, it was almost a knee-jerk reaction. "If you're going to treat me this way, then I'm going to act out so I deserve it."

Returning to *Banzai*, many with power like only to leave behind a happy, shiny history, so no mention of the raucous little newspaper was given in the yearbook. Thing is, though I was looking for credit for my actions at the time, I have to admit the memories are all that is important anymore. The concert was a damn good time, regardless of recognition. *Banzai* was done more out of boredom than for the history books. In a delicious turn of irony, though swept under the rug by "proper" students in charge of the school legacy, several issues were time-capsuled for the twentieth reunion. In the end, the students who actually enjoyed *Banzai* honored it.

The reunion was in my eyes a reminder of humanity and humility. No one was a god anymore; time had ravaged the few who might have believed they once were. Everyone had become adults; some got married, and some focused on careers. Some got divorced, while others had children of their own. A few hadn't changed much, but their arrogance or ignorance didn't faze me anymore. Instead, I felt a sort of pity. A little for them, and a little for society. There's something sad in seeing someone who never moved more than 90 miles from the place of their birth, who never traveled or got to experience a different culture. They maintain the same small town small-mindedness they grew up with, believing their idealized and isolated vision of the world is better than the real one.

Some of the ignorance I saw that night was willful; Oconomowoc had a lot of wealth when I lived there, and it was interesting to observe those children of privilege as adults. Most had low empathy levels, and they addressed social problems with a sense of, "Life is pretty good, I don't understand why people complain so much." They felt having been born into money meant they somehow earned it.

Catching up after twenty years was quite therapeutic; almost every old resentment I had ever held melted away immediately. I got to speak with people who had only been on the periphery of my awareness in school, and found many life stories entirely enthralling. Many had gone through the exact same emotions, fears, and anxieties; many had felt as secluded and awkward as me. Some had even skipped the earlier reunions, for the very same reasons I had.

The stimulus overloaded my senses; there were so many faces and names and nowhere near enough time to honor each person with a conversation. Some I have stayed in touch with, while others dissipated into the ether once again.

Going into the evening, out of everyone in my graduating class there was only one person I felt I could do without talking to, even twenty years later. Of all my antipathies, I wondered how many I had invented; who had I disliked because I thought they disliked me, and vice-versa? But regarding this one man, I couldn't escape the lingering feeling he was a douchebag, even if I couldn't remember a single specific reason why. I figured if I didn't bump into him, I would be entirely OK with that. What follows should be all too predictable.

I arrived at the reunion a few minutes before everyone was sitting down to dinner, where Brian Jones had saved my fiancée and I seats at his table. I pulled my chair out, sat down, and scooted my butt in, and directly across from me was the one person I wasn't interested in seeing.

He didn't acknowledge me, so I didn't acknowledge him, but I did stare intently and attempt to second-guess my emotions. Why did I not like him? Was I inventing an anger I should just let go?

It did make me smile to see he was going bald in the worst of ways; his forehead had expanded to the crown of his head, and he was desperately holding on to a few remaining wisps of hair. I focused on him through both the welcoming toast and opening pleasantries. I searched my memory for any negative he had done to me, and came up blank. Then, the house lights lowered. The reunion committee announced the start of a slideshow, one to honor classmates who had passed from this world into the next. Pictures of faces I once knew appeared, aged, and then disappeared forever. Each had a story of life, family, and loss.

Mere moments into the presentation, as many were watching with reverence the montage of our departed, my nemesis leaned in to the person sitting next to him and began talking: "So, this morning was great. I shot two under par on hole thirteen..."

And it hit me.

That's why I didn't like him.

He *was* a douchebag.

He had *always been* a douchebag, *was still* a douchebag, and would *always be* a douchebag.

Relief comes in many forms, and remembering why I had unkind thoughts about a fellow human being was as tasty as a cool drink of water on a hot summer day.

As of right now, I have no plans to attend another reunion. Despite the fact I genuinely enjoyed myself at the twenty, one gathering might have been enough. But you know what? If I ever hear the awkwardly balding douchebag, he who felt the need to discuss his golf game during our classmates' memorial, died? Well then, I might have to reconsider. Maybe I'll go just to talk about some mundane aspect of my life during his slideshow. Hell, maybe I'll even Bluto Blutarsky it up and cough "Asshole!" as his picture passes across the screen.

And I will smile as I do so.

10 – THE GAY DAYS OF BOSTON

After graduating from high school in 1988, I had absolutely no clue what I wanted to do with myself. Actually, I take that right back. I wanted to be either Sting, or a bass player in a heavy metal band. I just had no idea how anyone went about obtaining such a career, especially living in Oconomowoc, Wisconsin. Having been in a high school cover band didn't exactly lend itself to snagging a recording contract, and when it came to writing original music, we hadn't even tried. A possible lack of ambition may have played a role in our apathy, but more than that, we were entirely ignorant in the ways of writing unique material.

For reasons that escape me now, I didn't want to go to college. At least, not immediately. I had just left behind the rigid structure of authority and oppression known as public education, and didn't want to turn right around to re-enter it. Many teens view college as an escape into partying and carefree existence; having had such a shit time from 7th through 12th grade, further education sounded like more repression. The problem was, without college, what was I going to do with my time?

My parents, though not forceful, were firm: if I didn't want to go to college, I would have to get a job. Not a summer job, such as the ones I had been busying myself with through high school, but an actual job. My mother looked over the open positions list in the JC Penney warehouse; I applied for one and was hired.

Back then, Penney's held hidden ownership of a home shopping network. People would watch TV and order away to their heart's desire, not realizing they were getting re-labeled items from the company catalog. I became a packager for this division. Every morning I'd rise somewhere around 5:00 a.m., drive 30 to 45 minutes to Milwaukee, punch in, and receive a list of wares. I would walk the aisles of stock, pick what I could reach and wait for those on forklifts to grab the upper items. Everything would be taken to my station where I would box, protect with Styrofoam peanuts, and seal and label every purchase. The ready-to-ship article would be placed on a cart, and when the day was done, all carts were pushed to the docks to be loaded on a truck and shipped off around the country. I believe I knew five minutes into my first shift that this was not my idea of a fun future.

With every day came the same routine. Pick an order, pack an order, go on break, repeat. The monotony seemed destructive to the soul. At least to my soul, that is. There is a reason people get blind stinking drunk every Friday night; trying to blank out the previous five days of their lives is usually it.

There were those around me who hated every moment of their existence while at work. Others treated the job as if nothing more than a paycheck, and there were a magical few who had the wonderfully sunny disposition that allowed them to enjoy their jobs. They performed the daily routine happily, and lifted my spirits when I was less than enthused with my lot in life. I befriended an upbeat forklift driver named Rick; he became my lifeline to inner peace amidst the lifeless drones and angry workers. We would talk Monty Python and other such comedic gems throughout the day, and his presence gave me the focus I needed to maintain a sense of sanity while there.

One year in the warehouse was enough. I worked fall through Christmas, was laid off after the holiday, and was re-hired a few weeks later after I filed for unemployment, something done at my father's behest. According to him, it was another life lesson, more real-world experience. In my mind, I was nineteen and laid off from a job I didn't want in the first place, so filing for unemployment felt like taking advantage of the system. I thought I should just move on and find something to do with my life that actually interested me, so after working through the summer, that's exactly what I did.

In the spring of 1989, I applied to and was accepted by the Berklee College of Music in Boston, Massachusetts. Music still interested me, while regular college did not. Plus, working for a year gave me both a good foundation for the tuition and decent insight into the importance of focus. I was aware of several former classmates who had partied hard their first year away from home, and were thus removed from the college roster due to poor grades. Unlike some of my peers, my enlightenments came while earning a paycheck, not while paying tuition.

The only thing I remember about leaving for Boston is my mother crying. It comes to mind because I thought it so odd. I had no idea what empty nest syndrome was, and I was just leaving for school, not dying. As our home wasn't all that happy a place to be, I thought it a good thing to be getting out. Little did I know then that staying with my father was something my mother had done strictly for my sister and I. Fifty percent of her reason for being under his roof was now out the door.

I arrived at Berklee full of excitement and hope. Delusions of rock stardom shone in my eyes, and I believed the institution was the entrance to the world of music I desperately longed to join. As with much expectation in life, the letdown came fast, and hard. I discovered the school was more a technical institute than anything else, one teaching proficiencies rather than creativity.

It's entirely unfair to sum up my educational experience with one story, but I'm going to do it anyway. I took a course, Songwriting 101, where students were taught structure. The idea was to learn how to write a song for any medium, be it jazz, pop, or a thirty-second commercial. I was unhappy from the start, believing the whole point behind music was to lose structure, not enforce it; if you were creating a song, you did so with what was inside you and if that had you coloring outside the lines of conformity, so be it. I cite the Red Hot Chili Peppers as an example: in his autobiography, Anthony Kiedis states that when the band first started, they had no idea how to write songs. They wrote what they felt, and that was that. Later on, they learned about verse-chorus-verse-bridge-chorus pop construction, and began to use it. Personally, I find more originality and interest in anything and everything the band did from *Freaky Styley* through *Blood Sugar Sex Magik* than anything they've done since 1992. I didn't know why until I read Anthony's book, but that made it crystal clear. They went from outliers to the norm, which had them lose an intangible allure to my ears.

For the songwriting class, I wrote my pop-ditty and attempted my jazz standard. When it came to the TV jingle, I was struck with inspiration. While I in no way remember the melody behind my masterpiece,[1] I remember the title and a bit of the lyrics. It was either an ad for condoms or a PSA for safe sex and was called, *Baby on the Way*. The line retained in my mind is, "You slipped between her thighs, but didn't condomize, and now there's a baby on the way!"[2]

While I smiled at my little musical silliness, my professor did not. He, in fact, lectured me on inappropriate behavior in the classroom, as if I were in junior high and not an expensive specialty college. During his rant, he asked me, "What if the dean had come in at that moment? What if he stopped by to audit my class and heard that *filth?*"

"Fuck if I know," I laughed inside my head, but did not say. I sat and listened to the beratement with confused irritation, and let it go. Sadly, the professor did not.

Later that month, a teacher I did like pulled me aside and said the songwriting professor had been complaining about me to other staff members, and those other staff members were taking note. I couldn't believe it. I was attending an institution that purported being about expression, yet was running into someone petty and close-minded right off the bat. One song, and I was already on my way to becoming a pariah. The experience tainted my time there, yet at the same time sums up the school: a drummer named Barrett had the near exact same experience in Arranging 101. The professor lowered Barrett's grade for arranging his chosen song in a manner "Too abnormal to be commercial." What were they teaching, expression or conformity?

---

[1] Meaning "not masterpiece."

[2] Now you know why I'm no longer a musician.

While Berklee seems, in retrospect, to be a very decent factory for churning out technicians, I would argue it still failed on every level when attempting to nurture creativity. I still remember how good I felt when, halfway through my third semester, I realized, "I don't have to attend next semester. I can stop here and re-assess my life." That decision saved me thousands upon thousands of dollars and taught me there is nothing wrong with recalibrating your goals, even if it isn't the most socially acceptable decision.

The classroom aside, dorm life I did enjoy. I met many wonderful people who should have become lifelong friends, but have somehow managed to fade into the ether that is memory. Berklee had two dormitories at the time, and thanks to a curse of the gods I was placed in the off-campus Hemenway Building, an all-male dorm named for the street it resided on. While the sausage-fest aspect was irritating, the camaraderie was enjoyable indeed.

The place was a dump, but was beautiful to me in all its cramped, one-room glory. Three students were supposed to share each small space, but my West Virginian roommate Roy and I had fortune smile on us our first semester; our scheduled third never arrived. This was indeed a lucky break, as the room was barely big enough for one person, much less two or three. I never met the man, but I owe Ruben Scottomeyer a debt of gratitude for skipping out on his obligation to college. And yes, that was his name. My sister found it so absurd she named her first dog Ruben in honor of that missing man.

My room was on the fourth floor, and over the course of the first few weeks, a group of students from several rooms on the south side of the dorm became known as the "Fourth-Floor Posse." Silly? Absolutely. But in reflection, perfect. We were a tight band of idiots who bonded like young men are supposed to bond in such situations.

There was Estephano, an African-American Republican from Malibu. To be black and Republican was one thing, but to be a musician in a jazz school and have a conservative lean? That made him a minority in several different ways, especially among those who matched his skin tone. His roommate Rick was known for the entire year as "Condom," as he showed up as if in a 1980s teen sex comedy, with one suitcase full of clothes, and one full of prophylactics. Down the hall was a trio of cohorts: Chris, J.J., and Barrett. Next to them was a room with two students I cannot remember by name, but hilariously recall in description. By the luck of all draws, somehow two boys who were Goth before it was even called Goth ended up in the same room. They painted their windows black, wore all black, and pushed their beds together in order to snuggle at night. It is to the testament of a school of the arts two students could express themselves openly like that. People laughed and poked fun a bit, but overall accepted them for who they were. I doubt a college with football jocks would have been so forgiving.

I have no idea how friendships are made, but Barrett and I seemed to figure out early on we were going to get along well together. J.J. was another matter. He had two things going against him: a temper problem and a girlfriend out of his league. She was attractive, he was a goof, and while they made decent high school sweethearts, she began stretching her college legs immediately upon separation. She went to school somewhere across the state, and whenever he would call her dorm her roommate would say she was out with another boy. This drove J.J. insane. To make matters worse, her name was Muffy, and we all ran riot with that ammunition. J.J. stood vigilant over her handle the best he could; no one was supposed to mock the name or even allude to the idea it might have a double meaning, one rooted in sexuality and the female anatomy. Like a famous Howard Stern sketch, sitting around on a lazy afternoon, several of us started tossing out anything we could relating to "muff," just to get on J.J.'s nerves.

"Man, it's cold outside," someone would say. "I need ear MUFFS to even go to class."

"True that," another would respond. "Hey, you want to go to the bakery and get some MUFFins later?"

J.J. began to pout and scolded us, making me roll my eyes. I grabbed one of the many pornographic magazines laying around, opened it to a random page, and pointed at the lovely upside-down triangle the woman wore—this was in the days before the ubiquitous landing strip—and said, "You know what? THIS is muff! Deal with it!" I threw the magazine at J.J. and left. J.J. went ballistic. He had to be restrained to prevent him from chasing me. When he realized I was probably back in my room and out of reach, he destroyed everything around him, upending his desk and kicking the bathroom door in half. When all was finally calm again, Barrett, in a bit of inspired brilliance, got up, walked into the bathroom, closed the remaining half of the door, locked it, and took a leak as if nothing had happened. Several years after leaving Berklee and Boston, I received an update from the college; they sent out a journal listing current and previous students and what they were up to. J.J. and the company he worked for were listed, so I decided to check it out. After business hours, I called the company office and listened to the directory menu. J.J.'s name came up, and I pressed the proper digits to get his line. After his brief outgoing message and the ensuing beep, I yelled, "MUFFY-MUFFY MUFF-MUFF!!" into the phone for twenty seconds and hung up. I may not be coffee, but I bet that got him fired up the next morning.

As a collective, the posse would do silly and stupid things, such as going to the corner pizza shop at 2:00 a.m. wearing our bathrobes and pajamas. While others around us were drunkenly stumbling in from the bars, we would dine away in the corner, wearing slippers and attracting confused looks. Other stupidities involved several of us stealing away to other floors and making off with the fluorescent lighting in their hallways. Leaving our fellow students in darkness amused us, and tossing the lights out the window made for nice little popping implosions when they landed in the enclosed courtyard between the neighboring buildings. One of my favorite bits of entertainment was to leave food in the garbage can in my room, and then find mice in it after returning from class. The little buggers could get in when they smelled food, but couldn't scramble their way back out after dining. I would take the garbage can down to the first floor and tip it at the base of a door, allowing the frightened creatures to scurry under the crack and into some unwitting person's room.

Naturally, being in an all-male dorm at a school where boys outnumbered girls two to one meant very few of us were getting any of that wild college sex we'd heard so much about. Pornography was the interest of the day, and as Al Gore hadn't yet invented the Internet, free, easy access to smut didn't exist. A single television in the windowless dorm basement was available for student use, and one of my fondest memories is of a late-night porn-fest that was attempted. The absolute specifics of the evening are long gone from my mind, but the most important moment remains. The community room was separated from the stairwell by a small hallway. The television inside the community room was old school, with a knob and dials and no remote control. It was attached to an enormous and clunky 1970s-era VCR. One night, someone brought a pornographic movie to the community room. Word spread throughout the building quickly: get downstairs now, because the show is about to start. Fifty or sixty young men crowded themselves into the space and waited in anticipation. As we knew watching such content was against dorm rules, we placed two guards as lookouts; one stood at the base of the stairs, and I stood in the doorway to the community room. Should an authority figure arrive, signals would be given and the porn halted.

The event began with giggles and nervous energy; the video started amid hoots and hollers; "I'm sorry, I ordered a pizza, but don't think I can afford it... Is there any other way I can pay you?" It was every delivery boy's fantasy played out by a beautiful woman.

Naturally, when an entire dormitory of students disappears, those in charge notice. Soon enough, a resident assistant came inspecting, and from the base of the stairs my fellow guard signaled. I reached an arm inside the room and snapped my fingers, then gestured wildly, "Nix the tape! Nix the tape!" What happened next is something I will always remember fondly.

A fast-acting yet slow-thinking student leapt to his feet.

He darted to the television.

He turned the television off.

He sat back down.

The resident assistant opened the door to the community room to find fifty (or sixty) kids sitting in a pitch-black room, staring at a blank television screen.

If there were any way to represent the word "awkward" in the dictionary using the feeling in that room at that second, perfection would be indeed achieved.

There was a moment of utter silence, and then in a moment of pure genius, something so rarely achieved in life, a Canadian drummer named Pat Aldus firmly intoned, "So the bartender says..."

There was another second of silence, and then everyone just busted out laughing. Yes, the cleverest of covers, fifty (or sixty) young men had been sitting in a dark, windowless basement in complete silence, facing an extinguished television, waiting for a punch line. I believe we all got off with a stern warning on public decency.

(I probably shouldn't have used the phrase "got off" right there)

(Good times)

* * *

Money was always tight, and it was the enterprising drummer named Barrett who came across an advertisement designed to alleviate our suffering: we could donate sperm. The ad said they paid $35 a shot for something many of us were already shooting down shower drains and into tissue paper for free, and eyebrows raised in interest. The posse split somewhere down the middle on the issue; 50% said, "Fuck yeah!" where the other half played prudish and lied, saying, "I don't do that." Those of us willing to announce our private dalliances rolled our eyes; at that age, everyone masturbates, even Christians.[1]

A group field trip was organized, and sperm bank contacted. Those interested could attend at the scheduled donation time, between seven and eight in the morning Monday through Friday. We were startled and wondered if an afternoon arrangement could be worked out. It could not. The bank wanted donors in and out of the building before it opened for clients. No fraternizing with the ladies was the rule of the day, because they would either (a) discover just what miscreants were fathering their children, or (b) take an attraction to a donor and decide to get the sperm the old fashioned way. Okay, maybe not (b) so much, but the fantasies of college students are not too far off from those of pizza delivery drivers.

The group was collectively unhappy. Not only were many of us oft-times getting to bed around seven in the morning, but above and beyond that we wondered, "Who could pleasure themselves that early?" Yes, Virginia, there exists "Morning Wood," but that's generally a piss-on and it creates a different kind of release, one generally found on fetish websites. Worry ran high that no one would be able to perform at such an odd hour.

As money is still money, however, several of us decided to give it the old college try. Even if we failed flaccidly, we'd still have a laugh and a story to tell. A day was chosen, alarms were set, and bright and early one morn we subwayed our way across town.

There are letdowns in life, and there exists disappointment. I don't exactly remember what I imagined the place would be when gearing myself up for arrival, but a stale looking office building wasn't it. I had hoped for a bit of flair, or something somewhat seedy, but all

---

[1] They just cry during and pray afterwards; other than that, it's the same as the rest of us.

was cold, sterile, and professional. We were checked in, handed a plastic cup, and shown to an examination room.

Sadly, the best they did stimulation-wise was—no lie—the Sears catalog.

Again, I'm not sure exactly what my imagination led me to believe donating sperm would entail, but sitting in a doctor's office at seven in the morning attempting to achieve orgasm to bra and panty shots wasn't it. In the least, I expected the playful shame of videotapes or magazines a little more along the hard-core line. To make matters worse, they didn't even provide lubrication, something a necessity unless you're interested in chafing. Dry-jacking can be a painful experience indeed.

I struggled, and I wasn't the only one. I was actually the second person from the group to enter the waiting room after finishing, and I had taken thirty minutes. These weren't thirty minutes of "for your pleasure, ladies" blue steel. They were thirty, uncomfortable, "I believe I've made some wrong choices in life" minutes with at best a half-staff of embarrassment. To the janitor's credit, however, a side note of irony, or fun, is that when finished shooting my Mark Spitzes into the cup, I washed up using Ivory Liquid Hand Soap. Cute visual, I thought.

I wasn't alone in my difficulties; Barrett took forty-five long minutes to procreate into his cup, and others finished anywhere within the thirty to forty-five minute mark. The speediest member of our group was a tiny Cuban we nicknamed Rocco. He was in and out in under two minutes. Only our friend Peite proudly proclaimed he enjoyed the experience, and was having so much fun he decided to prop his feet up in the gynecological stirrups.[1] Peite was also the only one who admitted to having masturbated the night before, "in preparation." Only upon arrival the first morning did they tell us we weren't supposed to ejaculate for forty-eight hours beforehand, that we not deplete our reserves.

Over the course of several weeks, people rotated in and out of the donating process; I believe only Barrett and I went every time. Many were one-and-done; some gave several valiant attempts. When donating sperm, you need an extraordinarily high count of swimmers,

---

[1] Yippie-kai-aye, motherfucker.

as many die in the storage process. Sadly, we were all only average, and no one was hired on after the trial run.

Peite, by the way, was damned intelligent; I'd liken him to Oliver Wendell Jones from Bloom County. Somewhere in his teen years, a government body, CIA or FBI, I forget which, confiscated Peite's computer. They said he had broken into too many forbidden sites to be allowed to keep it. While at Berklee, I personally watched him break into NASA, right from his dorm room. He dialed up the phone company and cracked their code. Once inside the system, he routed his call through several countries to hide his location, and then ultimately phoned Houston. Peite then rooted around NASA until he found a way in.

At one point, Peite looked into changing our grades à la Matthew Broderick in WarGames, but that never came about. He set his computer up to call every single number within the local region and automatically make a note of any computer lines that answered. He was then going to figure out which one was Berklee's server, and hack into it. Maybe he ultimately decided that changing a series of grades would be too public, but I watched for a while as his computer dialed number after number in our area code.

I haven't talked to him in several years, but last I heard he was working for Richard Clarke. Peite's inquisitive nature always got the best of him, and one day after Berklee the government came calling once more. He'd been frisky with his computer again, and they had an ultimatum: work for us, or go to jail. As jail is always a shitty option, he went to work for The Man. An old professor friend of mine told me to Google his name, and then to click on images. Sure as shit, I found shots of him sitting next to people like Condi Rice and at the same table as Bill Clinton. I laughed heartily upon seeing such photos.

Though our grades never got changed, Peite helped me save money, that much I remember. For several dollars worth of materials, he was able to put together a hand-held tone generator. When used at a pay phone, it tricked the system into thinking a quarter had been inserted. I would dial any long distance number I wanted to, and when the recorded voice said, "Please insert five dollars," I would just press the device twenty times. This worked every single time, up until the one mishap when an actual operator jumped on and asked for the money to be inserted. I hung up on that occasion.

Donating sperm wasn't the only way to make money back then; medical research existed, too. Barrett, ever the eagle eye, discovered another advertisement, one offering cash to take part in experimental treatments. The medical world is always coming up with new pills with which to cure society's ills, and though I believe such things should be tested on prisoners, for some reason that's unconstitutional and a violation of personal rights. Such was my financial gain in college, as the only way to find willing subjects was to have those in need sign waivers and offer payment. Barrett and I thought it would be a place full of other college students, but when we arrived we found only the homeless and other such demoralized people milling around. Barrett bowed out immediately, leaving me to my own devices.

I had to go in two weekends in a row, each time arriving on Friday evening and staying in the facility for twenty-four hours solid. Bright and early Saturday morning, I was given pills. To this day, I'm not sure exactly what I took. The institution divided everyone into two groups: control and actual drug. You got either a placebo or the medication, and you had no idea which.

The first weekend was fine, save for the blood draws and boredom. After taking the pills, I had to give blood samples four times within the first hour, then every half hour after that for twelve hours. No technology existed to pop in one needle and then seal off the vein, they had to poke a new hole every single time. At the end of the day, I looked like a junkie, but felt fine. I figured I got lucky and received the placebo, or the drug was actually a decent thing to put on the market.

The second weekend, however, everything went wrong. It's all a haze to me now, but I remember Roy wondering how in the hell I got released in the condition I was in. At the end of the day I was shaking, with both a fever and the chills, was stark-white pale, and totally incoherent. I had signed myself out of the facility, gotten on a bus, and nearly passed out during the ride. When I made it back to the dorm, I startled everyone who saw me and went straight to bed. I slept most of Sunday, waking up only in time for dinner. Fortunately, by then, whatever was in my system had departed. I wisely decided I didn't need money that badly, and next time I was broke the payday wouldn't come at the expense of my health.

* * *

Though we were all poor and living in a male dominated school, alliances with females eventually came about. The miscreant "Condom" lived up to his name not by successes, but attempts. One cold winter day, he played the "Oops, I accidentally left my jacket at your dorm and walked a mile home in the zero degree weather" game, that he might get a second date from a girl he offended with his advances. Far as I know, it didn't work and he needed to buy a new parka.

Living in the dormitory and attempting to hook up with co-eds consumed more of our time than studying or practicing, and before the advent of cell phones and texting, placing a coat hanger on the door wasn't Hollywood invention, it was necessity. When someone got lucky, there existed no way to get quick word to a roommate: "I've got a live one, don't come home." So on rare evenings, you'd find you weren't welcome in your own room. You'd have to amuse yourself until either 3:00 a.m. (at best) or all night (at worst), finding either somewhere to wander or another floor to crash upon.

One such night, I found myself on the un-fun outside of the door. Sexual escapades were happening within, and unfortunately I wasn't invited to watch, coach, or film, so I decided to go for a stroll. It was late, and I wasn't in much of a social mood, so I meandered down Mass Ave. toward the St. Charles River and realized I had never walked along it.

The trail along the St. Charles River, at least in my neck of the Berklee woods, was depressed in setting from the surrounding topography. You had to find a set of stairs from the street down to the river, and once on the path while between two sets of stairs, you were trapped. Though it was nearing 2:00 a.m., the trail seemed well lit enough to be safe, so I made my way down and walked my westward route along the river.

This would be my undoing.

Approaching a set of stairs, I saw a man carrying a bike from the street to the trail. A quick mental calculation told me he would reach the river at the exact moment I hit the stairs. As he carried a bike, my hope was he would hop on and ride away. My fear was he would be a Chatty Cathy and strike up a conversation. Naturally, my baser instincts proved correct. I had an inner impulse tell me to head up the same stairs he was coming down, but I labeled it paranoia. Word to the wise, never neglect your niggling little spidey-senses.

Here's the thing with being in an anti-social mood: you generally feel guilty about being prickish. The bike-wielding man was actually very amiable, and we struck up a quick conversation. I began thinking, "I'm such a horrible person, not even wanting to say 'hello' to a fellow late-night wanderer." The man was, or claimed to be, a professor at either Harvard or M.I.T., one of the big-brain universities. Because of my guilt, when the eventual lag in conversation arrived I felt compelled to offer up a continuance.

"So," I asked, pointing at his bike. "You out cruising?"

"Actually," his reply began, "I was cruising you."

While physically I continued walking, my mind hit pause.

"Cruising... me?"

My cockeyed glance was enough to elicit a laugh, and an explanation.

"Oh, I figured out a while ago you aren't gay," he stated. "You're new to Boston, aren't you?"

Indeed I was.

"Well, after midnight, walking the river is a way for men to meet and hook up. Head off into the bushes, or someplace hidden."

"Funny," I muttered, furrowing my brow. "That's not mentioned in Fodor's Guide to Boston."

While I didn't mind getting hit on, especially considering it was me treading on his turf, what bothered me was the insistency with which he continued. As I was stuck walking until the next stairwell, he had ample opportunity to turn his charm on, and therefore not respect my state of being straight.

"So," he began. "Ever try it?"

"I'm no Mikey," I replied.

"What?"

"Cereal reference, never mind."

"Ever considered it?"

"Ever consider that every time the right-wing Christian agenda goes after your rights, your group argues 'biological orientation'?"

He hemmed and hawed, but had no real response.

I escaped further badgering at the next set of stairs, but I did not escape further attractions. Boston was a bit of a gay Mecca for me; I was approached often and began to mockingly shake my fist at the Heavens that I was so attractive to men, while my luck with women was sporadic at best.

In the dark ages before digital downloads and mp3s were used to sell music, Tower Records was a behemoth in the record industry. All was carried within its walls, from books and magazines, to music and movies. Of course, in 1990, movies meant big, clunky VHS tapes. Not nifty Blu-Ray or DVD discs. Being a poor college student, I'd often away into Tower Records to peruse the periodicals I couldn't afford to buy.

On one such visit, as I read my music magazine touting why the bass guitar I owned was inferior to the one displayed within its pages, a tiny fella approached me. His height fell somewhere between 5'4" and 5'6", and he was balding and had a dark, Mediterranean complexion. When he spoke, the accent was thick, distinct French.

He asked if I was a student, followed it with, "Where?" and became quite animated when I responded with "Berklee."

"Oh," he smiled, "You are musician! I am musician! I am student! We should jam together; play our instruments and create beautiful music for the world to listen to!"

While I'm not always a fan of my suspicious nature, his enthusiasm seemed a bit disingenuous to me. He continued to talk and began peppering me with questions. I answered him, but did so while continuing to read, never giving him my full attention and usually responding monosyllabically. He eventually asked for my phone number, and as I didn't have one, I told him to call the pay phone at the Hemenway dorm. It was listed in the student directory; if he were a student, he'd have access to it. If not, no loss to me.

Student or not, soon enough, the phone began ringing. My dorm room was back to back with the wall the phone was on, so several times a day someone would thump the plaster for my attention.

"Timmel! Phone!" would come muting through the wall.

"Male or female?" I'd ask, because there was always an outside chance it could be a girl, right?[1]

"Male, French!"

"Fuck him!"

"Copy!"

After two days, no one even bothered to ask me if I wanted to take the calls. The phone would ring, the answerer would hear an accent, and the phone would be replaced into its cradle. After two

---

[1] Wrong.

weeks, the French phone stopped ringing my way, and I was happy because of it.

I did finally find a willing female to date while at Berklee, and ended going out with an oboe player for several months. While we were together, I discovered I had happenchanced myself out of yet another homoerotic encounter. We were in her room, playing a game of kissy-face or something along those lines, when a flyer came sliding under the door and captured our attention.

I picked it up and read:

SECURITY NOTICE
It has come to the school's attention a man is posing as a Berklee student. He is either French or assumes a French accent when speaking and is of dark complexion. This man is not a student, and anyone coming in contact with him should notify the police.

I muttered, "Well how about that," and passed the paper to my female companion. She read it and gasped.

"That's him!" she shouted.

"That's who?" I asked.

He was, she explained, the man her roommate's boyfriend met, and met at Tower Records no less. Her roommate's boyfriend was also a student at Berklee and had taken up the Frenchman's offer of creating "beautiful music for the world to hear." He went to the man's apartment, shared some wine and cheese, and woke up on the floor with his pants around his ankles. The boyfriend stumbled away quickly, too incoherent to realize where he was or how to return police to the apartment later. He tried to make it very clear that he woke up before anything happened, and that the Frenchman was in the bathroom preparing himself, but the popular rumor became the man was in the bathroom washing up after the fact. Some people have called me overly cautious, but I'd say my suspicions of human nature have kept me safe my whole life.

At the end of the school year, we all made promises to keep in touch with one another, but life intervened like it always does. Of everyone, Barrett is the only person I still speak with regularly. When the next school year started, he, Peite, and I were the only three of the posse to return to Berklee. Regarding my love life, today I laugh nostalgically at what happened, but at the time the demise of my relationship with the oboe player wounded me. We decided to stay together romantically while apart physically over the summer; she was heading home to New Jersey, and I was staying in Boston. Naturally, her very first letter to me, landing in my mailbox within a week, was a "Dear John" notice. She didn't drop her bomb when departing, but didn't want to be bound to anyone while over the summer. Very confusing at the time, absolutely expected in retrospect.

The fourth floor did have a couple people who made a small splash in the music world. Abe Laboriel Jr. was already a phenomenal drummer when he entered the school, and several years after leaving Berklee I was watching Saturday Night Live when I spotted him playing for the musical guest, Seal. I dialed up Roy and within minutes my call waiting went off as Barrett called me. We were all watching and all amazed and proud. Several years after that, I saw Abe playing for Paul McCartney in Red Square, his famous Russian concert. Again, I was happy for my former dorm mate.

As said, I wasn't returning home. I had escaped my family and wanted nothing to do with going back. My resentment toward them had grown so deep that the following semester, as I was in an apartment of my own and didn't have to worry about the dorm closing for break, I skipped Thanksgiving. In a move of pure selfishness, I also declined to return for my paternal grandmother's funeral, she who had cared for me so often during my childhood. She had wasted away in a hospice, and I had visited her until she no longer recognized me. By the time I was in college, she was no longer lucid. When my grandmother died, she was no longer the woman I knew, and I didn't want to be a part of the procession if it meant having to see my mother and father fake it for public eyes. I felt I had already given my goodbyes, and felt that was more important than putting on a show.

Barrett decided to stay the summer, and he also felt loss that year. We lived in an exceedingly small one-bedroom apartment. It was all we could afford, and after living in the dorm, having a living room was like owning a mansion. Neither of us had a box spring or full bed, so we each threw a mattress on the floor and figured that was good enough for government work. The room was so small we were near stepping on one another constantly, which is why one event was so strange. One ordinary evening I went to bed after Barrett was already asleep. The next morning, I woke up and he was gone. I didn't think anything of it, figuring he either had to work or was off farting around somewhere. Several hours later, the phone rang; Barrett was on the other end. He was at home. Home, home. New Jersey, home. His mother had died. He got the call in the middle of the night, packed a quick bag, and jumped on an emergency red-eye flight. All without me waking up. I knew not what to say. To this day, the family has no idea what felled the mother Goodwin.

To pay the bills, Barrett and I each got a job working as security guards. Barrett patrolled a parking garage downtown and had to wear a full uniform. I was lucky; I did an overnight shift at a building that was supposed to be under construction, but they had run out of funds so I dressed casually. The builder's insurance provider didn't want anyone entering the structure, hurting themselves, and filing a lawsuit, so they hired guards. All summer I held two jobs; I loaded trucks in the early evening at UPS, then skateboarded the two miles home, ate, and then went off to the empty building. When school started, I kept this schedule as long as I could, then eventually gave up UPS and held onto the security position. Working without supervision, I figured I could do homework and practice at the building. I was right, too, until the place decided to save money by shutting off the power. The unfinished office I was in, already cold but once kept bearable by a single space heater, was now freezing and dark. Other guards sat in their car for their rotation, but I had no vehicle. I did two shifts in the pitch-black cold night then decided if they weren't going to respect me, I wouldn't respect the company. For the final few months before security was pulled entirely, I would show up at my scheduled time and replace the guard before me. I'd take the ledger, fill out all my rounds for the evening, then return home and go to bed. My alarm would go off an hour before the end of my shift, and I'd hike it back to the building to sign off and be replaced by the next worker. After masturbating, it was the easiest money I ever made.

When it came time to register for a fourth semester at Berklee, I took a pass and saved myself a lot of money and debt. With my free time, I explored the city. The Combat Zone is long gone from downtown Boston; when I lived there it was already in its dying days. Once a beacon of prostitution, violence, and drug dealing, only a few smut shops remained during my tenure. Peite, Barrett, and I would visit it when bored, and when we learned of porn stars passing through to sign autographs, I brought my bass down to be marked up. Barbra Dare was a delightfully warm person and enjoyed the process, taking pictures with fans for free. Tori Wells was bitter and bored. Someone ahead of us asked to take a picture and was scolded severely enough to have us hide our cameras in shame. Jamie Summers was just off-putting in general; she wasn't even a name star, yet was acting like a diva. I didn't like her much.

Several years later, with me living in Milwaukee and Beverly Hills 90210 a huge hit, the cute blonde with a button nose named Jennie Garth was scheduled to sign autographs at the local auto show.[1] My roommate at the time, Jim, and I treated 90210 as a home-cooked version of Mystery Science Theater 3000. We'd watch and shout our own dialogue at the screen, laughing at the silly teen soap opera. But when we saw Jennie was going to be in town, we knew we wanted to attend. Naturally, I brought my bass, and when I plopped it down for her to sign, she glowed.

"You really want me to sign this?" she asked.

"Sure do," I answered.

Then she noticed it had already been marked up.

"Whose are these?" she asked innocently of the signatures.

"Porn stars," I smiled.

Little did I know Jennie was a hard core Christian.

She frowned, signed my bass, and shoved it aside without giving me a second look. The bass was stolen several years later; the apartment was broken into and much went missing, including, and it still bothers me to this day, my Keebler Rainbow cookies. I remember arriving home and seeing the back window wide open, the screen torn. Then I noticed a blank spot where our television used to be. Frustrated, I went to assuage my anger with a cookie, and they were gone, too.

Goddamn criminals.

Anyway, Barrett, Peite, and I also went to the Combat Zone's rundown, old-school movie theater that had devolved into a porn theater. The idea being, it'd be damn nifty to see an adult movie like the good old days of porno chic, when X-rated movies made it to the big screen. The theater had been built in the heyday of Hollywood and was probably forty years old by the time we entered it. Though run down, you could catch a glimpse of what the place used to be

---

[1] Because nothing screams teen idol like "auto show."

when new. A chandelier hung from the domed, ornamented ceiling, and artwork was painted onto the outer walls. I was of mixed mind while there; on the one hand, it was nice, in a strange way, to see it still in existence and not boarded up or torn down. On the other hand, it was a dilapidated mess showing pornography. Sadly, while it might have been a theater by name, no actual film stock was present. The screen was illuminated via video projection, meaning we were witnessing grainy, poor quality porn thirty feet tall and seventy feet wide. Though that was disheartening, it was still neat watching a pimp in one corner send his prostitutes up and down the aisles. The women would occasionally stop to sit next to a mark, then either drop their head or gyrate a shoulder, depending on what he could afford. The other corner held a drug dealer offering wares. It was the first time I'd seen both businesses practiced so brazenly.

That we visited as a trio and sat together gave many of the regulars pause. They were loners, and this was supposed to be a place you went by yourself and minded your own business. When a man sat down behind us and a loud "ziiiiip" emanated from his seat, we made our way out of the theater. It was probably his jacket, but we weren't about to take any chances.

Also on the smut side of life, I was lucky enough to road trip it down to New York and visit Times Square and 42nd Street before Rudy Giuliani and Disney made that a family fun place. Barrett, his friend Michael, and I walked among the filth and smiled at the absurdity of it all. We entered a smaller shop that contained a live peep show and made our way to several respective personal cubicles.

The set up was as follows: the staging area was shaped like a protractor. The strippers were inside the half circled room with a flat back wall, and small, closet-like cubicles surrounded them along the curve. Inside each cubicle was a small, mini-window blocked by a drop visor. You put your token in, and the visor rose, allowing you to look in and talk to the two girls on display. They were bored, sitting on a couch and waiting for patrons that would pay them to either wiggle or do worse, depending on the amount. When one made her way to you, you negotiated; so much to touch a titty, so much to rub a butt. What you offered depended on how desperate and ugly you were.

Michael, for the record, was not ugly in the slightest. He was a tall, handsome black man and had women swooning over him with regularity. From our respective vantage points, Barrett and I watched as he wooed the women on display. Using muscles that I would say were fairly impressive, Michael put each foot high up on the opposing walls within his cubicle, then pushed his legs with enough outward force to both brace and lift himself to the point he could fit his manhood through the viewing slot. Though you were only supposed to negotiate enough to caress, Michael started receiving oral sex, for free, while Barrett and I laughed our asses off. I wish I could end the story with a funny account of Michael running out of tokens and the visor slamming down on his penis, but I cannot. The wise man loaded up the machine with all his money before ever attempting such a move.

That was it for my time in Boston. When spring rolled around a second time, I decided to move back to the state from whence I came. The big city was exceedingly expensive, and as I wasn't in school, staying just didn't make much sense. I didn't know what I was going to do next, but Dorothy was my name, and Wisconsin was my Kansas.

INTERLUDE

AFGHANISTAN, 2005

11 – DEATH BEFORE DYING

It began with a crying mother.

The night before my departure to Afghanistan, I was making a few calls; saying some goodbyes, receiving other well wishes, and going through standard motions of base touching before a trip. Though we humans rarely like to think of the worst that can happen in life, it is still sometimes necessary to dot all unfortunate "I's" and cross all tragic "T's," just in case. While discussing the trip with my mom, she eventually whispered, "What happens if you die over there?"

Sadly, distracted by packing, I forgot I was talking to a parent, not a friend, and answered honestly rather than carefully. "Fuck if I care. Throw me in a burlap bag and toss me in a ditch with whoever else the Taliban offed that day."

Silence followed, then a choke, and finally tears.

There is little in life more uncomfortable than the sound of a crying mother. Parents say they want to relate to you, to be your friend, but they cannot. The bond is too different than that of friendship. Parents like safety. Roses and rainbows. Eggshells to walk upon.

The next voice over the phone was my sister's, demanding, "What did you say? Why did you say that?? That's a horrible thing to say to Mom!"

That I wasn't thinking granted me little forgiveness.

I wasn't trying to be belittling or dismissive, I've just never understood the pageantry of death. When I'm gone, and all that remains is the shell that once was me, who cares what happens to it? Am I not to live on in memories and hearts? Such thoughts don't matter to loved ones. Death is about loss, and no mother wants to picture her child in a ditch while grieving.

Apologies were made and compromises reached. I allowed permission for a funeral, but insisted (in writing) on certain conditions. If I was not disfigured, the casket had to be open and a fake, Freddy Mercury mustache fitted upon my upper lip. As funerals are generally somber little slices of life, I needed reassurance mine would contain a little levity.

Not that I feared death on the trip. Just as with my tour of Iraq, my belief was death is for those who have moved beyond the drudgery of day-to-day existence on earth. At that juncture in my life—having recently been dumped and in the lovely pit of depression—I felt I had much more pain and rejection to experience before dying.[1] I believed life was exited by the comfortable, those who understood the silly and stupid nature of everything that transpired in the physical realm and were more amused than saddened by it. The downtrodden, such as myself? We suffered on endlessly. For all intents and purposes, I could have been a teenage girl, I was so emo.

If all trips begin with an omen, then the introduction to the flights with my traveling companion and fellow comedian Paul had us cursed by the Travel Demon.

Our travel plans had us flying commercial from the states to Germany, then transferring to military planes from Germany to Kyrgyzstan and ultimately into our final destination of Afghanistan. Attempting to check in at LAX for the first leg of our journey, however, we were told that while the Air Force made our

---

[1] And miles to go before I slept.

reservations, no tickets were actually ever purchased. If we wanted to offer up a personal credit card, the seats were waiting for us. If not? We were welcome to call taxis and head back home. How lovely.

If there is one thing to be understood about the military, it's that it is an enormous living, breathing, and messy organism. Everything is filled out in triplicate, and military logic is anything but logical. Liken it to a twenty-page, small-font legal contract; if a single comma is out of place, all gears grind to a halt and the document is rendered useless. Regarding the problem at hand, while it was obviously known that two comedians from the states were flying over, with shows having been scheduled, plane reservations made, and official military orders issued to Paul and I, somewhere along the way a break occurred in the chain of command and no purchase order enacted.

Naturally, a very specific itinerary, with a very specific timeline, had been set in place for us. We had to make it to Germany for our next flight, or we'd be stranded there. Panicked, we now had to pray our LA liaison would either be awake or be awoken by his cell phone to take our call at 7:30 a.m. He then had to get on the horn to Germany and pray someone with the authority to release funds was still in the office at 4:30 p.m.

After much back and forth between the parties in power, and well after the departure of our flight, Paul and I were rescheduled onto an afternoon airplane into Deutschland. To much amazement, we discovered that though we actually arrived in Germany much later than originally anticipated, we still landed a full two hours before our flight to Kyrgyzstan. Sadly, this meant nothing to the Air Force. According to regulations, passengers must be checked in and sitting in the terminal waiting area a full three hours before any flight. Flyers are not allowed to wander the terminal, nor relax in the USO lounge checking email. A passenger on an Air Force plane has to be in designated areas at designated times—three separate holding areas in all—before boarding a flight. If you have not checked in before that three-hour mark, the moment you cross it your seat is forfeit. You are then stuck waiting for the next available plane, which could be days away. So, while Paul and I could see that our ride had not only not taken off, it hadn't even boarded, we were not allowed to sit for two hours and wait for it. Because waiting two hours is apparently inherently unsafe and absolutely unheard of, and again, military logic is anything but.

Spending a day in Germany was not an awful thing, however, as we visited a Sound-of-Music little village, with Hansel & Gretel houses erected among enormous trees in the rolling hills of lush country. Considering a cliché can be a wonderful thing, then the phrase "truth is stranger than fiction" is the trump card of them all. I woke the next morning at 3:00 a.m., a little before my alarm, and it was dark and foggy outside. I stepped to the window, opened it, and looked over the blackened forest. As I breathed in the cold, wet early morning air, the radio/alarm clicked to life behind me.

And I was stunned.

As if timed by God, the opening notes to Rossini's *William Tell Overture* sounded lightly from the clock radio. If there are ever so precious moments in life, those hard to believe or describe, being in Germany, in a dark, fog-filled forest with William Tell playing... if you believed in the supernatural, you would almost feel the presence in the room with you, one as tangible as any physical form. The hair on my arms raised as I experienced goose bumps rippling across my skin, and I wondered how much of life is extraordinary outside circumstances acting their will upon us, and how much is self-invention inside our heads.

Paul and I caught our make-up flight, and thus spent an entire day without seeing daylight. We left Germany pre-dawn and flew against the sun ten hours on a windowless military plane to Kyrgyzstan, where we landed well into the evening. If the St. Louis Arch is the Gateway to the West, then Manas Air base, Kyrgyzstan, is the mouth into Hell. Manas is a way station, a pit stop between war or home, depending on your direction. Paul and I were going "Down Range." Iraq, it was explained, was "In Country"; Afghanistan was "Down Range." A subtle difference, to say the least.

We landed a little after 11:00 p.m., ate a midnight meal, took a two-hour nap and shuffled our way over to the loading zone for a 5:00 a.m. flight. Our transportation was a C-17 cargo plane, a cavernous tube filled with equipment making we comedians officially baggage, not passengers. As with any regular flight, a pre-liftoff safety briefing was given. When flying military, however, the extra information offered is worthy of note: "In case of a missile attack..." "If cargo should come loose and you have a crate of ammunition flying at you..." As flying into a war zone is serious business, everything was said in serious tones. So it was to our amusement that as our plane reached its cruising altitude, I spied our on-flight guide settling in among his multi-million dollar military computer and radar system and firing up a game of solitaire. Just another day at the office.

Hours later, the video game was off and his game face was on. In preparation for landing, instruments were checked and rechecked. Combat arrival is unlike any commercial flight; in a commercial landing, the nose remains high and the plane eases its way to earth, using wind resistance to gentle the impact as much as possible. When entering a war zone, no one wants to be an easy target for shoulder rockets or RPGs, so the planes remain high and fast for as long as possible, then nosedive in toward the runway, plummeting at high speed and leveling off at the last possible moment. The next time you hear of a crash during training, understand they were probably doing something very dangerous. With the military, even in peace can you die training for war.

Paul and I were flown to Kandahar, Afghanistan. The international military base erected atop the city's old airport was to be our hub for the coming weeks, but little did we know it would be our home for several days solid. When performing military tours in hot zones, you are generally flown to as many Forward Operating Bases as possible, staging multiple shows per day in order to entertain the largest volume of soldiers available. Sadly, our first day in, October 8th, 2005, this became impossible. For history buffs, that date will ring the memory bell of a great Pakistani earthquake; 7.7 on the Richter scale. Paul and I awoke to CNN announcing Donald Rumsfeld's decision to send military helicopters from Afghanistan across the border on rescue and relief missions. It was bizarre, watching helicopters on the news leaving a base, then looking out the window to see the event occurring live several hundred yards away. It was disappointing learning that with no spare helicopters, we had no way of being ushered around for shows and would be sitting squat a while.

Considering most Americans are not too geographically savvy, the earthquake did provide personal fodder. I had to explain to numerous friends and family members that Afghanistan is a country quite sizeable in nature, not sub-division tiny. People—my mother in particular—were emailing me incessantly, making sure I had not been killed in a devastation that had taken place nowhere near me. It's an unusual psychological phenomena, that the first thought after a localized tragedy is of your loved one regardless of the odds of involvement. The emails received made me wonder if it would have been appropriate for me to check in with friends in Bangor after Hurricane Katrina hit. "Hey, New Orleans got wiped out, and that's in America, like Maine is in America... So are you okay???"

At one point there was a glimmer of hope Paul and I could join a convoy to a nearby base and perform, but no space was available and we remained behind. I was told several hours later the group had been targeted, and I was disappointed to have missed it. The attack wasn't an out-and-out assault, but a suicide bombing gone wrong. A car laden with explosives made an end run at the final vehicle in line, but fortunately for everyone in that particular convoy there are few fanatics who are very bright; many foot soldiers in the fundamentalist world are young, and therefore easily brainwashed. They are told the reason they are poor/unemployed/didn't-get-the-wife-they-wanted is because of America, much the way Americans are told the reason they were downsized/dumped/not-ever-famous is because of illegal immigrants and gay marriage. Distraction from the root cause of a problem using the blame game is something done worldwide, and when dealing with suicide bombers any semblance of reason or rational thought they may have had is long gone by the time they are ready to take their own lives. The dimwitted terrorist fighting for "God" that day bounced his car off the back bumper of the bookend transport, lost control, and blew himself up as he was skidding away from the supply line. The stories of stupidity within the insurgent's ranks make soldiers laugh, but even a broken clock is right twice a day, and when a terrorist gets his shit together, people die.

The several day entrapment at Kandahar created plenty of time to learn about the area and conflict. I visited the TLS building, headquarters for the entire base and named for the "Taliban's Last Stand." It is the location where the Taliban went from oppressive assholes, governing their country through cruel means, to fragmented fuckheads scattered to the hills. The initial American rout of the Taliban was lightning-fast, and never ones to surrender, the final clump of terrorists banded together and holed up in one building. They fortified it, armed themselves heavily, and prepared for a fierce, final battle where no quarter would be asked or granted. They envisioned a room-to-room fight to the death and dreamed of killing Americans struggling to take the structure. Meanwhile, safely outside, those very American soldiers being salivated over looked at one another, asked, "How stupid do these idiots think we are," and called in coordinates. An air strike arrived and a new, ventilated roof, created. I laughed while standing beneath the missile hole and thought, "Well, we'll know Afghanistan is a truly free nation when illegal Mexican immigrants are hired to repair this."

I walked through the building, marveling at the charred-black inner walls still adorned with bullet holes from heat-exploded clips the militia had been hoping to fire at our soldiers. A flagpole had been erected through the point of impact, and the American flag flew high above the building. In a moment of personal honor, I was presented with a flag of my own. I tied it to the pole, raised it by hand up through the missile's entry point, and fluttered it in the light Afghani breeze for several moments. It was then lowered, folded, and given to me with a certificate of authenticity stating I arrived, supported the troops, and flew the flag where brutality once reigned. Not bad for a humble white boy from Wisconsin.

If the TLS building is where initial conflict ended, there had to be a place where it began. That location lay close enough that a fieldtrip gave me witness to the inception of what would eventually be known as 9/11. In the time between that Tuesday in 2001 and our invasion of Afghanistan, the most ubiquitous footage on television was of Osama bin Laden training angry insurgents on monkey bars. Said footage was shot at Tarnak Farms, ten kilometers from Kandahar. A convoy was created to drive out to look it all over, and though we were eventually allowed to visit the Farm, our trip was delayed by one day. The morning we were scheduled to stand in the aura of evil, evil acted first. Four international doctors were killed while treating displaced peoples at a refugee camp. The doctors didn't want military protection, because being associated with America and the West was "bad," and they thought remaining neutral would keep them safe. This bit of reasoning would be like me thinking I could stroll across the track at the Indy 500 on race day, because pedestrians are supposed to have the right of way. "Should matter" isn't "does matter," and though the doctors were only trying to help peasants, insurgents executed them. No one is welcome in the Taliban's world, a sad lesson to learn for those offering nothing other than good deeds. Safety concerns, along with—no lie—misplaced paperwork, waylaid our trip that day.

The following morning, after all proper forms were filed, our outing was green-lit and I piled into the point vehicle of the convoy as fast as possible. In any driving chain, the first link is the most susceptible to attack; the idea being that if you cripple the first car, all others following are trapped and wide open for violence. I figured that were anything to happen, I wanted to be front and center, my video camera documenting it all. Though no ambush occurred, my helmet did get put to good use when our Humvee hit a pothole so large it bounced me out of my seat and into the roof, cracking my head against the fortified metal there and giving me a serious case of the giggles.

The elation soon faded, as visiting Tarnak Farms and knowing who lived and schemed there was a somber event. It was also an eye opener, as seeing first-hand what America was up against in Afghanistan, I could understand the ill logic an angry and confused Donald Rumsfeld used when pushing for war with Iraq. "Afghanistan's got no targets," was his famous quote, and he wasn't lying. We bombed what we could, which was, if you remember the terrorist training videos, monkey bars. I'll type that again: We. Bombed. Monkey bars. A playground, if you will. America bombed the few buildings available, but overall, Osama's assholes were trained in the most primitive ways and under the most archaic conditions. The sensation of standing in a field of nothing, looking at clay huts and little else and knowing the people were so obsessed with America, a land so far away from them and full of technology they couldn't possibly grasp, that they were able to plot and fell two buildings in New York... it literally set my head to swimming.

Being trapped at Kandahar for several days also afforded me the depressing opportunity to attend a ramp ceremony. An American soldier had lost his life in an attack made on a patrol in the Afghani hills, and I was allowed to stand at attention and witness the loading of his flag-draped casket aboard the plane home. The Kandahar military base being an international one meant numerous nations stationed soldiers within its walls. France, England, and Romania are but a few of the countries represented, and the military uniform creates a brotherhood that surpasses all differences between governments. Every single unit available from every nation turned out for the observance, the majority having never met the deceased, as he was from a Firebase, a remote encampment out in the field. They turned out because though wearing a different uniform, they knew that somewhere parents were tearfully awaiting their child's arrival. They knew a friend of the fallen, a fellow soldier, would accompany the body all the way to its destination, look a mother, father, or wife in the eye, and hand over the flag currently covering the coffin. The ceremony is an event precious few civilians see, and one that left me with many emotional layers. Pride, regarding the honoring by all nations and soldiers. Embarrassment, like I was some sort of fucking tourist attending an event I had no business being at. Most of all, sorrow, over the loss. Every goddamn moment had me confused and moved in ways I don't like admitting to.

Fortunately, life has a way of making you laugh through tears, and at ritual's end I was given a respite from the lump in my throat. The soldiers in attendance were respectfully strong, standing tall with shoulders back but technically "at ease," as the stance is known. The call to attention was made, that the troops would exit the runway in an organized manner, and everyone snapped to. An inaudible command was given, and in true Keystone Cops fashion, many of the soldiers turned in different directions. Where all were supposed to turn to the right, some remained still, others turned left, and a few spun entirely around. No one broke formation, exactly, but they looked quite like the night-before-graduation unit from Stripes, unsure of what to do or where to face as they trained for their boom-chugga-lugga-lugga-lugga moment the next day. Though my heart was breaking, I had to smile.

After several days on one base, I was relieved to hear Paul and I would finally begin touring through the country. Traveling between FOBs[1] was a fun experience; while I still found Blackhawk helicopters the most fun form of transportation, the Chinooks I despised in Iraq proved to be quicker and more nimble than memory served. We would fly over very obvious poppy fields—whether or not they were growing wild or waiting for harvest and the opium trade was unknown—and mountaintops were skimmed at high speeds, that anyone hiding in a cave not draw a bead and knock us out of the sky. Two Chinooks had been shot down in the region in recent months. Fifteen Marines lost their lives in one, so reporters ran around excitedly, trying to get the biggest and best scoop on the

---

[1] Forward Operating Base: these are generally a little larger and better equipped than a Firebase, which is pretty much a tiny outlet used for quick-strikes against the enemy. A "Base" Base is the largest form of encampment, with all the bells and whistles including hospitals and restaurants.

story. Five crewmembers lost their life in the other, and the same reporters collectively said, "Five? That's not news," and shrugged away the importance of human life. Disgusting, but that's how the media operates.

Meeting soldiers overseas is always a funny experience, as "the grass is always greener" is their favorite game. I'd be asked where I just performed, and upon answering, defeated indignation would emerge from the questioner.

"Man," they'd begin, "I'd give anything to be stationed there. They get it so easy, while we're always under attack. They get Thai hookers flown in every week for sex parties, and we gotta jerk off in the porta potties. This base sucks."

That the base I'd just been at had uttered the exact same phrase concerning the camp I was currently in made me smile silently. The reality of the situation is the bases are all pretty much the same, and living on them is one big Groundhog Day: you woke up, ate, picked the dust boogers out of your nose,[1] did daily duties, ate, and went to bed. But, fantasy of the other keeps a soldier sane, I suppose.

Most bases were converted villages, and the soldiers lived in clay homes purchased by the American government. Discovering this, I asked one commander what his base cost and received a jubilant, "Are you kidding? It's a steal, only seventy-eight thousand dollars a year!"

My response was historical; "We're using *money* to buy land now? What a rip off. Didn't America used to get land using beads and smallpox?"

One of our first stops was the outpost of the fallen soldier whose ramp ceremony we had just attended. Paul and I were flown in around 9:00 a.m. for a 10:00 a.m. show. Everyone was asleep, as they had just gotten back from an overnight patrol where they searched for the insurgents that had killed their comrade. Tensions were high, considering the ambush and loss they had just faced, so the commanding officer informed us he was going to issue an order of attendance for the show. Such news made Paul and I uneasy, as not only was the current situation already not too ideal, but mandatory turnout brings in a reluctant audience. The show was to be

---

[1] Personal experience was this took several minutes and was repeated several times daily.

134

performed at the base headquarters, in what served as the recreation room; this headquarters turned out to be a small Afghani home, with the recreation room in essence a converted living room that was maybe fifteen by thirty feet at best.

Slowly, twenty tired soldiers with sleep-deprived eyes made their way in to sit wherever they could, which meant mostly on the floor. Some of the faces seemed so very, very young to me. Being nineteen or twenty might make one an adult by default, but when I think about what I was dealing with at that age, compared to the enormous stress and pressure those in front of me were living with daily? Words do fail.

Though exhausted and forced to be there, those twenty soldiers made a damn fine audience. Over the course of my act, they smiled, then laughed, then eventually applauded as their body posture went from rigid to relaxed. Their commander was a veteran, and he knew that sometimes youth has to be told how to deal with stress. Even though they had lost a brother in arms, someone most likely a close friend, they were still alive. Even if comedy seemed like the most inappropriate thing in the world, they needed to understand they still had laughter inside them. While initially I was wary of performing that morning, I believe that at the end of my career that show will remain the pinnacle of my time spent cajoling strangers into smiling.

After my twenty minutes were up, I introduced Paul. Considering how cramped the space was, I left the room and went outside. With thirty minutes to kill, I figured I'd wander the base and see what there was to see; I wanted to absorb a bit of what the men and women serving the country had to live with while there. Within ten minutes, I was approached by a hurried soldier and informed in somewhat panicked manner that Paul and I had to get out to the landing zone; the helicopter was on its way and it wouldn't wait for us. I quickly made my way back to the headquarters, paused to write a message of explanation, opened the door and signaled to Paul, then passed him the note. Paul nodded, and wrapped up his set a few minutes later.

Outside, after the show, he pulled me aside. "I didn't want to do this in front of anyone, but you need to be more mindful of your time from now on."

I was confused, and responded with a bewildered, "What?"

"If the show is going to be cut short, you need to be aware of how long you perform."

I was irritated, but remained silent. We had agreed to certain, set times up front; I did mine, then the circumstances changed entirely outside of either of our ability to control it. Had I run long and done thirty or forty minutes as opposed to my scheduled twenty, that would have been one thing. The show was being cut short; how was that in any way a reflection on me? That Paul's ego concerning performance time would supersede the overall importance—entertaining the troops—offended me. I rolled my eyes and let it all go, allowing Paul to feel good about scolding me and assuaging his embarrassment. He was the headliner, and on top of that had close ties with the booker who put me on the tour, so I didn't get into it with him.

To make matters laughably ironic, the rush order to get to the landing zone was needless panic. We ended up waiting, bored, forty-five minutes for our ride. Keep in mind, the base was very small and the landing zone was at best a three-minute walk or forty-five second jog from where we had been telling our jokes. In reality, we could have not only finished the show, but been anywhere on base, heard the helicopter echo in the mountains and met it before it even landed. But, as previously noted, the military likes it when you wait for flights.

As in Iraq, base-to-base travel became a blur. One location was notable for being within sight of an old, enormous fortress built by Genghis Khan; another I remember for its remoteness. Upon hearing we were traveling to the secluded Firebase, soldiers would laugh, clap me on the back and say, "Have fun with that." Though the country was "won," the most inaccessible of bases were still considered "behind enemy lines." While the camp with the fallen soldier was small, it still contained a series of individual dwellings within its walls. The most isolated base we visited was so tiny it was but a single structure, something similar in size to a fast food restaurant, and a lone contingent resided inside its walls. Paul and I were informed the Blackhawk would do a touch-drop; as soon as it hit the ground, we were to jump out so it could take off again. Despite the fact the entrance to the structure was less than 100 yards away, two armed Humvees mounted with 50-caliber guns met us. The soldiers manning them were exceedingly alert, and we were rushed into the vehicles and spirited away behind the blast walls quickly. Considering the size and location of the base—it being alone in a valley encircled

by mountains—I wondered how often they were attacked, and asked
if the insurgents ever did an all out surrounding of the structure.

"Yeah," the soldier answered. "Our translators started picking up
chatter on the radio about ten minutes before it happened, as they
got into position. See those black marks up on the hill?" he asked,
gesturing toward a hilltop speckled with black pockmarks. "We lit
that hill up like the fourth of July. Sent 'em scurrying like rats."

Boo-yah.

One thing the out-of-the-way Firebases had going for them was
independence; being on the front lines, they were far enough away
from central command to be allowed the courtesy of relaxed
regulations. Common sense and understanding the rules of tact
governed their style of dress, which could be a little unkempt without
a ranking officer barking at them to do pushups. As with any
institution: the larger the system, the bigger the bureaucracy. On our
home base, Kandahar, the rules and regulations were beyond silly at
times. One member of the Military Police told me without
exaggeration, "This base is out of control!" His reasoning? It turns
out there were soldiers who had in their possession, gasp,
pornography—some even had beer![1]

While I could understand the military not wanting drunken
soldiers wandering around in a war zone, the fact is: alcohol is used
to alleviate stress. Who has more stress than someone getting shot at
in a foreign country? The problem is their surroundings; Afghanistan
is an Islamic nation, and its laws forbid alcohol, just like meat used to
be verboten to Catholics. Which is too bad, because it could be
argued that half the militants wouldn't even exist if the Afghani
people could get a little buzzed every once in a while. Maybe if they
blew off steam by doing a shot or two, they wouldn't be a bunch of
unhappy dicks lashing out at the world around them and killing for
God. Oh, religion, is there any dictate you have that makes sense?

What makes no sense about the "no alcohol" mandate on
American bases is: I thought the bases were considered American
soil. It's what I was told when arriving; her flag flew proudly, and
soldiers abided by the governing rules of the United States. In
essence, by banning alcohol, we were capitulating in order to show
kindness to hosts that didn't invite us in. A tad hypocritical,

---

[1] To quote Colonel Kurtz, "The horror..."

considering we were supposed to be bringing them the right to free will and individual choice.

My two personal favorite—and by that I mean silly—regulations were: the 10-mph speed limit and the "No Bags in the Chow Hall" sign. The first rule seemed silly because everyone knows how exceedingly difficult it is to drive that slowly; most people drive faster in a parking lot. So to have to drive a mile or more across base and crawl along at 10-mph seemed amazingly frustrating. Especially considering speed traps actually did exist, and were enforced. Imagine signing up for the military, confidently asking to go overseas and work to both protect America and bring democracy to a nation, and the Military Police busts you for speeding. How rewarding.

The reason the "No Bags" sign made me smile was its location. It was displayed at the entrance of every mess hall, right next to the "If you AREN'T armed, you CAN'T eat here" sign.[1] While I understand the order was designed to prevent people from sneaking bombs in, it still seemed silly when I was yelled at for attempting to carry my camera bag in with me. I opened it and showed the civilian-contractor guard earning a great, tax-free paycheck higher than that of the soldiers surrounding her, my meager belongings, yet was still denied entry. I guess it made sense, though. Were anyone to have an actual bomb on them, there's absolutely no way in hell they could ever detonate it in the doorway or rush past her to explode it. I mean that literally; the woman blocking my entry that day was indeed built like an offensive lineman, only without the muscle.

One constant comment across every base visited, and something I remembered from Iraq, was something affectionately known as "Thursgay." A weekly ritual, local men across the region used Thursday to celebrate their right to enjoy one another physically, and repeatedly; it seems rural Islamic culture and Catholic priests share more traits than silly rules and the same God. Like a rest stop in America, every Thursday Afghani peasants paired up, wandered off into a field and did what comes naturally to your average San Franciscan. Every camp and base mentioned the practice, with many having armloads of the interludes on surveillance tapes. I was told at one location that the older Taliban prisoners actually staged a mini-

---

[1] Which is probably not unlike something you'd see at a picnic in Alabama.

riot when the army stopped placing younger insurgent captures in the same prison as them. The reason for the separation, it was explained, involved abuse of the younger prisoners so great that it generated a medical need for "having their anuses sewn back together." Ouch.

The funny thing is, it is not considered in any way to be a homosexual act. While there are absolutely homosexuals in any society, what happens every Thursday in the fringe of the Islamic world is considered normal behavior. Men having sex with men is "What God intended." Woman was created for baby making, man is superior, and was created for pleasure. So while women are married to keep the family name alive, men still slept with one another because it was the Godly thing to do. Confusing, yes, but what religion isn't when examined closely? I wish the practice were reported more widely, and fully believe the media is neither left nor right wing biased, just lazy. Maybe if Thursgay was front page and constant ticker news, fewer angry, uneducated young men would want to become terrorists: "Hey, hate America more than you enjoy controlled pooping? Sign right up!"

I don't write to attack anyone's belief system; those involved in such actions exist only on the periphery of the Muslim faith. What people tend to forget is that lunatics can be found within the borders of any organized dogma, and women are subjugated in many systems worldwide. In Greece, Christian women are not allowed to set foot on an icon of that religion, Mount Athos. The reason being, someone with breasts would surely distract the holy monks from their studies and no burden should ever be placed on men to control their thoughts or urges. No, it is far easier to discriminate and disallow the fair gender any pilgrimage to the sacred location. And I'll say this: you can tell me a thousand times the men on that island are chaste, and I will tell you a thousand times you are a liar. Buggery is absolutely occurring within the walls of those monasteries, as human nature is, has, and always will be *human nature.*

In Judaism, ultra-conservative Hasidic newspapers remove all traces of women from photographs before publication, as a picture of a woman could be seen as "sexually suggestive." Once again, the onus is not on men to see an image and control their response. In 2011, a photo of President Obama and his staff watching the raid on Osama Bin Laden's mansion exposed the belittling practice; the iconic image was printed in a Brooklyn newspaper, only after Hillary Clinton's image had been erased. I think I can speak for just about everyone with a penis when I say: if there is one thing Hillary Clinton has never been, it's "sexually" anything, much less "suggestive." Given that fact, the practice becomes nothing more than bigotry hiding under a holy guise.

My point being: anyone can read the notes about "Thursgay" as a reason to belittle one religion and champion their own, but that would be unwise. When searched for, actions can be found throughout history—as well as in modern-day society—that can shame and embarrass any system of devotion. It is my belief that instead of sweeping such events under the rug and pretending they don't exist, they should be broadcast and therefore ended. It is only through coming to terms with our failures are we allowed to move forward in life. This is true of all people and institutions, and should be embraced in healing, not shrouded in secrecy.

* * *

All along the tour, the insomnia I experienced in Germany continued to plague me. Every night I'd wake up somewhere between 1:00 and 3:00 a.m., be up all day, and then go to bed around 10:00 p.m. or so. Being awake in the wee hours of the night was nice, because most of the action the insurgents offered happened then; four evenings in a row the camp was shelled. Once, four mortars landed 200 yards from my place of lodging, a Johnny Lee Hooker boom-boom-boom-boom. Fortunately, with the Taliban being more concerned with bearding and boy-love than weapons training or showering, the combined attacks only damaged one British warplane and no one was hurt.

Standard procedure for rounds landing within the perimeter was for sirens to sound and a mandatory move into protective bunkers. I would use these opportunities to jump onto a computer, do laundry, or take care of some other activity that usually involved congestion. The night I did laundry was memorable. As the rounds came in and everyone woke from their beds to navigate into protective concrete cocoons, I gathered up my stinkables and waddled over to the washing machines. I figured they'd finally be available, as on two previous nights even at 4:00 a.m. all washers had been in use. I was reading, listening to the hypnotic chug of agitating clothes, when I heard yet another explosive thud nearby, and the tower guards open fire in response. I cautiously cocked my head toward the sounds, figuring the situation had to be relatively close at hand for guards to be shooting from the wire.

"NOT CLEAR!" The warning system bellowed. "CONDITION IS NOT CLEAR!!"

When it sounded, the announcement wasn't clear, either. The base PA system was more like a series of drive-thru speakers than a modern piece of technology, and words often came out garbled. Hours later at breakfast, conversation laughingly involved many people saying they only understood the word "CLEAR" and tried heading back to their barracks and into danger. An outsider might think it sensible to use two separate commands to relay information in such a case, possibly "SITUATION DANGER" and "CONDITION CLEAR," but sensibility isn't what fuels military regulations.

At the end of my scheduled stay in Afghanistan, it turned out returning to America was more difficult than leaving it. The initial flight back to Manas Air Base on Saturday cancelled on us, and Paul and I were told the next scheduled flight was on Tuesday.

Tuesday.

The person explaining this emphasized it for dramatic effect, "*Tee-uuu-sss-day.*"

On Sunday morning, if for no other reason than shits and giggles, we stopped by the terminal and asked about flights. The man behind the counter treated us like assholes; "What part of Tuesday didn't you idiots understand?"

Later Sunday afternoon, after spending time on the firing range—turns out I'm a damn fine shot with an M-4 and scope and got multiple headshots—the flight situation was mentioned to a Major who had befriended Paul and I; he about blew a gasket. Taking matters into his own hands, the Major called the terminal personally and was told, and I do quote, "Well, we had two flights take off earlier today, both pretty empty, but I'd say Tuesday is your best bet." Upon hearing of the two missed flights, I began wishing the terrorists would shell the base again, but only if they could take out air transport. The Major laid down the law: If any plane came anywhere near the base with seats on it, his phone was to ring immediately. An hour later, while sitting in the housing quarters, an angry call came in from our "Tee-uuu-sss-day" friend: "Get to the terminal, now! Where are you?! A flight is leaving NOW!"

Hmmm... but it was still Sunday. Suuuundaaaaay. For a day that wasn't supposed to have any flights, it seemed odd that three had so far passed through.

We hurried, but forgot that a flight leaving "NOW" in the Air Force meant it was actually leaving in three hours; once again, Paul and I sat and waited. Had we known what lay in wait for us in Kyrgyzstan, however, we would have just stayed put at Kandahar. The Travel Demon that entered our journey at its outset flew into full effect once we arrived back at Manas Air Base. According to our given travel plans, we were supposed to deplane, walk across the terminal, and board a night flight to Germany. Instead we found out the next scheduled trip west was on Wednesday. Now our commercial tickets back to the states were in jeopardy.

The travel pattern that cursed us in Afghanistan repeated itself; we missed several flights on Monday alone that we were never told of until after their departure. Our plight, however, was nowhere near as awful as others around us; Paul and I shared space with many people in more dire need of escape than we could ever claim to be. We spent time with a soldier who had already waited five days for a flight back to America, where his mother lay dying of cancer. There was one soldier in need of an operation, and another who had accompanied a fallen friend's body to America and was trying to get back to his company down range. The largest example of the clusterfuck that is military travel involved two soldiers, finished with their rotation. They had been trying to get home to family for almost a week, and had just flown from Bagram in Afghanistan to Manas in Kyrgyzstan. Once at Manas they were told to wait several days and catch a flight back into Afghanistan, but this time to Kandahar, where they could ultimately catch a flight to Kuwait. Basically, it was like flying from New York to Los Angeles, then to Chicago, for a flight to Phoenix. Military precision indeed. Paul and I may have been inconvenienced, but these people were being screwed sideways, which pretty much sums up military travel: It's a lot like date rape. You signed up for dinner, then woke up hours later sore, bruised, and confused. What's worse was the apathy everyone encountered; those working the terminal couldn't care less what happened around them. One giggled while telling me another flight Paul and I were waiting for had been cancelled, it was such a big joke.

My personal favorite waiting case, though, was the colonel trying to get back to his troops. He had been trapped for about a week and though he couldn't catch a flight, he was exceedingly upbeat and very friendly. We got to dining together, which was funny as passing soldiers would salute him, and I would say, "Damn, here you are getting all this respect, and I'm calling you 'dude.'" He let me get away with it, too.

Paul and I eventually became a running joke; people would erupt with laugher upon seeing us. "You guys are still here?" they asked. My response was that we were no longer guests, we had been deployed. I responded to the situation the only way I knew how, by growing a protest beard. I'm not sure it helped plane scheduling, but it did make me feel my frustration had a voice. An itchy voice, at that.

To ease the pain of soul crushing boredom, a trip off base and into the capital, Bishkek, was organized. The buildup was enormous; "You're going to find North Face jackets for five dollars! Cigarettes for five cents! And purses, oh, the purses! You're going to shop like a king for under twenty dollars." Purses? Under twenty dollars? Only three words could describe such a heaven: Best. Day. Ever. Like any anticipation offered—"You're going home"—letdown was imminent: "Flight's cancelled, back to your tent." Nothing was a bargain, not in the slightest. No cheap jackets, shoes, or purses.[1]

The military had four rules to follow while in town: 1) No visiting underground shopping malls, because they were unsafe. 2) No purchasing prostitutes, because it was against the law. 3) No consumption of alcohol, because the military is fucking retarded. 4) Use the buddy system, because two is better than one. Well, as I was civilian, not military, I was left to my own devices and decided to set off on my own. I don't know what I expected to find in the underground shopping malls—maybe the seedy underbelly of a society, with drugs, hookers, and unique pornography involving animals wearing diapers—but it definitely wasn't stationery and soap. Like the Starbucks-is-everywhere theme of America, every underground shopping mall had a dozen stores selling sharp looking writing materials and lovely scented body washes. These shops were very dangerous to the military, apparently. I could see why the underworld was off limits.

I figured a brothel would be too cumbersome to locate, so I wandered around until I found the more squalid section of town and

---

[1] Dammit

bingo, hooker row: all lined up and ready to spread disease. Of all the prostitutes I've been around in my life, which isn't too many but probably more than quadruple your average person, these were easily some of the most mannish. I actually wouldn't have been too surprised to find they were either operations gone wrong or outright transvestites, actually. Naturally, each refused to take a picture with me, which is a silly commonality among call girls. They all offer to blow you for fifty bucks, but won't ever capture a slice of life in photograph. Prostitutes actually get pretty huffy when you turn their services down, too. Oh, and I almost bought a bottle of vodka, if only to break the final of the four rules, but since I don't drink there was no point.

Dinner was also a bit of a disappointment. Not because Kyrgyz food is either delicious or not, but because of all the places to choose from, after everyone rejoined the group, we went to an Italian restaurant and ordered pizza. To travel all the way around the world to order pizza boggled my mind.[1]

The rest of the delay days were spent in boredom. On the plus side, extra comedy shows were added for those stationed or passing through the base. On the minus side, I kept begging to be allowed to bundle up in a protective suit and have video taken of the K-9 dogs attacking me, but no one would go for it. An email from a friend back in Afghanistan informed me Kandahar hadn't been shelled since our departure, which created the obvious joke: "The Taliban doesn't hate America, they hate comedians."

Eventually, a flight to Germany was found, and it was an actual military passenger plane, a nice change of pace from the cargo holds I'd grown accustomed to. Of our original stranded party, the colonel had escaped several hours earlier, and I believe the soldier on emergency family leave got on the plane with Paul and I, but my memory fails me now.

Overall, I'd give just about anything to go back. Whatever whining I've done, it's all for the fun of writing. The experience was absolutely a highlight of my life. I was able to meet many people, blow my vocal cords out performing shout-shows without a sound

---

[1] The pizza also cost twelve dollars, just like in the states. What a bargain!

system, and see a chunk of the world oft talked and reported about, but rarely seen by outside eyes.

In 2005, Afghanistan was just starting to slide; a shifting of troops to Iraq had insurgents getting frisky again. According to reports, it's only gotten more violent since then. When in power, the Taliban ran the country into the ground, ruling with religion over human rights and common sense. Today, we are doing our best to re-build it for its residents. Ironic, in a way, considering every election cycle our own ignorant fanatics take a book of fairy tales into the booth with them and vote against scientific fact and for ancient ideas. Either way, soldiers wearing the American uniform are in a foreign country, far from home, and building schools, hospitals, and roads. They are protecting women's rights and trying to provide clean water and democratic ideals to an entire nation.

All while being shot at and undermined by an angry minority.

If that doesn't deserve a magnet on your fucking Escalade, I don't know what does.

Special thanks to Robert L., Joe I., Major Bob M., and John P. for their guidance, safe keeping, and most of all company during my visit.

NATHAN TIMMEL

BLOCK IV

AGES 23 – 35

12 – I WAS A WHITE KNIGHT... ONCE

Liz Phair is a divorced woman.

I remember searching for her debut album in 1993. Few stores carried it, so to obtain *Exile in Guyville* I had to go to an overpriced indie shop and hand over a decent chunk of change. It was worth it. The album contained the voice of an intelligent, opinionated woman whose integrity seemed overshadowed only by her honesty. Naturally, I was somewhat smitten.

To my dismay, a few years later I read an interview with Ms. Phair, one where she spoke of her boyfriend—the man who would shortly be her husband. I do not recall direct quotes, but the content was: 'He played me just right. I was interested in him from the moment I saw him, but instead of pursuing me, he made me wait it out. He knew I was hot for him, so he toyed with me until I was about to burst. Had he just approached me outright, I probably would have lost interest.'

I nodded my head in acceptance and placed the magazine back on the shelf; never learn too much about your heroes, for they will always disappoint you. Gone was the independent, intelligent woman I admired. In her place was someone that did the thing I always despised in a relationship: played games.

* * *

I believe in cellular memory. The idea is: experiences we have do not leave us, they become ingrained in our DNA in ways we don't always understand. Events are not just infused within our mind, but every aspect of our being. From time to time, our emotions remind us of events that exist as recollections, happenings that were once all too real. A particular song can raise gooseflesh across the skin's surface; a specific geographical location causes chills down the spine.

I further believe you can never escape your memories or emotions, you can only acknowledge and co-exist with them. In the very least, you hope to overcome traumatic experiences through time and effort; returning to the scene of a horrific event can provide for amazing catharsis, if emotionally ready for it.

Every time I attempt to write about my twenties, I grow tense. My muscles tighten, and my jaw hardens. Though long removed from everything that happened, after so many years of silence I worry that when I finally spill my story, meticulous thought in examination will instead give way to an incoherent mess of emotions. That, and like anyone I don't particularly enjoy revisiting my failures or shortcomings.

I shouldn't be embarrassed by my past; logically, I understand I have nothing to be either proud or ashamed of. You live life by trial and error. Mostly error. You make as many mistakes as possible, that you may learn not to do so again. These mistakes most often involve romance. When you gain perspective in later years, you often wonder why you never saw it coming. That said, my twenties were wasted, tossed aside like a trifle.

In retrospect—the only way we actually understand anything—I now realize why I indulged in such self-damaging behavior. Though I never publicly acknowledged it, my parent's marriage was a disaster. I was raised in a household where my parents slept in separate rooms for most of my teenage years and the word "love" was never uttered under any circumstance. That said, I have never believed the past determines the future. Just because someone has been integrated in a situation doesn't mean they have to follow the same certain paradigms. Statistics say children of an alcoholic are more prone to becoming the like, yet some grow up to champion the fight against addiction; I grew up surrounded by infidelity and icy emotions, so I became a romantic to actively counter that upbringing.

I put women on a pedestal in response to what I saw at home. I opened doors, kissed tenderly, whispered "I love you" when I meant it, caressed, cuddled, massaged, made love, asked about a woman's day and listened to the answer, held hands in public, and gave gifts randomly. The problem is, quite often I chose the wrong people to approach with my affections. Instead of wooing women with healthy egos and self-confidence, I was drawn to those who looked upon romance as weakness, placing myself perfectly for failure and thus perpetuating my belief all relationships were doomed to fail.

When I was twenty-two I made my way to Milwaukee, Wisconsin. After three irritating semesters at The Berklee College of Music, I felt that instead of continuing in a direction that created unrest in me, I should audible up a mulligan.[1] Unfortunately, I didn't yet know what trail to take and I ended up in the refuge so many unfocused wanderers do, college. My high school grades had been sub-par, but grades weren't as important to Berklee as a deposited check, and they admitted me into their program. Once there, I improved my GPA ever so slightly enough to transfer to the University of Wisconsin, Milwaukee.[2]

While there, I did what many a college student does for money, I entered into the food service industry and began tending bar. When a restaurant on the shores of Lake Michigan opened a patio and expanded their staff, I was hired on to cater to customers wearing khaki shorts and Hawaiian shirts. The restaurant was an oddity in Milwaukee; it was a business with a great location, but Roxanne reputation. True money ate elsewhere, while white trash making their one special trip a year would pop in and believe they were dining like a Rockefeller; the restaurant was a magnet for those who use dining out as an opportunity to lord over and act above those serving them. I don't know that I started in the service industry with a lack of

---

[1] Combining sports metaphors is fun, isn't it?

[2] Motto: "We're like high school, with tuition!"

151

respect for the public, but working there surely challenged the idea we're all good at our core. I've long since thought that everyone in America should spend a year as a waiter or in customer service; civility and politeness would skyrocket if people got the flavor of humility on their own taste buds occasionally.

To amuse myself, during my entire tenure I poured one type of red wine; customers would order a merlot, cabernet, "your driest red wine," "your top shelf red wine," and I would reach for the same bottle every time. In four years, I never had a glass returned or received a single complaint. It was my own private revenge for being looked down upon.

A beautiful young cocktail waitress named Judy had already worked at the restaurant several months by the time of my arrival. Though cliché, I was smitten at first sight. Judy was a petite blonde; her head existed at just the right height for my chin to rest upon when we embraced. She had what a childhood nemesis of hers branded a snaggletooth, an incisor that was a little off kilter from the surrounding enamels that gave her smile an imperfection I found adorable.

I could attempt to create an embarrassing litany of other reasons I was attracted to her, but such lists are troublesome to write and tedious to read. Suffice to say, there are three ways men think of a woman at first glance. The innocent way is as a friend. We get a sense there is something worth knowing, but it is not of a physical nature. The second reaction involves carnality; a stirring in our loins creates a fire in us that demands we ravage the woman in the most passionate of ways. We are unconcerned with her name or personality, there is only want. Then there is the third manner of eyesight, where with but a fleeting look, a longing is created. We desire to trace the whole of the female form with our fingertips, gently caress skin, run a light thumb across an eyebrow, and brush hair back over the ear and cup the neck at the base of the skull. We imagine pulling her into us, that lips may brush lips and our nose nuzzle in her hair, breathing in the scent unique to her. It was with this third style of seeing I first observed Judy. From moment one, I wanted nothing more than to orbit her.

As Murphy's Law would have it, Judy had a boyfriend. Not just any boyfriend, her first boyfriend; Judy lived with her high school sweetheart, Jim. Together they had overcome his multiple infidelities, physical abuse, and sideline employment of selling (and sampling) drugs. In other words, they worked through all their problems thanks to her tolerance and acceptance, and Jim doing as he damned well pleased. So while my first instinct was that I wanted to be with Judy, the more I got to know her, the more I wanted to save her. I wanted to let her know she was worth better than she had, that she deserved more, and I would show her what love could be.[1]

Luckily, or unluckily, Judy looked at me sideways, also. Sometimes there is an amazing amount of guesswork involved in getting to know someone; other times intentions are crystal clear. I could read easily the intent in Judy's eyes. We became immediate friends, first spending time together within the safe walls of a group of co-workers, then gradually and with more and more frequency, were alone together.

I was immensely attracted to her, but couldn't muster up the courage to broach the subject of our mutual fascination. I both feared rejection and didn't know how to approach the boyfriend angle. My childhood and all the negative influences I had endured instilled in me an insecurity I didn't know how to overcome. Plus, on the surface of things, our friendship seemed solid. Given my parents relationship, the appearance of "peachy keen" was all I understood. That people were supposed to communicate their feelings was outside my realm of comprehension. I was both happy enough I was around her, and passive enough to remain silently in longing. After six or so months of ignoring the issue, however, Judy was strong enough to push everything into the light of day. She told me flat out she knew I cared for her, and she demanded I admit to it.

Admit I did, and Judy grew silent and said she had a lot to think about. She did not respond with emotional confessions of her own, and I was left dangling for several weeks. There are many awkward and hilarious moments in movies when one character says "I love you" and the other responds incorrectly or not at all. In reality, such a situation leaves he who has confessed pained and confused.

Fortunately for my self-preservation, Judy eventually decided she did indeed like me, too. Sadly, her emotional interest in me was nowhere near enough for her to leave Jim. Instead, we began an unhealthy, years-long and damaging sexual affair. We hid everything

---

[1] In reality, I probably wished to save my mother from her marriage; psychologists will have to determine that one.

from our friends, families, and co-workers. We were so good at it, that years later when everything became public knowledge, their shock was overwhelmingly genuine.

Judy was attracted to me, but didn't know how to respond to being in a relationship while wanting another person. To deal with her confusion, she kept very strict rules when we intertwined. Like a prostitute, she wouldn't kiss me during our liaisons; that would constitute emotional involvement and be considered "cheating." Judy would come to my apartment, have me undress her, then she would lay back and make statements like, "I'm just going to pretend this isn't happening" and allow me to have sex with her. A very romantic phrase to hear, and a great boost to my self-esteem.

For four long years we carried on in this fashion; she refused to leave Jim, and I refused to give up on her. We would capture an evening together, and then I would watch her rush back to him. Knowledge the woman that just shared my bed was returning to another man created immense frustration and anguish in me, but I could never walk away from the situation entirely. I attempted to end the affair repeatedly over the course of our awkward waltz, but failed miserably each time in an embarrassing pattern of abject idiocy. Every few months the anguish of being with Judy, while not having her, would grow to the point I would break it off. I would tell Judy I couldn't see her anymore; not as her friend, not outside of work, not at all. I even performed this action once immediately following sex, as I was going soft inside her. Before my climax, I had nothing but love for her. Immediately following it, the reality she was about to leave me hit like a ton of bricks.

No matter how often I was able to apply the brakes, however, like an addict white-knuckling for just one more fix I would soon capitulate and call her. I kept convincing myself there was one more gesture I could make that would allow Judy to see the light, or that this time I would be able to hold my emotions in check and achieve her level of indifference. Perhaps it was simple tenacity, like a dog with a Frisbee in clenched jaws, refusing to let go. Maybe it was an inability to accept loss. At the time it felt like something nobler.

In response to my pain and anger, I began throwing my cock into any warm hole it could find. As Judy considered her "real" relationship more important than me, I didn't consider it cheating. I flattered whomever I could and fucked them ten ways from Friday, in their favorite positions and shot my orgasm wherever they let me, in mouths or on faces, between tits and on or in the ass. I tugged hair and screwed women while standing against a wall. But I also kissed my conquest after she spit or swallowed, and did so passionately. I honored the gift of their bodies, cuddled afterwards, and listened when they talked. I may not have loved, but I cared, and I tried to use care as an excuse to justify my actions.

My favorite partner during this time was a hostess at the restaurant, a lovely woman named Paula. Paula was an olive-skinned stunner, with curly black locks atop her head. She was a unique blend from mixed parents, but my ignorance and poor memory prevent me from remembering which part of the Pacific Rim her ancestors hailed from. Paula was a good friend whose company I enjoyed, who also happened to be an extremely sexual woman. Paula and I had almost the same relationship as I did with Judy, only without the pain or confusion. Like Judy, Paula had several semi-serious boyfriends during our moments of intermingling. Oddly enough, however, whenever Paula was between relationships, she and I never became exclusive. Paula would be single a little while, eventually find a new boyfriend, all the while keeping me on the side around for extracurricular fun.

We also never had sex; Paula would only perform orally on me. I tried to enter her on a couple of occasions, but she always smiled coyly, closed her legs, and opened her mouth instead. Once, we were even both entirely naked in my bed; I finally had convinced her sex would be a fun change of pace for us. I got up for a half a second to grab a condom, and by the time I turned around she had changed her mind and instead went down on me yet again. This twist was in conflict with how Judy acted; Judy would only allow me to have sex with her. While she was dating Jim, I was allowed to perform oral pleasures on her, but the favor was never returned. To Judy, oral sex was too intimate an action, and therefore the greater of two infidelity evils. To Paula, penetrative sex was too intimate, and therefore the worse manner of cheating. One trait they did share was that neither kissed me, nor let me kiss them on the lips. Judy, while she was being physically unfaithful to Jim, refused to betray him emotionally. Paula, I believe, liked to feel a certain amount of control over the situation.

Paula and I had a bizarre system for hooking up while at work. At the end of the night when it was time to clean up, I would grab the recyclables or garbage and head out the back door to dispose of it. Paula and I would make eye contact, and she would then leave out the front. Paula would loop around to the back, and under cover of darkness go down on me beside the restaurant, outside of prying eyes. Sometimes she would stop by my apartment when working her day job and I was between classes; sometimes I would visit her. On occasion, I would simply pick her up and we would drive around while she did the deed, me dropping her off after finishing. More than once she performed her magic on me in the restaurant's coatroom during business hours. That was always... interesting.

Maybe Paula did what she did because she liked the power she had over me, the control, knowing I enjoyed the actions of her mouth. Maybe she just enjoyed oral sex, and I was an outlet for her. I was safe, allowing her to release a little tension and then return to the security of whatever relationship she was in. Either way, she was a kind and caring soul, and I always enjoyed her company regardless of whether or not we were being "naughty." Judy knew Paula liked me, so Paula and I were very cautious and never seen alone together. In spite of our vigilance, Paula still became Judy's internal nemesis; Judy obsessed over her, demeaned her at every turn available, and once told me that if she ever found out Paula and I had been together she would never speak to me again. A strange threat, I thought, considering that every time we were together she went back to Jim's bed without so much as a single consideration as to how that made me feel.

Despite my dalliances, only Judy held my heart. Though I tried to find solace in the arms and beds of other women, I always returned to her. The worst moment for my emotional well-being happened when I finally bore witness to the physical abuse Jim's hand delivered. He was working one evening, so Judy invited me over to play. It had been several days since I had seen her, as she had been calling in sick to work, and I was giddy in anticipation of the forthcoming physical interaction. When Judy answered my knock at her door, my excitement turned to horror and I could do nothing but stand before her in mute shock. It actually took Judy several seconds to realize why I was standing with my mouth agape before covering her purple and swollen eye; she had actually forgotten Jim hit her a few days prior. By the time I arrived, she was used to seeing her bruised face in the mirrors around her home, a place she planned on sequestering herself until her eye healed.

I was entirely unsure how to act; I was angry, hurt, and confused. I wanted to destroy Jim, and was disgusted Judy continued to remain with him over me. That she treated the situation as if it were absolutely normal created immeasurable frustration in me. Seeing her so wounded made me long for her all the more, and I desired to protect her and keep her safe from harm. Despite my anger and pleading, she still wouldn't leave him. As was the basis for our relationship, I could not tend to her emotionally, so I did my best to treat her wounds physically. Defying all logical responses to seeing her abused, her touch still brought out an erection in me, and we had sex in a reclining chair that night.

Everything came to an end between them when Jim lived up to his personality flaws and read Judy's diary. She left it out; he picked it up and paged through it, growing angrier by the moment. Inside were all the sordid details of our liaisons, with active accounts of positions they never attempted and descriptive details of the two orifices below her waistline that I had entered, one of which he had not.

Jim exited the relationship immediately. He read the diary while Judy was at the restaurant, packed up many of his things, and left that night. Though she had forgiven him for several past infidelities, he was unwilling to forgive her but one. In a note or angry phone call, he told her he had been planning to leave for months, and everything in his actions suggested it to be true. They had been fighting more and more often; she was spending more and more time with me, leaving work, coming to my house, and returning to him sometimes as late as four or five in the morning. When she would ignore my beckons and go straight home after work, he wouldn't even be there, he himself staying out until all hours of the night. It was a relationship in tatters. Yet a year later, in a random verbal altercation, Jim re-broke Judy's heart by telling her he was hurt by her betrayal because he had been preparing to propose to her. Though nothing in that statement rang true, she believed it above all else, and became re-morose over her loss. I thought it a cheap shot, taken from a point of fanciful memory of their history, not the reality of what I saw.

One thing always bothered me about the spark that sent Jim running was Judy having left her diary out. That Jim would read it is merely another chink in his already pockmarked armor. Judy said she trusted him to respect her privacy and claimed shock by his action, but for her to write out all the sordid details of our exchanges and then place it in public gave me pause. Though she said she loved him, and no doubt she did, sometimes people know they have to exit a damaging situation. By having an affair with me, journaling the details, and not concealing the evidence would be a very passive-aggressive way of quitting the relationship without having to take responsibility for her actions. A Pyrrhic victory, if you will, with devastating emotional cost for those involved.

With the thought she had consciously left the diary out for him to read, I believed it would be our time to shine. I was wrong. We continued on as we always had, physically engaged in private, platonic in public, and emotionally entangled overall; Judy didn't want to be seen by our friends as someone that jumped from one relationship to the next. Plus, no matter how much I made myself available for her, Judy was convinced Jim would return. They were, in her words, "Perfect for one another."

How we finally ended up together involved games and manipulation on my part. Though I'm not proud of it, I was willing to do whatever it took to finally hold Judy's hand with all the world watching. While I had always been quite reserved regarding the conquests I had while waiting for Judy, I felt it was time to take one pursuit public. There was a waitress I believed I could bed, and I told Judy that if she wasn't willing to be with me, then I was going to chase this new doe. The waitress was just out of a relationship and only required casual fun, so I made myself available, and we spent an evening together.

Gossip runs rampant in any restaurant, and within a week the waitress hung out with Judy and Paula. Paula told me about the powwow first, and it was surreal, like something out of a soap opera. Here were three women I had been with in one manner or another sitting in conversation, each thinking they were the only person to taste me. Eventually, the waitress got around to describing our night together. Paula didn't mind, and in fact laughed it off inside her mind while remaining cool, calm, and collected on the outside. When Judy described the gathering, however, she said hearing of me with another woman made her physically ill. It was the straw that snapped the camel's spine, just as I had hoped. Though for years I had to endure her return to Jim's bed, my straying ways hurt her self-esteem, and she said it was time for us to be exclusive, and visibly so. I was overjoyed, because I was ignorant. I didn't realize the difference between her ego wanting to remain un-bruised and her heart making an active decision to be with me. In the end, I see that she never did actually choose my side; she just didn't want to lose.

Judy, though always at odds with Paula, moved in with her and found great power in having sex with me in Paula's bed. Later, when Paula moved out, I suggested we have sex in the new roommate's bed. We did, but Judy didn't like it. There were no emotions involved, no empowerment, and thus we remained away from then on.

Though we were now dating, I was not allowed to meet her family. They despised me, so our union was kept secret from them. That I didn't meet them in our initial years makes sense; we were carrying on illicitly, so to have me in the same room with blood relations was too confusing. After their relationship ended, Jim, the ten-year favorite and heir apparent to the son-in-law throne, ran immediately to her parents and cried "Betrayal!" He told all who would listen how her affair ruined everything, neglecting all the while to mention his own straying ways or pugilistic actions. Judy never edited this tale. So eager was she to wear her scarlet letter and allow Jim his sordid affairs and swinging fist, I was deemed the unwelcome outcast. That I never forced her to tell her family the truth was a sign of my own weak self-esteem.[1]

Despite all my complaints, I still enjoyed our time together. When we became public lovers, all our friends said it was a union that made nothing but sense; they had thought we would make a great couple for years. The easiest way to explain our relationship is to say that we just gelled well together. There were no fights; there was no drama. I was now completely loyal to Judy, so much so she actually inspired probably my greatest prank to date.

The eatery we worked at was corporately owned, and it had, I forget specifics, between thirty and fifty restaurants nationwide. The Milwaukee location is gone now; mismanagement from both above and at the local level saw to that. One man who helped drive things into the ground was a new general manager, someone sent in to "turn things around." He entered with big ideas and a bigger attitude. He

---

[1] Only in one moment of honesty did she tell her brother Kerry she was seeing me. In ways I will always be grateful for, instead of judging, berating, or condemning her, he told his sister to follow her heart. If I was good to her, then that was all that mattered. I was never able to meet, or thank, Kerry for that kindness.

also arrived with a wife, a woman who happened to have a fine palate for hard liquor.

Within his first week of employment, the wife showed up at the restaurant pie-eyed and stumbling. Though obviously intoxicated beyond the point of service, she sat in the lounge and demanded drinks from the cocktail waitress on duty, Judy. It was their first meeting, and Judy questioned whether or not she should serve someone so smashed.[1]

It was a bad move on Judy's part. The wife threw a fit, her GM hubby got involved, and Judy was fired.

Just like that.

I was both furious, and immediately inspired.

I quickly made my way to the office and obtained several items: a box of corporate stationary, a box of corporate envelopes, a list of every single restaurant owned by the company, and most importantly, the corporate home office location.

My scavenger hunt complete, I drafted a letter, the lyrics of which I do not remember but overall was a little ditty sung in the key of revenge: "Due to recent events at our Wisconsin location, spouses of general managers are not allowed to consume alcohol while on company property, and are furthermore not to be on company property for any reason while inebriated." No names were mentioned, but the gist did exist; something happened in the city of breweries involving the new GM and his wife.

I had a friend who lived in the same California city as the corporate office, so I made up my thirty (to fifty) letters, sent a package to mi amigo, and she plopped them into a mailbox. Within days, every restaurant in the chain started receiving said memo, on corporate letterhead, in a corporate envelope, from the corporate zip code.

That it was a fake was no doubt determined rather quickly. But for the few hours or days between reception and double-checking, it had to have been believed true. Regardless of the eventual reality coming to light, everyone in upper management all across the country knew the wife in Wisconsin was a boozehound who needed to have tracks covered by her husband.

I quit a few days after the letter was mailed.

---

[1] That was six, count 'em, six "s's" in a row. Boo-yah.

I believe the GM was fired within the year.

Judy took her newfound unemployment as an opportunity to go back to school. She enrolled for classes, then decided to study abroad for part of one semester. For several weeks, she traveled through France and Italy, drawing, sculpting, and unfortunately for me, meeting men with exotic accents.

When she returned, Judy was different. She was on edge constantly, easily agitated. She was less affectionate and somewhat distant; many of my physical advances were met with a brush off rather than mutual embrace. Had I more life experience under my belt, I would have understood the signs of guilt and confusion for what they were, but they weren't even on my radar. Even when she started communicating with a Frenchman she said was "just a friend," even when she told me she sent him money to help pay his phone bill because their cross-continental conversations were so expensive, at no point did I want to even begin to open my eyes to the truth: she had been unfaithful.

Judy's behavior changed so much that when Milwaukee hosted its annual Harley festival, she began acting out. She was drinking more, and then started exposing her breasts to strangers as payment to sit on the back of their bikes. I was at work when she called to tell me of her girls-gone-wild ways; her voice was aglow and I could picture her smiling as she spoke. I grew silent. I remember sitting with the phone to my ear for several long seconds, wondering how to respond. The words that came out of my mouth surprised even me.

"Are you trying to get me to break up with you?" I asked quietly.

I didn't know where the question came from, but it was all that made sense. She was drinking more, constantly lamenting her return to the states, and now flashing her breasts in public. Meanwhile, every little thing I did was far from magic; in fact, Judy lashed out at me in anger with surprising frequency, something she had never done before.

If my question was surprising, her answer was sobering. "I don't know," Judy whispered.

Over the course of the next ten minutes, she explained to me that she jumped into our relationship too quickly, that she needed to be alone to get her head together, and that she wasn't going to date anyone for the next two years.

"I need to be completely independent," she said.

All I could muster up in response was, "I love you."

I felt those words should be enough, that like in many a Hollywood movie, love would emerge victorious over all evil. With but the uttering of the phrase, she was supposed to see the error of her ways and change her mind.

She did not.

And like that, we went back to square one. When you watch a horror movie, you know where the killer is; you scream, "Don't go in that room," but the characters on the screen do not listen. Much like one of those doomed actors, I was trapped by my emotions and allowed myself to reside in the background of Judy's life once again. We returned to our old pattern of not dating openly, while still having sex on the sidelines. I convinced myself this was just another stage to the game, and thought all would eventually be well again; hell, we had acted out the majority of our relationship in this fashion. It was par for the course, the two of us, intractably circling around one another, unable to escape.

I lavished whatever gifts upon her I could that final summer. A computer, a TV, a radio, and when fall reared its colorful head and she needed it, a loan for her college tuition.

At the same time, unknown to me, she carried on her friendship with the Frenchman. After hearing she was now single, he decided that what they had wasn't enough and gave Judy an ultimatum: either date him, or never speak to him again. Judy came to a conclusion quickly, and when she told me she was giddy with excitement: "I'm going to date him!"

I have no words to explain my emotions at that moment. Not just because of what I was being told, but the manner in which the information was presented to me remains insensitively shocking to this day. Not only was she animated and happy, she was surprised by my shocked reaction. I wasn't happy for her, I was actively upset. Heartbroken, as the sensation is known.

Judy grew angry with me; wasn't I her friend? Wasn't I overjoyed she found someone? I should be high-fiving her and hugging her in all our nonsexual glory! I reminded her that she was supposed to be single for two years, and she looked at me as if I were crazy. Like a window-licker, I had assumed we would spend those two years dancing our silly dance of together/apart, and then end up entwined again.

I remember very well what happened after that, and if I thought I grew tense when first attempting to write out this tale, the hesitancy in me now is murderous. Every fiber of my being calls for me to lie, to make up a fanciful ending where I stoically accepted my fate and walked away like a man, but that's not what happened. Instead, I made the embarrassing and illogical choice to hold on.

The next day, I was taking a shower. I wasn't so much washing myself off as standing under flowing water, dazed by the previous day's information and wondering if it was all a sick dream I would soon wake up from. Without warning, a power washed over me. My entire body tingled, and a force from outside me spoke inside my head, saying, "Tell her, now. Tell her everything, and win her over." I did not so much walk, but something influenced my body for me, moving me from the shower to the dining room to retrieve my phone. Naked, dripping wet and energized by an unfocused electricity running riot through my body, I called Judy at work and vomited up my emotions. I told her how I felt, how I had always felt, how I wanted to meet her family and charm the resentment they felt for me out of them, to show them how much I cared about her and could use that to win them over. Most likely, I babbled unintelligibly for several minutes before Judy got a word in edgewise.

"I have to go," she whispered, her voice a mix of caution and indifference. "We can talk about this later. Pick me up after my shift."

I was slightly humbled, but not defeated. I immediately dressed my best, went out and gathered up a dozen roses, and navigated my way to her workplace. Judy came out, gave the roses a resigned look, and we drove to her house in near silence.

Once there, we went into her room and she told me to have a seat, she would be right back. She turned to leave, then paused. Judy turned back, reached down and scooped up a pile of handwritten letters sitting on her coffee table, and bundled them up.

"I don't want you reading these," she explained.

While I understood Jim had betrayed her trust, to confuse his actions with my honor was irritating and made me defensive.

Judy asked her roommate for some privacy; was there somewhere she could go for a little while, so we could sit in the living room? Judy's bedroom was a place for intimacy and privacy; to me, it was a room we made love in. To Judy, it was an area I was no longer welcome. Little did I realize this at the time.

We retreated into the living room, where she told me it was over. We could be friends again in a few months, if I wanted to be, but we would no longer be lovers. She had moved on.

I kneeled in front of her, and begged. I put forth the same demand as the Frenchman, saying that was unacceptable; I couldn't be just her friend, I wanted us together. Judy shrugged, at a loss for words.

I laid my head in her lap and cried. Not movie tears, where everything is touching and people look beautiful as a single wistful tear rolls down one cheek, but sloppy, mucus-inducing, body wrenching sobs.

Judy stoically stroked my hair, and when I was finished, showed me to the door. She told me to call her again when I was ready to talk; I told her, not in anger but anguish, that that moment would never come. I didn't have it in me to be friends with her. She reiterated to call her when ready.

And that was that.

Five days later, I turned twenty-nine.

Happy birthday to me.

* * *

For the first two post-Judy weeks, I didn't sleep or eat. I lost thirty-five pounds and on four occasions cried so hard that I threw up stomach acid. I read stories of war veterans, men who had lost limbs and awoke at night to phantom pains, scratching at limbs long since dust. It made me wonder how long I would itch for an empty bed and missing person. Over the course of the next few months, through our mutual friends, I discovered that not only had the Frenchman come to visit, he had done so over Christmas. He got to both meet and spend the holiday with her family, people I had never been allowed to meet or interact with. They began talking marriage almost immediately; Judy wanted to move to France.

My first step toward healing, then, was to carve myself out of the lives of our Venn diagram friends. Given I had lost friends through geographical displacement my whole life, I departed the clique quite casually. To this day, I do not regret or feel even the slightest bit bad about it. I told everyone it wasn't enough to ask them not to talk about Judy, seeing them reminded me of her. I have to admit, part of me was confused by the continued loyalty they threw her way. Given her infidelity and theft—repayment of the tuition loan was something that happened in several small installments, then stopped abruptly, leaving my bank account slighted—it seemed to me they shouldn't want to be around a person like that. But, we all live our own lives, and rarely do we decide our friends based on their actions concerning others, we see in them how they treat us. Since I didn't want to make demands or place anyone in the middle of anything, I opted out. I couldn't live my life with the ghost of Judy around every corner, her image in every friend we shared, ready to draw memories out of me and set back the healing process every time I inched forward.

I also started seeing a therapist, a woman named Roberta, who was beyond helpful and informative. She rightly realized that my torment over the loss of Judy was rooted in something much deeper, and we worked to find it the best we could. For the first time in my life, she got me talking to my family. Like most people, when I entered my teen years, I did so surly. I took resenting my family to unheard of levels and by the time I got into my twenties, ignoring my mother, father, and sister felt as natural to me as breathing. When I was twenty-five, my parents mixed it up in an enormous release of the problems they had been neglecting for years. It was Christmas, which was an especially nice touch, and my mother was in the kitchen, screaming and smashing dishes. My father was either throwing her clothes out onto the lawn or around the house, details are sketchy. I was in my room, wondering why the hell I had even bothered coming home to visit, when one of them finally shouted out the "D" word. My mother was already living in Madison part-time—she had gotten a job there and came home on random weekends—and with both kids out of the house, there was no need to put on appearances anymore. Freedom was a William Wallace reality my mom felt was within reach, and after serving a quarter-century sentence of unhappy, she went for it. Whether or not either of them looked to me for approval or emotional support during that time I do not know; I was as neglectful a son as I could be when they might have needed me. So as you are trained, so as you become. But, with the prodding of Roberta, I finally talked to my parents. I discussed our always moving, my always losing friends, the icy chill surrounding their marriage, their infidelities, anything and everything I could think of.

During one conversation, my mother mentioned something in passing, a sentence almost an afterthought to whatever her focus had been. She said that other than the one instance when I was six, my "abduction," she could not recall a single time when anything other than extreme physical pain caused me to cry. That moment aside, no amount of emotional duress seemed to create any stirring in me; in moments of stress or emotional hurt, I was even keeled to almost the point of stoicism. To Roberta, this gift of information was a godsend. It explained much about my current state of mind, and fueled her approach in helping me. It meant everything I was going through wasn't entirely about Judy; she just happened to be the catalyst for a release of twenty-nine years of pent up emotions. Judy represented every friend I had ever lost, every bedroom I had to abandon.

With this development, I discovered that losing Judy was my way of proving exactly what everyone feels about themselves at some point in time: "No one will ever love me." It wasn't enough for me to believe such silliness, I had to verify it and in Judy found a woman willing to help me achieve certainty. Roberta gently explained situations I was too wrapped up in to understand clearly, such as why Judy didn't remain with me a while after Jim left her. At the time, I saw his departure as my opening; now it's all too obvious how myopic that vision was. Judy turned to me not out of want, but desperation. I was her rebound; the fact we had been together for years before the opportunity to use me didn't matter a whit. The hardest thing for me to accept when Judy eventually left was: she never chose me, she fell on me. I was more than willing to brace her descent, and she was all too happy to have a warm body to cushion the collapse. Once she dusted herself off and was able to stand upright again, she walked off; that she did it by shifting into the arms of another while we were together was a nice twist in karma's favor. I may have thought I was justified in being the other man while she was with Jim, but in the cosmic scheme of things, cheating, is cheating. I was a part of a betrayal regardless of circumstance, and it came back to haunt me when Judy was ready to escape our relationship. To her, it was only natural to find someone new before releasing someone old; she never had to be alone, she never had to feel unloved.

About eight months after our final night together, while driving down Prospect Avenue on Milwaukee's east side, I passed Judy. She was walking along the sidewalk, hand-in-hand with a man I did not recognize. Though I had been making considerable progress with Roberta, not only the sight of Judy, but the sight of her with yet another lover, brought home all the pain I had been working so hard to escape. On an emotional bender, I called Judy and asked her if she would attend a therapy session with me, so we might talk in a neutral environment. She was agreeable, so I picked her up before my next meeting and had an eye-opening experience. Judy spent the entire hour alternately angry—upset with me for still being hung up on her—and silently defensive. She was so negative, the following week Roberta asked me as gently as she could, "What did you ever see in her?"

I asked Judy only one question the entire hour; why did she leave? Her two-word reply and the only explanation I've ever received was, "We're incompatible." She expanded nothing beyond that, and on the ride home admitted to attending the session for two reasons: one, to hear what lies I was telling my therapist, and two, to tell her side of the story. Considering she said precious little when given the opportunity, to this day I have yet to understand why she joined me that day. I did discover, however, the Frenchman broke up with her after only several months; a cross-continental relationship just wasn't going to work for him. Instead of re-considering her once-wonderful plan of being alone and independent for two years, she leapt right into the arms of yet one more man. I silently hoped he was wiser than I, and that he knew what he was getting into.

Maybe this next memory has absolutely nothing to do with anything; maybe it is an encapsulation of our entire relationship. Whichever side it lays on, it is a niggling little thought that always fires across my synapses when my mind wanders to Judy. On January 26th, 1997, the New England Patriots met the Green Bay Packers in Super Bowl thirty-one. U2 had just announced a world tour in advance of their album *Pop*, and when halftime came around, I made mention they would have made for a fantastic mid-game show. Judy was offended. Though neither xenophobic nor "rah-rah America!" in any way, shape, or form, Judy stated the idea of an Irish band playing at the Super Bowl was absurd.

"The Super Bowl is an American ritual," she stated. "It needs to be a celebration of American music and traditions."

We actually got in a mini-argument over the idea, which I found entirely confusing for two reasons: one, Judy wasn't into football, and two, Judy really liked U2; we actually attended their PopMart concert at Camp Randall several months later. I couldn't understand why allowing the biggest band in the world to play at the biggest sporting event in America could be a bad thing. In fact, I thought it made nothing but sense. Judy adamantly argued otherwise, and we left the situation at a stalemate.

Turns out, I was right. In 2002, U2 was asked to play the Super Bowl halftime show, and not only was it the most watched halftime ever—ratings normally dipped during the game break—in 2009, Sports Illustrated rated it the best halftime show of all time. So maybe Judy and I actually were incompatible; I was ahead of the curve, and she behind it. This could, naturally, be a hindsight of self-justification, but as said, the memory refuses to leave me.

Though I was alternately angry and upset for years by the termination of the relationship, today I no longer blame Judy for anything as I once did; I understand all too well the decision to pursue her was always mine. I made myself available, and though she never chose to be with me, she also didn't want me to be with anyone else while she was alone. I fully believe that she did like me for a while, but she loved Jim, and that made all the difference. Though I rationalize my pain by saying it was influenced and enhanced by childhood trauma, I cannot deny the emotional damage I felt when I realized I was but an afterthought to her. As painful as the breakup was, however, the fact of the matter is someone like Judy is all I was ready for at that stage of my life and immaturity. I fully believed I was second best and deserved to wait for her, which proved futile.

I learned two things from the relationship, first and foremost that you can never "save" anyone emotionally. People choose to be in a situation for a reason, and the onus is not on you to rescue them from it. When I set out to prove to Judy she deserved better than a man who cheated on and hit her, I was trying to convince her of something she didn't fully believe. Likewise, while I had friends who flat out told me that she was using me and that I should walk away from the whole mess, I refused to listen to them. She could not be saved from Jim; I could not be saved from her. A vicious cycle, yes, but we all learn at different speeds.

The second thing I learned involves maintaining shared power in a relationship. Part of the problem in any failed relationship is a willingness to wait for the other to see in you what you see in them. By giving yourself up to waiting, you are giving up power. Power, above all else, should be shared equally between any two people interested in eyeing the horizon together. If you are ever the stand-by friend, the best friend that does and says all the right things, the one you've seen come out on top in so many a Hollywood movie, you are wasting your time. Your heart can convince you otherwise, but you're wrong. You'll always be wrong, as you've already lost by treating yourself as second best.

A weak foundation holds no house. If a relationship begins, even if only for a mere moment a merger is sparked by power and games, then no matter how much truth you pour into the union you will always be sailing towards disaster.

Just ask Liz Phair.

13 – THE CHARMED LIFE

You do it out of love.

There is no other reason to become a comedian. No other reason to drive the countless hours in your car, a toilet paper "manpon" wedged in your ass crack to catch sweat the best it can.

(Truckers may be the assholes of the highway, but they do hold certain wisdom)

You arrive at the hotel to find there is no reservation in your name. Why? The comedy club has double-booked comedians, meaning they scheduled two comedians for the same week in the same slot. Unfortunately for you, the other one checked in first. You shake your head and roll your eyes, not understanding how double booking happens; ever go to a football game to discover three teams have shown up to play? No. When the NFL sets their schedule, it's two teams per stadium. Yet somehow, booking two comedians for the same slot happens more than it should in the world of stand up.

Things eventually get worked out—"you'll share the week!"—and you make your way to your room. Though January weather is pounding the Midwest City you're in, it is colder in the room than outside the building. Oh well, at least you weren't sent packing.

Might as well shower, get some steam going. A pungent rusty waterfall exits the faucet as the pipes bleed free a confession of their rarity of use.

Let it run; things will work themselves out.

(Would that it were this easy in life)

Water goes clear, lift the tab to start the shower. An over-calcified nozzle shoots streams everywhere, like a penis with a morning-after-sex cum clot sending hot piss to the floor, not the intended target.

(That's what happens, ladies, it's not our fault)

Showtime arrives; the crowd looks nice. You take the stage and wave after wave of smoke hits, chokes you, and gives you images of coal miner's black lung. You inform the audience, "If Madonna can say 'a cigarette is a disgusting thing to put in your mouth,' and she's had Dennis Rodman's rod in hers, that tells you a thing or two about how awful smoking is." They laugh, but don't extinguish their cancer sticks.

For the entire time you're on stage, you smile a genuine smile. It's somewhat meditative, empowering and relaxing at the same time; audience laughter sounding like a chant, "Ohm..."

The show ends, so you head to the door and shake hands as the audience shuffles past. Eventually, an overweight white guy with a beard and confederate hat offers a racist joke.

"You can use that in your act!" he suggests, laughing.

You force a smile through gritted teeth and wonder what the hell went so wrong in the person's life that they thought it appropriate to approach you with such hate.

Head back to the room; it's still cold, but at least now you smell like an ashtray. Like any drug, the stage is a high that offers little in the way of lasting effect. The alone becomes palpable.

Turn on the television and Queen Latifah is on Letterman, the pinnacle of all talk shows and your dream.

The Queen says she likes skydiving; your mind immediately spits out a zinger: "That's brave, trusting a parachute to hold that much weight. Then again, the army drops tanks out of planes."

Fair, but nowhere near funny enough for an audience.

Oh well.

You do it out of love.

* * *

Were I a meticulous person, I'd be able to tell you the exact date I first took the stage as a comedian. Sadly, such records are long lost from my memory.

I was about to graduate from the University of Wisconsin Milwaukee, lived in the city bearing the same name, and had no clue what I was going to do with my life. I was aware that a bar downtown, The Safe House, held a comedy showcase every Thursday night. It was an open microphone, meaning amateurs were the mainstay of the evening, and if you wanted to get in front of an audience in Milwaukee, you went there first.

I attended a show, talked to the person in charge, and signed up for the following week. I couldn't tell you anything about the routine I performed other than I remember doing really, really well. I "destroyed," as comedians say to one another after an exceptional set. I got off stage full of confidence and amazement; "I can do this," I thought. "No one ever destroys their first up, I must be a natural!"

Naturally, I tanked and heard crickets during my next several performances. So much for the lightning-fast start.

Regardless, I was hooked. Laughter or not, I knew I wanted to perform, to turn my ideas into words and hear those words generate laughter. I flashed at an instant back to both sitting in the movie theater watching *Richard Pryor Live on the Sunset Strip*, and listening to George Carlin's album *Class Clown* for the first time. My life seemed to make sense.

I struck up a friendship with a fellow novice comedian, a father of three named Mike Marvell, who told me of a comedy club, Stooges, not far from his house on the south side of the city. Mike had been spending time there, researching the local scene, and encouraged me to follow suit. Stooges is gone now, and has been for years, but looking back I realize it was a very happy accident I stumbled into starting my comedy career upon its stage.

A fiercely independent and comedy-intelligent woman named Joey owned the club, and coming up under her tutelage was both informative and energizing. Joey cultivated young comedians, a rarity back then and even more so today. She encouraged me, talked to me, and gave me the ins and outs of the comedy business. I was a nobody, a neophyte barely able to walk on my two wobbly comedic legs, but she treated me like I belonged. I wasn't charged entry to shows and was almost ordered to badger the professional comedians passing through her doors for information about the business. They were doing what I wanted to; I was told to pick their brains as best I could.

Stooges was a family business, with Joey's son Andy tending bar and her daughter, Cindy, the head waitress. This created a welcoming atmosphere, one unlike a company where the employees have nothing invested in the establishment or its future. Every weekend, I'd go to the club to watch and learn, watch and learn. I saw many different comedic styles, digested each performance, and examined how each performer got laughter in their own way. Even more relevant to my growth, I did my best to understand why they failed when no one laughed. The most important thing I absorbed was the idea to talk about myself on stage. I discovered the comedians I liked most were those I learned about, the ones who talked about their lives and interests. When their set ended, I felt a sort of bond with them. Conversely, when a comedian got up and cracked wise about traffic, the weather, or other non-personal topics, even if I laughed and enjoyed myself, I likened them to Chinese food: an hour later and they were disappeared from my memory. I watched with interest as a comedian from New York came to town and began telling subway joke after subway joke. Even knowing very little about the process of crafting a routine and presenting it to an audience, I knew early on she was in trouble. Milwaukee had no subway system, and therefore no foundation for her set. The audience sat politely through material that didn't interest them, and the woman grew more and more nervous as no laughter reached her ears. She was not invited to the club a second time.

At the time, Wisconsin's capital, Madison, had two comedy clubs. Each held an open microphone every Wednesday night. The single most important thing to a developing comedian is stage time; the more you perform, the better you get. Every Wednesday, I'd drive to Madison with a couple friends to perform five minutes at one of the clubs. Thursday I'd visit The Safe House for my fix, and Friday and Saturday I would be at Stooges, hoping to get a guest spot on their shows. After several months of this routine, Joey gave me a shot at hosting an entire weekend.

The general format for a comedy club is to have three comedians per show: host, feature, and headliner. The host goes up first and performs for ten to fifteen minutes. The audience is typically settling in, and there are distractions as drinks are ordered, coats are removed and shuffled around, and appetizers delivered and munched on. The host takes the bullet for the evening; it's his job to grab everyone's attention, make the club announcements (such as drink specials, calendar dates of upcoming shows and the like), and then hand a warmed-up audience to the feature act. The feature, or middle, has the cake slot. The audience is focused, and he'll do twenty-five to thirty minutes and be off the stage before they can get too drunk, tired, or rowdy. The headliner, or closer, is what every comic shoots for. You get to be on stage for forty-five to fifty minutes, sometimes even an hour, and you are the top dog of the evening. You also get paid the most, which is always a nifty little bonus.

I did well enough that weekend for Joey to put me into her rotation, and about every six weeks I was hired to host. After three or four weekends working the club, I got my first compliment. I remember clearly the kind words tossed my way as if they were Mean Joe Green's football jersey. I walked off the stage following a set full of laughter and was so happy I wasn't even paying attention to the feature comedian. Chances are, I was riding an ego high, thinking, "What do I have to learn from the guy on stage now? I can get laughs. The audience loved me!" Joey walked by, and without pausing her stride or even looking at me, shot "Good job on the announcements" my way. Not, "You were funny tonight," or "The audience really liked you," but "Good job on the announcements." It took a half second to process, but then I laughed as she departed. The announcements were in fact my job. Though I had gotten laughter, that was secondary to my duties. Joey had in effect both told me, "Well done," with the subtext, "Don't get cocky." It knocked me back into place, and I turned my attention to the stage to see what I could learn from the person who was both performing more time and getting paid better than I was.

Over the next two years, I bumped into people on the brink of becoming gods. They would in no way remember me, but I was lucky enough to either guest set in front of or host for Dan Whitney, Lewis Black, and Dave Attell. I got to absorb the differences between creating a character, a persona, and being the same person both on and off stage. I learned that there was no right or wrong way to approach comedy; it didn't matter if you were a fictional construction, such as Dan Whitney's Larry the Cable Guy, an exaggerated extension of yourself, like Lewis Black's performances, or just 100% you, like Dave Attell. Each performer did what felt right to them, and it worked in turn. I also was lucky enough to see these men have some non-stellar sets, something I'm guessing happens very rarely these days. It was eye opening to witness, and taught me to never rest on my laurels. Audiences can be quite fickle, even to the most famous.

Sadly, over time, I began to understand an unfortunate truth: Joey was a rare breed of club owner. Joey paid attention to what was happening on her stage and cared about comedy as an art form. You would think that would be the only way to run a comedy club, with passion for the craft itself, but that's hardly the case. Unfortunately, there are three basic types of comedy club owners: those who love comedy and respect it, those who half listen to the audience for laugher without caring if the person on stage is using stolen jokes or base material to get their laughs, and those who don't pay attention to comedy or the audience, who opened their club on a whim because they didn't want to get "a real job."

It took me eleven years to finally have an epiphany, which means it took me eleven years to realize something I always knew: comedy is not like the business world. When dealing with corporations, if you have a fantastic résumé full of excellent references and you interview well, you have a decent shot at getting hired. Not so in the comedy world. I have been booked in more rooms by people saying, "Well, you wore me down with your persistence" than I have by those saying, "I looked over your press kit, watched part of your DVD, and think you'd be great for my club." Sadly, that means attrition has gotten me further in the game than talent. It means by incessantly emailing and calling people, I finally got work. I was a mosquito that would not go away, so they decided to hire me to shut me up. It also means someone who never gets laughter, a comedian with few stage skills and bland jokes, can do the same thing and end up on stage disappointing customers spending their hard-earned money. It is by disinterested owners I generally get asked, "How were they?" after my set. It means the owner wasn't paying any attention to either my act or the audience response. While I understand any business is a difficult thing to run, with employees to manage and a non-stop barrage of problems to deal with, at some point, time should still be made to bear witness to what is happening on stage. It has been the bane of my existence when I have done very well at a club, yet had difficulty returning because the owner was too "busy" sitting at the bar watching boxing or in their office drinking beer and playing video poker all night to pay attention to his customers.

Despite my complaints, I cannot say there is a right or wrong way to run a club. For all her comedy knowledge, Joey's club eventually went under. Conversely, many clubs whose owners have more business sense than a love of comedy do very well. These owners generally run their rooms based on how much they like the comic off stage; they want to get drunk and stoned after the show and if you don't do so with them, you have a hard time getting re-booked. To date, I've rarely had a problem returning to a room where the owner was present, interested in what was happening, examined each comedian to grace their stage, and listened to audience laughter. I have had limited problems returning to rooms where the owner was more interested in liquor sales and gave little thought to the comedians they hired. Naturally, I have had many problems returning to clubs where I didn't feel like doing lines of coke with the owner.

My purpose here isn't to be overly negative or say there is an established adversarial relationship between comedians and club owners, I just want to make clear that comedy is a rough goddamn business. I could write pages upon pages of horrific story after horrific story involving this industry; I have been fired after driving hundreds of miles to a show because the headliner wanted to work with his friend rather than me. I have gotten emails from bookers at four in the morning, where they admitted being intoxicated and said they "didn't get" my act as they watched my DVD, and I was once hung up on by a club owner who said, "Oh you fucking guys won't leave me alone" after I explained I was a comedian doing a follow-up call on a press kit I had sent. Yes, heaven forbid a comedian call a comedy club owner looking for work.

The two worst cases of treatment I can think of actually occurred over back-to-back weekends in my life. Though the first is a bit of an extreme, it still sums up the lack of support a working comedian occasionally has to deal with. I was in the middle slot of a three-person show, and when I walked up on stage I was met with the ear-piercing cry, "Bring it on, motha-fucka!" That someone was so intoxicated to bellow at a comedy show did not surprise me; live comedy is a realm of entertainment where drunken louts have to be dealt with on a semi-regular basis. The source of the screeching on that particular occasion, however, did make me tilt my head to the side like a dog riddled with confusion. In front of the stage was a table of ten women, all dressed to the hilt, all white, and all easily aged sixty and above. "Grandmothers' Night Out," if you will. One was so drunk she was doing a head bob, as if in eighth grade history class and staying awake was a chore in and of itself. This woman had been the source of the high-pitched screech of obscenity.

I asked her to repeat her war cry, as I wasn't positive my ears were working correctly, and once again the live-action Mrs. Howell shouted, "Bring it on, motha-fucka!" I arched an eyebrow, said, "Ok then," and started my show. The woman randomly bellowed the same refrain several times throughout my time on stage, and after giving her the benefit of the drunken doubt for a couple of interjections, I slammed her hard and the audience roared their approval. Though I don't remember what I said, the woman realized she was fighting a losing battle, stopped shouting and proceeded to doze off and drool lightly out the side of her mouth. Through the rest of my act, two tables in the corner did their best to "contribute" and derail the show with shouts and inter-table talk, but I simply ignored them; when they realized they weren't going to become part of my show, they shut up.

After I exited the stage, the headliner, Adam, was introduced. The wealthy dowager awoke from her nap, and if I thought she had been belligerent enough to warrant getting kicked out during my set, what happened next was unlike anything I'd ever seen. When Adam hit the stage, he too was met with a new high-pitched cry from the elderly woman. It wasn't a random offering as had been with me, this time she took one look at the person walking to the microphone and knew exactly what to scream.

"Bring it on, nigger!" echoed above the welcoming applause the host had called for, and the room went silent. Not "nigga," which could have been considered *marginally* more appropriate, as if she was possibly trying to be hip and use street slang, but "nigger." As bright as a day in July and as loud and proud as Alabama Man might bellow, she let it fly in front of the entire room. It wasn't said as a challenge, but more a hoot, like the full-blown cheer of someone looking to have a good time.

To say the audience was stunned would be saying too little; there are rare times when you can make two hundred people gasp collectively and hold their breath, and this was one definite way to do it. Adam, to his credit, handled the situation with as much grace as possible. He didn't lose his cool and blow up at her, but he didn't let it go. His first response was a measured, "Excuse me?" to which he received a second, "Bring it on, nigger!" Adam asked why she thought it was an appropriate thing to say, or if she was playing or believing she was somehow relating to him and her response was yet again, "Bring it on, nigger!"

Given that the room was filled with as diverse a cross section of Americana as possible, and that a certain tension filled it from the instant her first racial slur was shouted, anything could have happened. Still, Adam kept control of the situation and did his best to move on. The club, believe it or not, made no move to have the woman removed or quieted. In the corner, meanwhile, the two tables of white trash I had ignored grew loud again, to the point Adam could do nothing but wage verbal war with them.

Within five minutes, everyone was talking amongst themselves about what was happening, shouting "Shut the fuck up" at either the racist woman or the two tables in the corner. People were also yelling at Adam, who was doing his best in trying to deal with a room spiraling out of control. In the midst of this battle, the manager of the club carried a note to the stage and handed it directly to Adam. He read it, then resumed his attempts to quell the crowd. Eventually the table of women left, and did so to a chant of "Na-na-na-na, hey-hey-hey, good bye" from the entire audience, save for the two drunken tables in the corner, who continued to shout random shit throughout the rest of the evening with no action being taken by the club. Adam worked his contracted time, eventually closed his set, and the audience gave him thunderous applause for his efforts.

After all had ended, as Adam and I stood by our for-sale wares, every person that walked by us issued an apology on behalf of others. They apologized for the woman and her racial slur, for the staff that didn't intervene, for the drunks in the corner... everyone was contrite except those who should have been. The exiting audience was also curious. Many remembered the note being passed to the stage and asked Adam what it said. They wondered if the police were being contacted, or if he was given insight as to how the drunks and racists were being handled. He passed on answering, and instead tossed out vague little lies; "It was about something I had asked about earlier," "Oh, nothing important," and the like. When all was said and done and every member of the public had left, I asked what the note really said. What I was told floored me: "Let it go and move on," was written in bold strokes on the folded piece of paper. A black man who had just been called a nigger in front of a room full of people, and three times no less, a man doing an amazing job of handling the situation in a club that was doing nothing to police its customers, well, he was handed a note telling him to let it go and move on.

I had never heard of anything less supportive; 2008 suddenly felt a lot like the 1950s.

To the manager's credit, somewhat, she eventually admitted to being in the wrong and said she was sorry for the note and much of the situation. Evidently she and the bouncers were unaware of what had happened, assessed the situation incorrectly, and made the decision to intervene inappropriately. But that didn't make it right. An apology follows an accident, and to not have the comedian's back in a situation showed an incredible lack of faith in Adam. I couldn't believe she had taken the note up there in the first place and was angry on his behalf. I also wondered what I'd do if anything like it ever happened to me.

The neat thing about life, then, is when you look at a situation and wonder how you'd react if it were presented to you, sometimes you are given the opportunity to find out.

The very next week, headlining a show myself, in a different room in a different state, I took to the stage a little after 10 p.m. I should have been on stage at 9:30, but the 9:00 show had been delayed a half an hour. A birthday party of twelve was exceedingly late, and the club was more interested in catering to the needs of that one party than punctuality. Such an action immediately set a poor precedent; upon arriving, the birthday party realized the show had been held just for them. Even if they didn't openly understand the power they had, they did grasp on a subtle level just how important they were. While this might humble and embarrass some people, such is not the case with those who arrive drunk. Some bars and clubs will cut off intoxicated customers, but others will just serve, serve away. The birthday party did Jell-O shots all through the opening act, and by the time I hit the stage, all were slurring and shouting.

When I was introduced, "That's my brother's name!" was yelled up at me.

"Your brother is named Nathan Timmel?" I asked, and got a giggle from the audience. It was a gentle enough response, but enough to start the table off and running.

The birthday party was restless; they were talking to one another loudly when I wasn't acknowledging and attempting to quiet them, and shouted incoherent crap back at anything I did send their way. Instead of being witness to a bouncer or club employee kicking them out or quieting them down, I would look over to see them being served even more alcohol. They were all members of the Army, and as I was in a military town, surrounded by military bases and the club itself had called for a toast for those that serve, I was placating as nicely but as firmly as possible. I never have a problem slamming a group that won't shut up, but neither do I start a fight when hopelessly outnumbered.

So, it was to my stunned anger when, thirty minutes into my set, I was handed a note from the club owner: "Please stop talking to them and move on with your act."

I couldn't believe it.

I felt defeated.

I had just taken two flights across the country, rented a car, and driven an hour to find I was neither staying in a hotel nor any private place of lodging, but with an employee of the club. Not just any employee of the club, like, say, a nubile twenty-four year old blonde waitress, but a seventy-year-old grandmother. A woman with an analog television and an enormous old-school cable box atop it, an apartment filled with old-person clutter, and one with that ever-present nursing home smell. After all that, here I was, standing in front of a group of people who never should have been let in the door in the first place, let alone had the show held thirty minutes for their arrival or been served more alcohol, and I was being told I was the asshole. Had I an established career, I would have apologized to the people who had come out to see comedy, told the club to fuck off, and walked off the stage and out the door. Fuck the pay; if I could have afforded the professional repercussions, I would have eaten the time and money. Instead, I remained on stage for another twenty minutes, doing my best to remain as professional as possible given the circumstances.

Unlike the time I was witness to Adam being blamed for club failure, I was given no apology for the rude behavior or lack of support. I was, in fact, told, "The other tables complained and I had to give out comp tickets because of that group." According to her, this was somehow my fault. The final straw on my irritated back came from the doorman, who shook his head in resigned confidence to me; "Those people, I tell you, they came in a couple weeks ago and did the exact same thing."

Of course they did.

Despite my complaints, it was still worth the trip. It's actually always worth it. That event occurred on a Friday night; both shows on Saturday were amazing. Good audiences, big laughter. No matter what I've gone through, from sleeping in my car at 3 a.m. in the middle of an enormous road trip, being hung up on, ignored, or told "I wouldn't hire you if it meant finding Osama Bin Laden,"[1] it's all still worth it. From time to time I may have questioned what I'm doing, but I've never doubted I've made the right life choice. Standing on the stage is electrifying; knowing my words and ideas are causing an audience to have the response of laughter is an amazing high. It's an endorphin rush unlike anything else I've ever done, be it skydiving, sex, rafting class-five whitewater rapids, being flown in a Blackhawk Helicopter in a war zone, surfing... stand up comedy still trumps all. I got into performing just as Judy was gearing up to leave me, and the ability to write and joke about having been cheated on and dumped was immensely therapeutic. I used to call my hosting duties "Fifteen minutes minus pain," as I was near suicidal during most of that period of my life, yet would be entirely OK while on stage.

I've been lucky enough (and worked hard enough) to move from the opening to the closing slot in many clubs, and that's what makes it all worthwhile. In my mind, I've never been paid a cent for my time on the stage. The clubs may hand me a check because I performed, but to me, the money is for the time I spent traveling to the location or sitting in my hotel room waiting for the show to start. To me, the paycheck is for the downtime, the time between my shows. For the

---

[1] This is an actual quote, said to me in 2007. It came from the worst kind of club owner: The Failed Comedian. Something inside them snaps when they give up on their dream and go to work for the other side of the business. You think they'd enter into the position with compassion and understanding, but generally The Failed Comedian is an awful, bitter person. The man who tossed that quote my way admitted he never watched my DVD, he said he didn't feel he had to because he "didn't like [my] headshot." On the flip side, there are former comedians who become club owners because they wanted to settle down and raise a family; these clubs are generally wonderful to work, as they have a nurturing edge to them.

actual act of standing on a stage and telling jokes? If I were a millionaire, I'd be doing that for free.

To stand on stage, however, you have to get hired, and that's the biggest struggle to the unknown comedian. Even harder than writing new material is getting booked. Rejection is constant, and you rarely get to actually hear the word "no." More often than not you just get ignored; I've sent some clubs promotional materials for upwards of three years and never heard a peep in return.

The fastest way to get ahead in comedy is to get a TV credit. Clubs and audiences alike enjoy the validity the phrase "As seen on" gives a performer; it makes it incredibly easy to get hired. Say you have press kits from two comedians: The first says, "A nationally touring comedian for ten years," has positive testimonials from twenty club owners, is a published writer, has credits such as morning radio shows with huge followings and consistent play on Satellite Radio, several worldwide tours in support of American troops stationed in Iraq and Afghanistan, and three compact discs under his belt. The second résumé is from a comic who has been performing for a year and a half, yet has been on television once. Truth is, the second comedian will get hired before the first a majority of the time. While such a move might make sense for advertising purposes, it's not always a wise thing. A few years after an incident I mentioned earlier, the club owner who rudely hung up on me ("Oh you fucking guys...") lost his club. Instead of hiring funny comedians, he hired only those who had a TV credit. They charged more, but many couldn't get laughs, and bad word of mouth bankrupted his business.

* * *

After several years of struggling in the industry, I worked with a comedian who had been on the road for fourteen years. We were on the same gig in the middle of nowhere, a one-night show in a bar, and in him I saw my future. I didn't like it one bit. The idea of being fourteen years into my career and working some Podunk bar in some Podunk town frightened me. I resolved then and there to move to Los Angeles and give "making it" a go. I figured the ever-elusive TV credit would help me avoid an unwanted future.

Luckily, I already had a support team in the city; a good friend and fellow comedian Bryan had moved to L.A. a few years prior. Following him had been another good friend and fellow comedian,

Baxter. The three of us had road tripped it from Milwaukee to Madison for years in search of stage time and had become close in the process. Regrouped, Baxter and I got an apartment in the same complex as Bryan, who then got both Baxter and I industry jobs with a company that represented filming locations.

Movies and television shows are filmed in two places: on a movie studio lot, or on a real location. For example, instead of building an office or hospital set, sometimes the production will just rent a working office or hospital and film in it after hours. The company I worked for acted as a liaison between properties and film productions; the property could sit back and collect a paycheck without having to do anything, and my company would take a percentage for brokering the deal. My specific title was Site Rep, short for site representation. My job was to sit on a property in use and make sure the production adhered to the specifics in the contract signed. Basically, I was a babysitter, and "No" was the main word in my vocabulary. Production companies are notorious for doing anything they can to get the "magic shot," and they can sometimes do so in damaging ways.

"Hey, I got an idea," I'd hear someone offer. "If we knock a hole in that wall, we can stick a camera in it and get a great angle on this scene!"

"Yeah... no." I'd interject in a low, Bill Lumbergh drawl. "We're not putting any holes into the walls today."

Such interactions would repeat themselves throughout the production's duration.

My first day of training was hilarious; a Michael Mann television show had rented out an entire floor of office space in a building my company represented. They were going to build it out to look like a police station, and then use it as a permanent set. I was excited; before *The Dark Knight* came along, *The Insider* had been my favorite film of all time. I watched it obsessively and couldn't believe my first day was going to be on the same set as its director, the aforementioned Michael Mann.

On my day of training, the production team was on the roof, thirty-five stories in the air. They were considering filming a scene up there, wanted to see what the view was like, and how it would play for the show. One specific instruction was hammered home to me: do not allow anyone to set anything on the ledge of the building. If something somehow got knocked off and fell thirty-five stories?

Even the littlest of items could pick up enough velocity to injure or kill someone.

As I meandered my way around the rooftop, keeping a respectful eye on everyone, I saw Mr. Mann place his beverage on the ledge of the building. I paused. My supervisor was downstairs monitoring the floor the rest of the production was working on, and I was left to my lonesome. Even though I hadn't been told, I still knew etiquette probably meant it wasn't my place to approach the most powerful person on the set and speak to him directly, but being new I didn't know where the chain of command lay or which of his underlings to approach. I kept staring at the mug on the ledge, the words, "Anything falls off the building and it's all over" echoing in my head. After a quick hesitation, I mustered up some resolve and approached the group of executives having their creative discussion. I stood on the outside of the circle a moment, and then in true "One of these things is not like the other" fashion, they took notice of me waiting awkwardly and turned their heads.

"Hiya," I said to Michael Mann with a gentle wave. "I was hoping we could get that drink removed from the ledge. Wouldn't want it to go over and all."

All eyes looked from me, to Michael Mann.

He looked from his drink, back to me, then chose his words carefully.

"Fuck off."

He returned to his conversation, paused, then looked back at me and kindly added, a gentle tone in his voice, "With all due respect."

I nodded my head, thinking, "Fair enough" and left. The funny thing is, "Fuck off" might read harshly, but he had said it so gentlemanly I wasn't offended in the slightest.

A few minutes later, one of the assistant directors came over and apologized, saying they didn't realize I was with the property and that I was just trying to keep everything safe. I laughed it off, because, as said, I wasn't offended, and I thought in fact it was a neat first-day story for any job. I eventually, for the record, spent time on several Michael Mann projects, and he was quite kind. He once even shook my hand in vigorous thanks for a favor I had granted the production. Even so, the story of our first encounter became a lovely running joke at my place of employment.

* * *

Productions work long hours; it wasn't uncommon to spend sixteen hours on any given day getting the right take on a scene. I would regularly come home exhausted, crash for four hours, and have to get right back up and head back to the set. On a couple occasions, I stayed at the property and slept on the floor, figuring it was better to try and get a little more sleep there than to waste an hour driving to and from my home, showering, unwinding, and finally falling asleep in time for the alarm to go off.

I moved three times during my time in L.A., my final apartment having been found on Craigslist, which always represents an eclectic sect of Americana. I had responded to an advertisement, "Roommate wanted," and the young, in-her-twenties woman and I seemed to hit it off, so it was agreed I would sign the lease. On the very moment I did so, before my pen had left the paper, she spoke some very curious words to me.

"By the way," she began, "I like to keep a... toy, in the freezer. If that bothers you, let me know and I can put it somewhere else."

The pregnant pause between "a" and "toy" led me to believe she wasn't speaking of Han Solo in carbonite, so I asked Bryan's new bride about the idea of a frozen, glass "appendage" being used for fun. Her response was an off-handed, "Well, cold is a stimulus, I guess." Yeah, that or a starter kit for necrophilia.

Either way, my roommate was a very nice person, but one that battled depression. Finding a roommate wasn't the only thing she used Craigslist for; the "Casual Encounters" section was an exceedingly popular bookmark on her computer. One week, no less than five separate men made their way into her bedroom.

Whatever emotional baggage she had been carrying all came to a head early one morning. I had just worked an enormous shift, around twenty hours I believe. By the time I got home at 2 a.m., I was exhausted beyond words. I stripped to my underwear and crashed hard. I don't know how long after I had fallen asleep everything happened, but I awoke to a knocking at my bedroom door.

"L.A.P.D.," a voice said. "Is anyone in there?"

"Um... yeah," I responded groggily.

"I'm opening the door," the voice informed.

"Okay."

The door opened, and backlit was the silhouette of a uniformed officer. I heard movement in my apartment behind him, a scuttling of many people fussing about. A firefighter walked past the police officer as I started to rise.

"What's your name?" the officer asked.

"Nathan," I responded.

"Nathan?"

"Timmel. Nathan Timmel."

"You live here?"

"Yes."

"Did you know we were in your apartment?"

"No."

"You didn't hear us?"

"I work long hours and was just out cold, sorry."

"So you didn't know your roommate attempted suicide tonight?"

"Uh... no."

"Her boyfriend called us. She's being taken to the hospital right now. It looks like an overdose."

By this point, I had gotten up and walked into the apartment proper; every cupboard door was wide open and the flashing red lights of the ambulance outside flickered off the living room walls.

"Do you know if she has any pills stashed anywhere?" he asked. "We need to know what she ingested."

I apologized, but didn't have any information for him.

The officer took a quick statement—nothing much, as I had no clue as to what happened—and gave me the name of the hospital my roommate was being taken to. After that, everyone left in haste to the next emergency, leaving me standing, in my underwear, confused and curious.

I wandered around the apartment a bit, tidying up, when I walked by her bedroom door. Lying on the floor was her cell phone. It hadn't crossed my mind until that point, but as soon as I saw the phone I realized someone had to call her family. Though it was early, maybe four in the morning, her family lived on the East Coast and might be awake.

I cautiously picked up the cell phone and did a quick search for words like "Home" or "Mom." I don't remember what I called, but I did end up with her mother on the other end of the line. It was an uncomfortable phone call, to say the least. I introduced myself, then hesitatingly gathered up the right words to offer.

"There's no easy way to say this," I began, "but the reason I'm using your daughter's phone is the police just woke me up with some disturbing information. I guess she took some pills, tried to take her life, and is being taken to the hospital."

I offered the name of the hospital, then paused. I awaited tears or sorrow.

I received irritation.

"Again?" the mother accused. "Bah. Well, at least they're taking her to a decent hospital this time. Thanks for calling."

She hung up.

Alrighty, then.

I went back to bed, fell asleep, and eventually got up and spent the day hanging out with friends. Retelling the tale, when I got to the part of the story when the officer asked if I knew where her pills were, my friend Frank arched an eyebrow and said, "Did you ask if he looked in the freezer?" If there is a definition of "Comedic Timing" in the dictionary, that's it right there.

My roommate, for the record, recovered nicely, moved in with her family for a while, got married, and seems to be doing much better these days.

* * *

I didn't move to Hollywood for location work; I was still interested in comedy, comedians, and the artistic scene. To my distaste, the city introduced me to a new breed of person: the backslash. I didn't particularly like these people, and found backslashing one's purported talents was something used far too often in self-description in Los Angeles.

"I'm a comedian/actor/model," a business card would state.

"I'm a model/voice-over artist/comedian/actress."

"Comedian/sketch-comic/monologist/actor/singer."

It seemed the more titles you could cram into your name, the more important you felt. The longer I lived there, the more I wanted to say, "You forgot waiter" at the end of their multi-pronged lists. When asked what dream I was chasing, I would just respond, "Comedian."

"Nothing else?"

"Nope."

Comedy was all that interested me; I didn't burn to become a movie star or get my own TV show, I just wanted a few TV credits, that I might continue to tour, but get better pay and bigger gigs. I also didn't want to be mediocre at several things; I preferred to excel in one specific area. Many backslash people I met weren't very good at their chosen fields. They couldn't get laughs to save their lives, yet they kept right on saying they were comedians. Their acting skills were non-existent, but they called themselves an actor, because getting noticed at all cost was important to them. My naivety was charming to many of my peers, but despite their mockery I subscribed to the axiom, "Jack of all trades, master of none" regarding their methods.

I was also a rarity: I was a comic who had been touring the country and getting paid to perform. Many of the comedians I bumped into were seven-minute wonders, people who jumped from coffee shop to coffee shop, reciting the same jokes repeatedly. I actually know of several people who didn't write a single new joke in the entire five years I lived there. I also discovered something disgusting when I moved to Los Angeles: the "bringer show." Now a staple at many clubs across the country, Los Angeles is the origin for making the comedians provide all the paying customers for a show. The rule was straightforward: if you brought five customers, you got five minutes on stage. I'm not sure who had this clever idea first, but they severely damaged the state of comedy across the country. They took the concept of originality and talent and reduced it to popularity. If you had more friends, you got more stage time, regardless of how awful a performer you might happen to be. While it is important for comedians to promote their shows, shouldering them with the burden of bringing an audience is a bit much. Imagine being hired at McDonald's and being told, "Okay, we'll give you shifts, but only if you make sure all your friends and family eat here. If they don't? You're fired." Fortunately, just as he had helped me find gainful employment, Bryan had lived in the city long enough to make some good contacts. He did his best to get me put on a few shows, even though I could do nothing to fill any seats.

One room was in Santa Monica, off the 3rd Street Promenade in an alleyway. While waiting for a performance to start one summer evening, a Hispanic family ran by Bryan, his girlfriend Natalie, the comics Mike Black and Craig Coleman, and me. The father was carrying his young daughter, who was crying.

In his best English, the man yelled, "He attack my girl with knife! Help us!"

He pointed, and our collective heads turned as one to see a man down the alleyway wearing a trenchcoat and swaying erratically. One hand was splayed wide and the other tightly fisted, as if holding something. He was disheveled and looked homeless, a very likely scenario given the area.

Without missing a beat, Bryan yelled, "Timmel, come on!" and took off after him. Natalie dialed 911 and tried following the family with the injured daughter. I shadowed Bryan. Craig and Mike said, "fuck that" in nonverbal body language, and stayed put.

As we moved closer to the man, pale yellow neon shining down from a store light offered forth the familiar glint of steel; a knife was indeed in play tonight. Bryan and I exchanged a cautious glance; what were we getting ourselves into?

The man made a stabbing, "Stay back, I'm dangerous!" gesture and ducked into a cubbyhole that contained no exit.

Knowing that in nature a cornered animal is where it's most dangerous, Bryan and I held back. Our plan was to observe from a distance, wait patiently for the police, then bravely point at his hiding place when they arrived.

Stabby, however, wasn't about to sit around waiting for the men in blue. He darted at us and made a break up the alley as we backed off. Not wanting to let him out of our sight, we continued following several paces behind for half a city block, but then something snapped in Bryan. Maybe it was the fact his brother was a homicide detective; maybe he just decided he'd had enough of the nonsense and decided to go all in. Whatever the reason, without warning, Bryan ran right at Stabby and readied to take him down; Stabby realized it was game on and decided to sprint. Bryan kicked out to trip him, and unfortunately was more Charlie Brown than Kung Fu. As if Lucy had pulled the football away before him, instead of tripping Stabby Bryan missed wide and high and stumbled to a near fall. He then looked to me to make sure I was still following and not doubled over with laughter; I was probably doing a little of both.

Stabby was not laughing, and turned to swing at Bryan. Whether it was with his knifed hand or balled fist I couldn't tell, I just knew everything had just shot up a notch in the danger department. I'd like to write that something poetic crossed my mind, such as "In for a penny, in for a pound," or "It is in these moments we define ourselves," but I'm pretty sure the only thought I had was the very benign, "Oh, fuck." In my mind, I saw this escalating to damaging levels, where one of us, and it looked like Bryan, was going to get hurt.

Fortunately, Bryan dodged the swing, threw the off-balance Stabby to the ground, and I caught up in time to jump on him.

I ground my knee into Stabby's back and pushed his face into the concrete. He squirmed for a little while, then finally began to calm. When he did so, Bryan stood up to take a breather from all the excitement and took a step back to take everything in.

Out of nowhere, as if he'd been by our side all along, Craig appeared, shouting forcefully, "That's right asshole! You STAY down!"

Bryan and I exchanged disbelieving looks: really, Craig? After all the danger had been removed from the situation, you were jumping in and acting like a hero?

Naturally, in that moment, the police helicopter we didn't even realize had been following us flipped on its spotlight, illuminating me dead center in its stare. I immediately envisioned myself on a bad episode of "Cops," the shot of me kneeling atop a homeless man in a piss-drenched alley, a bright light blinding me. This was not how I wanted to get my first TV credit.

The local bike patrol arrived quickly and took Stabby into custody, taking our statements and letting us know an ambulance had arrived for the young girl. Sadly, she was apparently the fourth person Stabby had cut that night. I have no idea what happened to her, or any of the others attacked.

* * *

Bringer shows aside, The Improv did hold occasional auditions for comedians new to town. I performed at one, did well enough, and was allowed a second audition. At said second audition, I took to the stage with five well-rehearsed minutes. I'm glad I had prepared, for as I grabbed the microphone, I looked down at the audience to see one couple acting extremely frisky. A buxom woman was sitting on her fella's lap, and they were kissing and having a grand old time. It wasn't overly distracting, so I started in on my jokes. My punch lines worked; the audience started laughing. After thirty seconds, my mind started nagging at me, telling me there was something I was missing in the couple. I glanced down again, doing my best to both see under the spotlight, while not looking like I was trying to see under the spotlight. The woman seemed improbably familiar. She was blocking the man's face, so I couldn't get a bead on him, but I could swear I knew her. I continued my set, now fully on autopilot, where my mind was thinking about the woman as my mouth went its own direction and handled business. Somewhere around the two-minute mark, it hit me like a flash.

"Holy poop on a stick," I thought. "That's Gerri Halliwell."

My mind started doing celebrity math, and I realized that if the gossip rags were right, the lap she was sitting on was one owned by Jerry O'Connell.

Glancing down again, I saw that not only was I right, he was laughing heartily. My ego did an eyebrow raise; I was making a couple celebrities laugh. Nifty!

After the show, I was lucky enough to meet Jerry O'Connell, and he said he really enjoyed my act. Over the next several years, I bumped into him on random movie sets while at work, and he always looked at me with a furrowed brow.

"I recognize you," he'd eventually say, "but I don't know from where."

I would then remind him he saw me at The Improv, and he would smile and laugh and shake my hand.

Over the course of my years in Los Angeles, I got to meet or even talk with a handful of celebrities. Though it may seem obvious, the main thing I got out of the experience is the idea they're all just people. Some are kind and grateful for their success, others are prickish and off-putting. It is what it is. There is no magic formula for fame, and considering some of the rich assholes I've bumped into, I'd have to question whether or not karma exists in the slightest.

My second audition at The Improv didn't just go well in my mind, the club observer thought so, too. I was given a phone number and told I could call in my availability every week. If they had an open slot, I had a shot at getting on the stage. I was damned happy, until I realized that I was one of 1,345 comedians in the same situation. Beyond my auditions, I never graced The Improv stage again. I called dutifully for five years and never once was called back.

So it goes.

The Improv is one of three big-name comedy venues in Los Angeles, and while I never took to the Laugh Factory stage, I did spend a decent amount of time at The Comedy Store. Bryan ran a Tuesday night show, and he was kind enough to let me host it. I met a few people, made a few friends, and then on a few rare moments was called and given a slot on off nights.

The Comedy Store is on the infamous Sunset Strip, at the base of the Hollywood Hills. Parking is both limited and fairly pricey in such places, and the only way to avoid giving your wallet a beating was to park hell and beyond up in the Hills. Most roads had posted tow zones on them, and if there's one thing Los Angeles doesn't joke about, it's a tow zone. The L.A.P.D. makes bank off yanking cars, and in an area such as the Hollywood Hills, filled with multi-million dollar homes, a watchful eye is constantly upon such areas. Towards the top, however, side streets have street parking, most likely because few people want to hike a quarter mile straight up to retrieve their car. I climbed it every time. I'd drive up the steep slope of Queens Road and leave my car where I could find space. Returning after my show, I used the walk as exercise for the mind. Passing the houses hidden behind gates and expensive shrubs, I looked for inspiration. The town was full of money and success; the neighborhood I parked in was proof positive of it. I would daydream as I climbed, using the houses as focus: "This is attainable."

I generally went home feeling good after a night at The Comedy Store.

Maintaining that positive attitude in L.A. was trying. In the time I lived there, three people I met began their comedy career, got a slot on television, and gave up doing stand-up all together. So the one thing I moved to the city to achieve, others did with less effort and follow through. I understand the industry better today, but it was incredibly frustrating to navigate at the time. The simple fact of the matter is, a lot of comedians on television are cast for their niche, not their comedy. Programs have a certain number of demographics they want to cater to, and they look for people who fit those needs. Funny or not is secondary in such decision making processes; look trumps talent in initial Hollywood discovery.

Talent, then, keeps you in the race. Jack Nicholson may have gotten a lucky break with *Easy Rider*, but incredible acting made him a legend. The three comics who got on TV while I watched from the sidelines did so too soon in their careers. Each had a solid seven-minute set, yet little else. They didn't have the skills to perform at comedy clubs, they didn't have screenplays to sell, didn't fit any available acting needs, and were thus run though the machine and put back out to pasture. When that didn't sit well with them, they just moved on, either willingly or begrudgingly.

But, not everyone walks away despite their lack of talent. When I went to Iraq to perform for the troops, I was lucky enough to work for an organization founded on the sole principle of providing laughter to American soldiers. The focus was comedy, and comedians were screened for abilities and talent. Shows were billed as "All Headliner" performances, meaning only seasoned veterans were used. At that point in my career, I had been touring the country for years and had been in front of hundreds of audiences and thousands of people. I could alter my act to meet many standards, from clean to dirty, political or personal. Over time, a comedian learns how to adjust as needed. This is what the organization wanted: adaptability. Could the performer meet the needs of any audience? The answer had to be "yes," because entertaining the troops was the only thing of concern for the organization. Profit was not even on their radar; if any government stipend for travel was available, the organization up and turned it over to the performer. Therefore a $200 stipend given to the organization became a full $200 to the comedian for their efforts.

When I got to Kuwait, I met a military liaison that spoke of an upstart agency interested in military comedy contracts. The agency already provided musicians, but was putting a foot in the laughter door and had sent a couple joke-slingers over. The liaison noted, with disappointment in his voice, their comedians were not very funny, and they spoke of a stipend much, much lower than the government had paid. So while the agency was handed $200, the performer was given $50, with $150 padding the pockets of agency owners.

I found this interesting, to say the least.

After spending a few months in L.A., I began hearing open-microphone comics—those just getting started—boast of going on tour to both overseas and across America. I now knew who the upstart agency was finding to take the $50 fee and could only think, "How sad." The comedians were both hurting their development and stigmatizing comedy. By jumping in over their heads, they were trying to tell thirty minutes worth of jokes when they couldn't generate consistent laughter for five. The young comedians also couldn't adapt, as they didn't have enough material to do so. If their regular shtick wasn't working, they had no fallback position to try. So American audiences would be bored and upset enough by a bad show enough to avoid comedy for a while, and soldiers deserving of actual distraction from their daily problems were forced to sit through a bargain basement performance.

A couple years after my first trip, I was offered the chance to return to Iraq with another batch of comedians. Unfortunately, my trip, and every tour the organization had, fell through. The organization that employed me lost all its contracts to the upstart agency that, in effect, told the government, "The stipend you offer is too much. We'll do it for less."

By playing with the money early on, the agency gained leverage; a $200 stipend became $150. The comics would still get their $50, with the agency "only" pocketing $100. The agency gained more on the back end by scooping up a greater volume of tours. Because that is the corporate nature of war, right? "How can I use the conflict to *my* advantage?"

I understand how this happens on the governmental end. The accountants are only looking at numbers on a ledger, and when larger vs. smaller dollar amount arrives in front of them, smaller wins. Sadly, in the world of thousand-dollar toilet seats and $700 hammers, the decision-maker in this case probably saved the equivalent about of five toilet seats for the fiscal year.

The damage done in terms of entertainment value, however, was immense. The agency known for musicians and cover bands was plucking from the comedy world the same seven-minute wonders that did not have the skills to shift their routines for content or environment. Comedy is a craft that involves progression; like anything, you become more qualified the more you practice. Those not entirely ready for the dynamics of a professional show should never have been sent to entertain those that deserve much, much better. The comedians may act out of purity of heart, but there is a world of difference between an amateur and a professional. Using amateurs shows an unfortunate lack of concern for soldiers in need of entertainment and distraction.

I must be clear, though: it's not about the money.

If the military wants to save money, it can call for volunteers. I and many others would go over for free; it is an honor just to be of service. But I refuse to carry a company using the war for profit on my shoulders; to be involved with such an act is unforgivable. I want nothing to do with it.

* * *

The longer I lived in Los Angeles, the less time I actually spent there. Comedy clubs across America were still hiring, and it was very rewarding to travel to one of those and be paid to perform for an hour. The option was remaining in L.A. and being told I could do five minutes if I brought ten paying customers in. Ten paying customers who would each have to buy two overpriced beverages to boot.

In the end, Iowa accidentally saved me.

I was within its borders, and one night, through a series of happenchance circumstances, a young woman ended up in the right audience, in the right frame of mind, and saw me. Though I left immediately after my show and we never spoke that evening, she would still end up changing my life immensely.

INTERLUDE

IRAQ, 2009

NATHAN TIMMEL

14 – A SECOND SUNSET IN THE SAND

This time, I forgot to tell my mother.

Several years earlier, while readying myself for a trip to Afghanistan, I accidentally made her cry. Mom was worried about my safety, whereas I had no concerns. I trusted I would be fine 'n' dandy on my trip and was so callously indifferent about her worry, it upset her mightily. So about three weeks out from another trip to the Middle East, while chatting casually with my mom, she asked a question and I responded, "Well, I'll still be in Iraq then."

"What," my mother said flatly.

Though "what" is generally a question, there was no inflection suggesting inquiry in her voice. Mom was pissed. Though I had known for months a trip to the desert country of heat and camels was coming, it somehow slipped my mind to inform her.

A stern lecture from an angry and unhappy mother followed. Though I was being chastised, I couldn't help but find it hilarious. A son forgetting to tell his mother he was happily headed into danger? Most amusing! To me, anyway.

Not so amusing was the time spent on a cramped airplane; the trip to Kuwait took three flights and over fifteen hours. Exhausted and sore from the ordeal, I met the two other comics scheduled for the tour in the Kuwait airport lobby, and together we waited for our transport to the military base.

Landing in any foreign territory, you don't immediately notice subtle differences in culture. The big differences—dress, language, body makeup, and skin color—are obvious. Little things might not register right away, but when the pieces fall into place a light bulb goes off above your head. In Kuwait, what took me a second to process was that everyone smoked, and they did so everywhere. Unlike America, where an active fight against the tobacco industry has been ongoing for decades, Kuwait held a 1950s mindset towards the habit. While big tobacco was continually losing ground in the United States, overseas it marched forward unabated. In many nations, it is still a point of pride to puff a Marlboro Red over any local brand. Designated smoking areas were actively posted, but they were mostly ignored. People—men, actually; if smoking was something women did in private, I was not witness to it—smoked where they wanted and no one enforced any regulations. The Burger King[1] trays were dotted with burn marks, and cigarettes were tossed to the airport floor just as casually as could be. The positive aspect of all this is: if we don't get the terrorists with bombs, hopefully we'll kill them with cancer.

Two hours passed as we waited for our contact, and irritation set in. Luckily, in an international airport used by American military, there is always a friendly face about. I struck up a conversation with a couple soldiers looking for someone from the same flight I had arrived on, and they were from the base we comics were headed to. They recognized one of the contact names we had, and one kindly called him for us. We were told to wait by Starbucks.[2]

Walking our way to the meeting point, I passed an American man holding a sign with three names on it. I had seen him milling about the lobby, but as none of the names on his placard were ours, I didn't give him much thought. His cell phone rang as I passed, and he began a conversation as I left earshot.

---

[1] Of course there's a Burger King in Kuwait. Driving through the country, you see many signs of Americana, though sadly few of them involve the best we have to offer.

[2] *Of course* there's a Starbucks in the Kuwait International Airport. Who doesn't want a nice, hot coffee when it's over 100 degrees out?

When we arrived at Starbucks, I noticed the man looking in our direction and walking over. When he got back within range, I heard him say, "They're right here? I don't see anyone looking for me."

He paused, and looked at us.

"Are you guys comedians?"

"We are," I told him.

"Going to Arifjan?"

"Yes."

"I found them," he said into the phone.

Our contact's name began with the letter B, and when looking to see why he had the wrong names, B took a closer look at his orders. Every date, on every form, was for the month of June. Sadly, it was now July, meaning B brought the previous month's documentation, names, and pictures with him. While it is somewhat amusing, having the wrong orders meant we couldn't get on base and into our beds; we had to wait outside the gate for over a half an hour while B called in for an escort.

As we waited, one question I pondered while examining the barren landscape was: would you rather be poor in heaven, or rich in hell? Kuwait may be one of the most oil-rich nations on the planet, but all you can do is shuffle from air-conditioned location to air-conditioned location; the desert climate leaves little worth doing outside. Kuwaiti citizens, much like Alaskans, receive a government stipend just for existing, but that's something I'm not sure is worth receiving if you actually have to live in Kuwait. Maybe I should phrase the question sexually: would you rather date a beautiful, yet prudish woman, or a Plain Jane that's a wildcat in the sack? Beauty looks good on the arm, but better in the bed is probably superior.

After our escort arrived and we were finally allowed onto the base, as I undressed in my ten-by-six foot room—one with air conditioning auto-set so low I eventually had to open my window to the 120-degree heat and let the two fight it out—I made an unfortunate discovery. Several days before departing I had taken a softball to the leg. I was helping my girlfriend Lydia with batting practice; I lobbed them in, and she knocked them out. Save for the last ball, that is. That one she didn't launch out of the park so much as into me. My right leg, to be specific. Just below the kneecap. A knot swelled to generous proportions, which I iced and elevated, and eventually the bulge subsided to a healthy little lump. All was well, until I spent an inordinate amount of time seated on an airplane.

Spending fifteen hours sitting meant whatever was left of the leg-swell drained into my foot, creating one exceptionally puffy appendage. My heel became a lovely Prince-purple, as a decent volume of blood had decided to pool there, and my shoe no longer fit. This was not an exciting development.

I hobbled over to a recreation room to lie on the floor and elevate my legs. I scooched my butt up to the wall, lay my legs extended up said wall, then set my watch timer for thirty minutes. Fatigued, I began nodding off, followed immediately by accidentally snoring myself back awake. I noticed I was doing so to the amusement of a cadet working on her computer across the room, but was too tired to be embarrassed.

After the allotted thirty minutes passed, my foot was a little more normal, though still quite squishy to the touch. I hoped it wouldn't turn into a problem.

Our first show was the following evening, and it was as botched as our pickup; once again, B proved that you can keep a government job with the barest minimum of effort. At 1:00 p.m. we gathered for what was supposed to be a simple day trip to visit another base in Kuwait, Ali Al Saleem.

Entering the van, I asked in a clear, slow voice, "Is our show at the base we're going to, or here on Arifjan?"

"Huh?" B responded. "Your show is tonight."

"I know that," I informed him. "But is it on this base, Arifjan, or the one we are going to?"

"Oh," B said thoughtfully. "It's here."

And that was the last of it, until we got to Ali Al Saleem at 3:00 and were told, "OK, show's at seven, you have four hours to kill."

The other two comics and I looked at one another, unprofessionally dressed in sandals and shorts, unshowered and scruffy, and wondered just how stupid B was.[1]

We were performing outdoors—which is never good for comedy—and when the start time arrived an audience of approximately four people was waiting patiently. Ali Al Saleem is a large base, and it is sometimes difficult to market a show in such places. While there is very little to do, people still enter routines, and advertising becomes exactly like it is in America: something to ignore.

---

[1] Very.

Posters promoted our arrival, but they blended in with every other activity being pushed. An email had been sent from recreation officers to all soldiers, but soldiers receive spam just like the rest of the world, and spam is usually deleted unopened.

I decided to throw myself on the grenade and go up first. My idea was that once the people milling about saw someone yapping away at them, they would be curious, meander over, and have a seat. Like the opening of a spigot, the instant I spoke into the microphone, ears perked and people flowed toward the sound. I might not be the most famous thing to ever take the stage, but in that environment, I was something different. *Something* was happening, something out of the norm, which is always good in the eyes of a weary soldier. While 100 posters were placed in every corner of the camp, only at the show's inception did the event become tangible.

Having done military tours before, I was able to cater my set to the audience a little. I started throwing out little nuggets of inside information on military life to draw everyone in. One such tidbit was how some men of the military refer to female soldiers overseas. As the military is generally a sausage fest, women have all the power when it comes to mixed-gender liaisons. It's basically a buffet for women, which irritates rejected men. Therefore, some of the fairer sex in uniform are referred to as a "two-ten-two." In the states, they're so ugly they're considered a two, but when they get to the Middle East, they're in such high demand they become tens. Their ego soars like an eagle, but when they return to the states, they're crushed as they become twos again.

Cute, but I gave women their revenge using the same term, telling the men they're labeled the exact same way. In the states, they're two inches and last two minutes. In Iraq, they're suddenly ten inches and last ten minutes! But when they return to America...

The speech flowed the same way every night; up front, men laughed and howled. After the twist, women were pointing fingers and giggling. And I loved it all.

Fortunately, I never have to cater my act to any audience to the point of pandering. I do my best to relate to people on their level, but ultimately my comedy is personal. I tell stories of my life, such as the interactions between my family and the like. It's an act I can carry with me anywhere, one that need not depend on surroundings, such as jokes about traffic. All too often I've seen a comedian get in over his head while relying on the crutch of pretending to relate to the audience: "Boy, isn't traffic crazy here in..." and where a generic city would normally be inserted—Miami, New Orleans, London, Belfast or Berlin—in Iraq, what could a comedian say? "Boy, the traffic sure is crazy here in Tikrit?" Such a comment would not go over well in a war zone. The issues soldiers deal with is not "crazy," it's deadly. Improvised Explosive Devices exist in random locations, and Humvees don't wait for red lights.

Kuwait out of the way, we were told to gather at 9:00 a.m. the next morning for our foray into Iraq. At nine on the dot, B showed up in a panic.

"Your flight got moved up, we have to get there NOW," he stressed.

We hurried, he sped, and we arrived at the flight line with plenty of time to spare. Too much time, in fact. So much time, that as we sat and waited, B checked on our situation with the woman in charge.

"Well, they moved your flight from ten-thirty to one-thirty," B told us. "I'm leaving. Call if you need anything."

I was handed a slip of paper with the contact information for our next stop on it, and like a ghost, B disappeared.

The instant he left, the woman he had conferred with approached us and said, "You know, he screwed up. Your flight was always at 1:30, he just wrote it down wrong."

Of course he did, and then he blamed her for his mistake.

Lovely.

Flying into Iraq five years after my first visit was an event involving contrast. Five years ago, I stepped off a C-130 cargo plane and into a war zone. Everyone was in body armor, everyone was armed, and military vehicles were everywhere; Bradleys, Humvees, and tanks surrounded me.

This time, when the back door of our transport opened at Al Asad Airbase, two soldiers and an entertainment rep—not a single one in body armor—waited for us out in the open, and they waited with two standard, off-the-lot trucks, with no extra plating or bulletproof glass on either.

Such changes were a testament to the job being done there. I'm not going to go on record and say the country was safe and that I'd walk around Baghdad at night, but the threat of danger had lessened. Last time I visited, several bases came under some form of attack. Whether it was a single rocket launched randomly over the protective barrier or several mortars lobbed inside the perimeter, violence was ever-present. By the end of this visit, however, nothing had happened. No sirens sounded, no alarms blared, no attack occurred. Sectarian brutality between clans is another issue, but Iraq was getting safer for American soldiers.

In fact, it was so "safe" in Iraq in 2009 a serious issue threatened the men and women of the military from within. The first time I visited, in 2004, soldiers exhibited a sense of anger and resentment over their deployment. Anti-Bush graffiti adorned every bathroom at every base, and people were unhappy. In 2009, the pervasive mood was resigned acceptance. The unhappy was still prevalent, but in a way that was more, "This is life, it sucks, and you deal with it." It felt like a loveless marriage, one where the spark died long ago, but inertia kept everyone wrapped up in the union. Such a situation creates a stress that is slow to simmer, but when it boils, it explodes. Though it wasn't making the news in America, three bases in a row told me they lost more servicemen in the first half of the year to suicide than to terrorist attacks or gunfights.

The standard suicide followed a pattern: a nineteen to twenty-one-year-old kid away from home for not only the first time, but for an extended period of time. He went over while in a relationship, maybe did the "panic engagement" to have a lifeline to hold onto, and then he got dumped. Heartbreak involves actual physical pain, and if you've never felt it, you're lucky. If you add the mind-numbing life of being trapped in a situation where every day is the goddamned same to the bodily stress of heartbreak, and do so in the mind of a nineteen-year-old, you have a recipe for disaster. Few teenagers have the capability to envision a better future when their immediate surroundings are horrific, and their emotions are haywire. I remember being entirely unhappy at that age, and my life was fucking fantastic by comparison.

Sadly, the military is responding in a typically out-of-touch fashion. Every commercial break on every Armed Forces Entertainment network had at least one ad addressing the situation. Naturally, the ads confronted the problem sideways and offered help that was ass-backwards from reality.

"Friends should be vigilant!" they warned. "If you or someone you know is contemplating hurting themselves, talk to your chaplain!"

Are you fucking kidding me? "Talk to your chaplain" is the cork that will stop the epidemical wave of suicides in the military? It's as logical as saying, "Jesus will help you pray your gay away." Some problems are real, and real problems need real solutions. No recently dumped teen wants to sit with a priest and talk out his problems. At nineteen, you don't understand that life is full of options, especially not when you exist within the hell of monotony. The person that dumped you becomes the end-all be-all to your life. No one will ever love you like she did, no one will ever understand you like she did, and you two were just oh-so-perfect together...

The truth is, if one partner doesn't work out, another will. It's a fact.

What the military needs to do is take anyone on the verge of suicide, anyone right there up against their wit's end and about to eat the barrel of a gun, furlough them for ten days to Thailand. Place a jumbo pack of condoms and $200 in the palm of their hand and say, *"You're fucking nineteen years old, go get laid like a nineteen-year-old! Go fuck your ex right out of your system!"*

Will that cure the pain?

No.

But it will let the kid know there is still fun to be had in the world without the Jane Doe that broke his heart, and it will act as a stopgap between the time he might do something stupid and the period in which he begins to heal.

If that seems too extreme, the military can take little measures. Pornography is currently blocked on the Internet service that soldiers use. While this is understandable at public kiosks, many servicemen (and women) have laptops used in the privacy of their own barracks. People have needs and urges; if the military would allow them their God-given right to masturbate using something other than the imagination, I guarantee it would boost morale.

As tragic as one tale was, I have to admit to having felt disgustingly inspired by it. As always, it began with a teenager. He was chatting on Skype with his girlfriend, who was back in the states, and things were not going well. No one is sure if she admitted to falling for another boy, or if she just broke up with him because she couldn't wait any longer, but the end result was the same: he was shocked, and heartbroken. Try putting yourself in his position; imagine being that lonely, desolate, bored. The one thing you're holding onto is the idea someone loves and is waiting for you back home. Then she appears on screen, right there in front of you, and says she just can't wait anymore.

In a moment of pain, anger, and confusion, the young man shot himself. Not back in his room, after writing a note, and not after acting emo for a week, sulking and moping about. He acted in the moment. He stood his Twisted Sister ground, said he wasn't gonna take it, and showed his love the magnitude of her actions. The boy killed himself with the webcam still rolling, and a shocked and no doubt permanently damaged girl thousands of miles away was powerless to do anything about it.

While it is an absolute horror the boy took his own life, I consider it grotesquely poetic the girlfriend had to witness firsthand the repercussion of her actions. To me, his response was like the painting of a great work of art, or the composing of the most beautiful symphony ever heard. "You'll be sorry you left me" is all too often an empty threat, or one used to threaten an ex with action against them, but not in his case. This kid showed the world that if you're going to do something exceedingly stupid, you have to do it with flair. Damn if I don't give him kudos for that statement.

* * *

Al Asad was one of Saddam Hussein's premiere air stations, and also home to a notorious piece of history. His son Uday was legendary in his day for cruelty; he existed only to cause pain. Uday was the head of Iraq's Olympic Committee and was known far and wide to torture athletes who did not perform up to expectations. He would take entire families hostage, using them as motivational pieces: play poorly and lose your wife or child.

Dead center in Al Asad was Saddam's soccer stadium. Inside, all practice and torture took place under Uday's watchful eye. The best athletes in the country were sent there to train, and not all returned home. Uday's seat was in the center top row, where he would sit, gun in lap, randomly shooting at players' feet like it was the old west.

Today the stadium crumbles. The grass of the field is long dead and has been replaced by the ever-present sand the climate demands. Kiosks line old vendor slots, and bootlegs of American movies and television shows are sold where people were once murdered as a form of motivation.

Outside Al Asad, I visited an old Iraqi fighter jet, one laying in ruin on the perimeter of the base. Saddam was stupid-smart, meaning he had ideas, but didn't think them through. Saddam always placed jets on the edges of his air bases and would cover them in camouflage, leaving them hidden from his enemies. The plan was: if and when attacks were made on the base, ha-ha! The planes would be safe!

Which would work wonderfully, except when America attacked, we bombed the shit out of the runways, control towers, and any building around. So... great, you've got some planes sitting in the desert that can't take off or communicate with one another. Swing and a miss, Saddam, but thanks for playing.

We left Al Asad on a Marine "Phrog," a CH-46 helicopter, which is a smaller version of the twin rotor Chinook. Hazy morning conditions meant we spent five hours waiting for clearance, because not much flies when the sand is kicking. Regarding the Marines, we were told, "These fuckers will fly in anything. If they're grounded, you know it's bad out."

Flying over barren desert, it was safe enough to allow us to take pictures standing with the airships guns. "Just don't fucking fire it," the gunner commanded. When we got within several miles of a city, however, the gunners resumed their posts.

The body language of our escorts changing from desert to city was a fascinating metamorphosis; both went from a slumped-shoulder casual stance to vigilant attention. Their eyes scanned back and forth, ever alert, and the muzzle of their guns followed, tracing all movements. A city is host to many nooks, crannies, and alleyways, and each holds the promise of danger.

On certain flights, I was given a headset and cracked wise with everyone. When the conversation turned serious, I understood without prompting it was time to keep my comedic mouth shut.

"White car to our left," one pilot announced calmly.

"Already targeted," the gunner responded.

"Looks like he's got something sticking out of his window."

"Can't tell what it is, but there's no movement."

"Copy."

When the pilot announced the possible threat, I turned my untrained eyes to the side and saw only traffic; there was a multitude of autos driving back and forth on a busy Iraqi thoroughfare. Only after several seconds of scanning was I able to lock onto the white car. By that point, however, had it been a danger to us, it would have been too late. The fact the gunner had assessed the target I couldn't even find and had done so before being alerted to its presence impressed the hell out of me. The car turned out to be no hazard, as it was just hauling something that didn't entirely fit in the back seat, but for a good twenty seconds, the driver had no idea his car was ready to be lit up by a hail of 50-caliber gunfire.

Every time a helicopter flies in Iraq, it does so in tandem with a partner. If one runs into trouble, the other is there for either attack or evac, depending on what the situation calls for. I rode in both the lead and second chopper over the course of my visit, and each time protocol was the same: the lead chopper flew a direct route, with the second swaying gently side-to-side behind and a little above it. It was both comforting and hypnotizing to witness, as the follow chopper swayed lazily, like a cat's tail on a living room floor. They were always watching, waiting to pounce should the need arise.

Many bases in Iraq are like small, self-contained, gated mini-cities. The last time I visited, most places had only tents standing. Fixed structures were few, and conditions were minimal. This time, many amenities were available. Fast food restaurants, small mall-like shopping areas, and even the occasional movie theater now adorned once-vacant lots. In 2004, meals were served under a canvas roof; in 2009, I ate in air-conditioned luxury. Not that the food improved, even if military food is actually more tedious than bad. The same menu was offered day after day, and it's probably easy to go a little insane in such situations. "Let's see, do I want a tuna salad sandwich for lunch today, or chicken salad? If I have tuna tomorrow, I can have chicken today, and then again the day after tomorrow..."

Though it was unusual to see a Subway or Taco Bell on a base in Iraq, it's probably quite nice for a soldier to have that occasional option. The restaurants aren't the structures we see in cities here. Fast food locations provided for the military are more like mobile homes you'd see at a state fair or amusement park. You ordered, then ate outside or back in your room. Considering the DFAC (dining facility) kept limited hours, Taco Bell works well for a soldier on duty past dinner.

Camp Ramadi, however, was nothing like many of the lush bases we visited. Everything was rustic in Ramadi, and that's putting it nicely. Life is hard. Marines lodged in old Iraqi barracks that are in worse repair than most inner-city apartments. Where Al Asad was known as *Camp Cupcake*—not only because the geography of the base suggested an inverted cupcake, as it rests in a crater looking like a muffin top, but also because it contained many nice amenities— Ramadi exposed the harshest of conditions soldiers lived in.

Al Asad's freestanding structures had protective barriers, but they were pristine and stood several yards back from any structure. In Ramadi, the barriers showed their wear and tear, with crumbling cement revealing it had been tested and withstood whatever had been launched its way. The blast shields also hugged any building they were meant to protect; they weren't twenty yards from a building, they were snug up against them. A mortar or rocket would have to actually hit a structure dead on to do any damage. To miss by even two feet meant the barriers would take the hit and protect all. The protection was necessary, as at one point during the peak of conflict, Ramadi held the "honor" of being the second most-attacked base in Iraq.

With literally nothing to do, notice of a comedy show had everyone interested; troops were grabbing the best seats long before show time. I was excited to give a good performance, but the evening got off on a hilariously awkward foot. The opening comic that night purchased a Cuban cigar earlier in the day, and smoked it before going up. There is a reason Cuban cigars are legendary, and one of them is their intoxicating effect. So, that day the opener didn't eat much at dinner, didn't drink enough fluids, and then puffed on a Cuban cigar; he couldn't have put on a worse pair of Bad Idea Jeans[1] had he tried. With a combination of hunger, dehydration, and Cuban smoke in his system, he hit the stage a rambling, incoherent mess. At first, the soldiers weren't sure what to think and wondered why they were being subjected to such a shitty comedian, but as time passed, they realized his disorientation wasn't part of his act and grew amused. I stood side-stage, hissing his name as he went ten minutes past his allotted time before finally grabbing his attention. He maintained lucidity long enough to bring me up, botching my name while doing so. By playfully mocking him in my opening comments, I was able to say what all the soldiers had been thinking: "What a doofus that guy was."

On the morning of our scheduled departure from Ramadi, a small sandstorm blew in and canceled all flights. I say small, only because

---

[1] "Now that I have kids, I feel a lot better about having a gun in the house."

that is what I was told. From my perspective, it was full-fledged and powerful. The sky was so red it felt like being on Mars. It entered my pores, and several people outside wore surgical masks to protect their lungs. If I even cracked my mouth for a moment, it felt like I was drinking powder and I could feel the grit across my teeth as if checking pearls for purity.

At one point the sun was entirely eclipsed by sand and I could stare right at it, seeing only a haze of an outline. Commenting on that, a soldier reminded me I was standing in the middle of a "nothing" storm; the fact I could see fifty yards meant it was tiny. Many enlisted told me stories of not being able to see their hand in front of their face, or the hood of a car from the windshield. On those days, the only thing to do was hunker down and wait it out.

Being trapped meant an extra day of wandering through buildings, and I was lucky enough to meet one of the base commanders. He explained that part of the reason conditions were so poor at Ramadi is because the base is one of many being shuttered by the military. Within six months of my visit, it would be no more. Instead of maintaining it and repairing barriers, they were walking away from everything like a foreclosed home. What's funny (or sad, depending on your point of view) is this fact seemed to matter little to the corporation known as Halliburton. KBR, as is its technical name, continued to place bids on nonexistent contracts to repair the base.

"Your roads need repair," the rep would say. "We can fix them for ten million dollars."

"No need," the commander would respond. "We won't be here long enough for it to be worthwhile."

"Um... how about for five million!"

The commander I met laughed as he spoke of repeatedly shooting them down, but to the "ultra-patriotic" corporate heads of KBR, profit is king. They were more than willing to do a multi-million dollar repair of a road, even if it would be useless soon.

Despite that commander's ever-cautious use of American tax dollars, waste is still prevalent in the military. At Camp Bucca, a $26,000,000 American-made sewage treatment plant sat idle because there wasn't enough waste to operate it. The plant was built at the same time a temporary detention facility was created, and my comedy troupe became only the third set of civilians ever allowed inside the "prison."

Prison is in quotes, because public relations was the most important thing in Iraq at that moment. Having won the war, winning hearts and minds was front and center on the American agenda, and that was done through attrition; Blackhawk gunners dropped "Candy Bombs" when they saw children, sweet treats not unlike the chocolate GIs handed out in WWII. Such actions were meant to win over the future generation. Kindness, explanation and education were the tools used to win those too old for chocolate.

Kindness, and, of course, sleight-of-hand.

After the disaster that was Abu Ghraib, Camp Bucca became the go-to place for captured insurgents. As "prison" has a negative connotation, "detention center" became one label used in description, but the most common was TIF,[1] "Theater Internment Facility." At its peak, Bucca held 21,000 detainees, and those 21,000 detainees were watched over by less than 6,000 American troops. With that many people pooping daily, the sewage treatment plant had enough waste to hum along nicely. In 2009, Iraq was building its own prisons, with America slowly turning control of all detainees over to them. The center at Bucca was emptying out, and no people meant no waste, meaning America essentially built a $26,000,000 structure for temporary use.

In some cases, detainees leaving behind the barbed wire walls were doing so in good standing. Many inmates arrived for reasons somewhat out of their control, as insurgents threatened Iraqis as much as they did Americans; a typical peasant was brought into a terrorist cell through the use of intimidation.

"Tonight, after dark, you will go to this spot, and dig a hole," an insurgent would tell a farmer. "If you do it, I will give you one thousand dollars. If you do not, I will kill your family."

So the farmer would go and dig the hole.

Meanwhile, the insurgent would approach another peasant-class Iraqi citizen: "You will go to this hole, tomorrow night, and run wires from this point, to this point," with the same threat against his family following the instructions.

So, the second person headed to the hole with wires.

---

[1] Pronounced "tiff," as in, "the couple got into a tiff over his idea to bring another woman into the bedroom. 'Just to liven things up,' he stated."

If those two completed their tasks, on the third night, the insurgent would take his IED and complete the cycle.

Sadly, more often than not the first two people were those captured by American forces, leaving the actual insurgent remaining free. The peasants could not be let go, because they were technically a part of the cell, but their role in things was better understood by 2009. They were no longer lumped in as one with actual religious zealots, were allowed family visits, and had the ability to learn to read and/or master a skill. Where Abu Ghraib was about living in squalor and setting Guinness World Records for "stacked naked inmates," Camp Bucca was created for education and reform.

Those interned for minor offenses are taught both woodworking and farming skills. More importantly, they are taught to read, which is a key component for a bright Iraqi future. By teaching a person to read, they are able then to apply a more critical thought process to life. Thus, when an Imam or cleric from a violent school of thought tells them the Koran says they should be living a life of jihad, the peasant can then open the book and decipher it themselves.

Not all captured have innocence in them, however. Those with absolute hatred were housed within the barbed wire and high fences, and their anger was so great that escape tunnels were once discovered. Said tunnels did not head away from the prison; they were being dug into the camp proper. The insurgents didn't want to get away; they wanted to emerge within the walls of the camp itself to kill more Americans. Those are the people so consumed by fury, they spit on soldiers and create piss and shit bombs to toss their way. Even though they are treated to three square meals a day and the same medical care as every American soldier—better medical care than many American citizens receive—they remain hateful and violent. All the while, our soldiers remain stoic. They do not react when insulted, nor do they strike inmates when spat upon, because taken out of context, the story or a picture of an American guard defending himself against an attacking detainee would spark outrage among many in the Muslim world.

Fortunately, there just might exist a thing called Karma in the universe. When Iraq takes full control of these facilities, there will be fewer and fewer insurgent prisoners. Iraqi guards are blithely matter-of-fact in assessment of how they are going to deal with the militants. Ask an Iraqi guard, "What do you plan to do with violent insurgents when you take over?" and you will receive a bored shrug in response: "Kill them."

There are times I absolutely wish the American prison system worked this way. I don't think the death penalty should be used as revenge or as a deterrent to crime, it should be used because some people don't deserve to breathe air. Rape a woman? Molest a child? Torture someone because you're a sociopath? A bored shrug should be all that's given as the switch is flicked that you may ride the lightning of an electric chair.

Camp Bucca was my favorite base, if only for the "holy-fuck-is-it-a-small-world" moment that happened. Walking through the chow hall at lunch, I glanced down and saw a familiar face. The Wisconsin National Guard was in charge of the base during my visit, and Wisconsin is where I spent most of my formative years. I hadn't seen the fella in about four years, but Chad, a bartender from a comedy club in Wisconsin, was sitting in his Army garb, eating.

He was a little disappointed, because he had seen my poster and wanted to surprise me after the show, but seeing him first was better, because I had a story I could pull out on stage and embarrass him with.[1] Chad had been engaged back when I knew him, but never got married. About four months out from their blissful day, Chad's fiancée brought up one of the issues they would have to deal with. I'm not sure if it was the catering, invitations, DJ, or band, but it doesn't matter. What matters is how Chad responded, because he offhandedly tossed out, "Oh, didn't I tell you? I moved the wedding date. I didn't think the one we had was going to work out."

I repeat: Chad told his bride to be, casually, *four months out*, that he had changed their wedding date. The fact I said they never married should explain full well how that worked out for him.

* * *

As always, events blurred together by the end of the tour. Bits of note that amused me involve the little, larger, and enormous. On the small side of things, when arriving at Camp Basrah, I was amazingly amused by the fact my private quarters had a Winnie the Pooh welcome mat in it.

---

[1] It's good to be king.

On the larger aspect of life experiences, when traveling for extended periods of time, I tend to stop shaving and document my freedom using a travel beard. This means that several days into any trip, I have a decent scruff going, and on a military base, it gets attention. Male members of the military, as one might expect, are clean cut and clean shaven. All save for one small segment, one that wears their hair thick and grows their facial hair to match: Special Forces. These are men who wander into the wilderness and disappear for days and even weeks at a time. Regular soldiers don't know exactly what they do, but on many a base they are looked upon with wary eyes. I remember well the first time soldiers started giving me a somewhat wide berth when I attempted to walk among them. It was a Master Sergeant that finally explained my way that when I looked scruffy and walked with an air of indifference concerning protocol, it was believed I was indeed a member of Special Forces. To combat the confusion, I started walking with a goofy smile on my face so no one would fear me, then feel cheated when seeing me telling jokes that evening: "Hey, I thought that guy could kill me with his pinkie finger, but it turns out he's just some pussy civilian!"

Finally, regarding the most mammoth of life experiences, when traveling between two bases on a C-130, a question came down from the cockpit: "Any of you guys wanna fly the plane?"

There are moments in life where you think you heard something, but aren't exactly sure and request it be repeated for clarity. Being asked if I wanted to fly a plane was definitely one of those moments.

In full candor, I'm positive I was allowed behind the stick for two reasons: one, the plane was 100% empty. There was no risk to anyone or anything, the only cargo aboard being three expendable comedians. Two, the pilots know their shit backward, forward, inside, and out. No matter what I did behind the stick, there was no way I could crash the plane before they could re-assume control, if need be.

So there I sat, in the cockpit of an enormous military plane with everything under my control. The sad thing about trying to describe such a feeling is that words do fail. I know exactly what pure joy is, because I've been skydiving and ridden in a Blackhawk helicopter. Pure joy is your body feeling alive, tingling with excitement as if just having achieved orgasm. I know love, laughter, and anticipation. If asked, I could describe each sensation to the point Helen Keller could understand it. But flying an airplane without any warning or training? By comparison, that was almost too wonderful to comprehend.

A transparent, teleprompter-type screen was placed in front of my eye-line; on it were a series of graphics, circles, lines, and numbers. The pilot explained the graphics to me and said my goal was to keep the big circle centered over the little circle. He then intoned, "She's all yours," and released the controls. Touching controls in front of you and feeling several hundred tons of metal move under you is an almost orgasmic sensation. If I nudged the stick left, the entire plane would sway left immediately. If I fingertip-pushed down, we swooped sharply. The plane was big, but she was sensitive. Just like a fat girl mustering up the courage to ask a boy to prom.

I'm not sure if it's the way the human mind is wired, or just me being a little off, but it kept crossing my mind to push into a nosedive. Not to endanger anyone, just for the fun of doing so. Sort of a, "Well, you're test-driving this puppy, let's see what she can do" feeling. After the fifth time the devil on my shoulder whispered how exciting it would be, I started feeling almost guilty. I knew I wouldn't do such a thing, but damn if some part of me wasn't interested in seeing what would happen if I did.

* * *

The tour finished where it started, in Kuwait. We boarded a Blackhawk in Iraq and sped south across the border in the best taxi a person could ever hope for. Flying hundreds of feet above the surface, the scenery remained the same, yet changed at the same time. Iraq's economy is a mess, whereas Kuwait is oil-rich. The highways in Iraq were sand-blown, like a North Dakota plain in winter, nature's substance of choice whipping across the man-made intruder. In Kuwait, though all still looked of sand and waste, the roads stood out as having been maintained. Power lines appeared, and they too looked first, not third world, in quality.

Not wanting to leave us on a happy note, B tried one final time to damage our trip. He didn't meet us at the landing pad; another representative did. The man was kind, and began reading our itinerary to us: "Ok, you'll spend tonight, tomorrow night, then..."

And we interrupted him.

"Two nights? Um, we fly home tomorrow."

"Really? B didn't arrange any transportation for tomorrow."

We shook our collective comedic heads, which was all we could do. Transportation was eventually arranged for our actual flights home, but it was still a testament to the incompetence that was B that we had to explain our orders to the people that issued them.

My trip ended as it started, with an injury. The Middle East, it goes without saying, is hot. It is a desert clime, and temperatures easily reached upwards of 120 degrees during my visit, which isn't horrible considering it was regularly warmer the last time I visited; I still have in my possession a photo of a thermometer reading 140 degrees from that previous tour.

Such sunny situations can create a not-so-fresh feeling in the darker regions of the human body, and suffice to say, I succumbed to an unfortunate affliction the region offers to unsuspecting visitors. Basically, my pores bled free so much sweat that I returned to America with what could best be described as severe case of "Adult Onset Diaper Rash."

Seeing a physician for such an ailment was hardly flattering, though when scheduling the appointment, for half a second my mind flashed to the comedic value of saying "woman" when asked my preference in a doctor. Embarrassment and ego won out, however, and I asked for a man to tackle the unfortunate task of examining my red flesh.

Upon meeting my white-coated new friend, I apologized in advance for what he was about to look at. He laughed, and was kind, gentle, and professional; he told me looking up my heroin-hider was no different than looking into my ear, considering how often he researched both orifices. In fact, the situation was so casual for him, he tried to make small talk as he examined me.

I did my best to respond, but as I had never spent time in either a prison or fraternity, having a man finger-tickle my balloon knot was new to me, and not altogether exciting.

It was diagnosed I did indeed have chaffed skin betwixt my cheeks, and that I would need a medical gel to go above and beyond the duty any over-the-counter cream could handle in healing me.

Sadly, in hearing this news, Lyds immediately pulled out the "We're not married yet" card, meaning it was not within her obligations to help apply an ointment to my nether regions. I showed her the still-visible welt on my leg, reminding her of all I'd gone through for her, but she was not swayed in the slightest.

Oh well, apparently no good deed ever *does* go unpunished, especially when dealing with the animal known as woman. Maybe one day I'll dial Lyds up on Skype. That'll show her.

BLOCK V

AGES 36 – 40

15 – DOES ANYONE ACTUALLY MOVE TO IOWA?

I was thirty-six years old the first time I saw my father smile.

He had just started dating a woman in Oshkosh, Wisconsin, and I was performing at a comedy club not too far away. They came out to a show, we did a little meet and greet so I could get to know her a little, and they made their way to a table. As they visited with one another, they flirted and giggled and interacted with ease. Within moments, my father smiled, and the visual hit me so hard I was stunned; *I was seeing my father happy.* It wasn't just that he was happy, I was shocked because I realized I had never seen him that way before. From childhood through my adult years, I had adapted to the idea my father was at best stoic, or at worst, morose. Given the tumultuous relationship he had with my mother and the eleven years spent alone after their divorce, to see him smiling while interacting with his new girlfriend—or any woman for that matter—I would have been less surprised had I seen a monkey driving a car.

With a quiet clarity, I understood that in my youth my dad never looked at me with eyes of indifference, he watched me with a mix fear and caution. He had been raised in an environment of physical abuse and contempt and knew he wanted to succeed where his parents had "failed," so to speak. My dad didn't want to damage me, as he felt he had been damaged, but didn't know how to be a father himself. He never learned about the process of parenting through familial osmosis, and I had come along much too quickly for him to mentally prepare for the challenge of fatherhood. Instead of raising me hands on, my dad backed off and let me figure everything out on my own, stepping in when he thought necessary.

* * *

Living in Los Angeles kept me fairly unhappy.

At the time, I was pointing fingers and decrying a system I felt kept me down. Looking back, I understand the only thing holding me back was me; I wasn't ready to play the Hollywood game. I harbored a Midwest naiveté that believed if you worked hard, stood on stage and showed a modicum of talent, you'd be recognized; I never once considered any social aspect to the business.

Everything in Hollywood operates on the idea of "heat." To manufacture heat you have to network, and from almost everything I discovered networking involved a lot of late night drinking. I've always enjoyed being social, but when it comes to the constant wear and tear of hanging out until all hours in the morning just to maintain the "right connections," I am an absolute failure. Without those connections, nothing happens in Los Angeles.

"Heat" is something that builds around you; it is nothing you can force. For example, were I to approach an agent, look him directly in the eye and say full of confidence, "Hi, I'm Nathan Timmel. If you sign me I will get the job done," the agent would walk away, annoyed at having been disturbed. I was witness to several incidences like this and gave it a shot or two on my own, always with the same result. If that same agent, however, were to sit down at Starbucks and hear two strangers converse, one saying, "I saw this comic, Nathan Timmel, last night. He was pretty funny," that agent would be all over his phone, screaming at assistants: "Who is this Nathan Timmel

I'm hearing about?! Why don't we have Nathan Timmel on our roster?? Nathan Timmel is the future!" Again, I have observed such interactions.

To keep my ego from being annihilated through rejection, I spent half the year working outside California. I would fly to Madison, Wisconsin, where my mother still lived, and use it as a staging point for comedy clubs scattered across the Midwest. One slow Saturday night on a sojourn in Iowa, only twelve people made comedy their entertainment choice of the evening. Being that Iowa and Wisconsin are neighbors, the instant I finished my set, I walked off the stage and out the door, pausing only to get paid. There was another comic on after me, and I figured it would be better to get a jump on the drive home over hanging out and mingling with the non-crowd of customers. That decision could have been disastrous, if not for the tenacity of one woman in the audience. On that particular Saturday in June, an Iowan named Lydia decided she needed to get out of the house and have a laugh. Though I had no way of knowing it at the time, when I left the club before the show's end, she was watching from the audience and disappointed by my departure.

Several days later, I received a MySpace friend request. MySpace, for those that don't know, was a social networking site that was "cool" after Friendster became "lame," and was "lame" after Facebook became "cool." Though as a comedian I probably should have been collecting as many online "friends" as possible, I never blindly accepted requests. I found that too many people out there had their own agenda, and nine times out of ten I was entirely uninterested in their marketing attempts. The friend request I received from Iowa, however, had two things going for it: the hometown listed on the woman's profile was twenty minutes from where I had performed, and the woman herself was stunningly attractive. Or at least she was online; I had already discovered that many people altered pictures for publication on the Internet, that they appear much more thin/attractive/desirable than they actually were in person. I fired off a quick note to this woman, the aforementioned Lydia, "Nice to meet you. Are you friending me because you were at a show this past weekend?" and that was that.

Until, that is, I received a reply in my mailbox. She had indeed been at a show, and enjoyed what she saw. I responded to her reply, and back and forth we started to sway, each exchange growing in length just a little. As the emails grew longer, the time between them shrank. A mere four days later, I opened up a note to find ten digits awaiting me. Lydia had been to a concert, drenched her brain with alcohol, and mustered up the courage to ask me to call her. Not wanting to disappoint a (supposedly) beautiful woman, I dialed her up. I didn't hold on to the number for five days to "play cool," nor did I pretend I hadn't received the email until the next day so I wouldn't seem over eager; I wanted to call, so I did.

Over the course of five hours, we had the most bizarre, no-holds-barred conversation I'd ever had. This wasn't "So, what kind of movies do you like?" giggling, it was everything-on-the-table honesty. I had never in my life had a first conversation like it. Hell, sometimes I had been in mini-relationships of a few months to a year that never approached the depth to which Lydia was willing to descend. But the thing is, I loved it. She wasn't trying to impress me, put on airs, or falsify who she was; neither was she laying out her cards in a brash, "take it or leave it" manner. I got the sense she was stating, "This is who I am; I am looking for someone to accept me as is."[1] We finally said our goodnights somewhere in the neighborhood of four in the morning, and as I sat back in my hotel bed to take it all in I wondered, "Who the hell is this woman?"

Lydia was a person whose life was in unfortunate flux; she had recently started a new job (one which left her in tears on the first day and proceeded to remain unsatisfying for several months), lost her "second-mother" aunt to ovarian cancer, was witness to her eighty-three-year-old grandfather undergoing surgery for an abdominal aneurysm, broke up with her boyfriend (an event that resulted in him shouting insults at her over the phone for the better part of an hour), started seeing a therapist, gone on depression medication, and lost all but one of her friends. The last statement is the most important, in terms of how she happened to arrive at the comedy club to see me.

Girls can be exceptionally cruel. In adolescence, they create cliques that are impossible to breach and are generally lorded over by a single queen. Sometimes, if women do not graduate from the mentality they learned in junior and senior high, they will carry this thought process with them into adulthood. In Lydia's case, she was a small cog in a gear that revolved around recreational volleyball; the controlling force of this social circle was a tiny woman who had a

---

[1] Lydia has a habit of using semi-colons when she speaks.

severe Napoleon Complex named Mindy. One frustrated day, Lydia butted heads with Mindy, and as if fourteen-year-old girls and not young women, Mindy put the word out to the group: "It's Lydia or me, choose." Only one person remained by Lydia's side, and when that friend wasn't around she found herself isolated and alone.

Several weeks after her banishment from the "in crowd," word reached Lydia that Mindy was having a gathering. Depression sank in. Everyone she used to hang out with would be there, laughing and having fun, while she would be secluded in her condo. Desperately needing to get out of the house and away from that situation, Lydia called Kristine, the one friend who had refused to choose sides after the immature display of behavior by Mindy. Kristine agreed to forgo the party and attend a comedy show with Lydia. So it came to pass, a series of unfortunate events brought Lydia to the comedy club, on the very week out of the year I happened to be in town.

After getting to know one another for two weeks online, Lydia and I chose to meet in person. We each wanted to see whether or not the spark we shared via the telephone would translate into in-person chemistry. I was constantly on tour in the Midwest and was easily able to drive to her tiny town for our date. As I parked out front of her condo, I called to let her know I had arrived. Lydia made her way down three flights of stairs, and as she did so windows lining the front of her building allowed me quick glimpses of this woman I'd agreed to take to dinner. When she finally got to ground level and opened the front door, I thought, "Oh wow. This could be very good." Lydia was as beautiful as her pictures. Sandy-blonde hair rested gently below her shoulders, she was taller than many Hollywood leading men I had bumped into, and she wore a wide, nervous smile. I was smitten almost immediately.

We hugged hello, and she apologized for jabbing me with her chin, something she described as "too pointy." I hadn't noticed the supposed defect, but thought all features rested symmetrically well upon her face.

The two of us retreated to her condo, where her new kitten Simon, a gender-confused little gray fur ball, ran between my ankles as I walked in. During my entire visit, he howled for attention as if the most neglected kitty on the planet. In contrast, Lydia's full-grown cat, Pandora, was an aloof and skittish creature with brown and black fur speckled with dandruff; she darted into hiding immediately upon my arrival.

While being given the grand tour of her two-bedroom condo, the bookshelf gave me pause. Though littered with much in the way of fiction and business management, the top row contained many offerings on romance and self-reliance. The titles were standard fare, and may as well have screamed, "So You Just Got Dumped," "Why Your Friends All Left You," "I'm Isolated and Cry Myself to Sleep," or "You're Going to Die Alone." My brow furrowed slightly, but I wondered if these tomes were helping Lydia be as honest with herself as she was with me. Instead of playing games, the death-knell of any union, she was communicating, openly and honestly. I liked this.

While we talked, Lydia couldn't stop fidgeting; her nails were nonexistent and looked like they were attacked to the nub regularly. I did my best to put her at ease, but we quickly retreated to a bar so she could get a drink or two in her and relax.

Dinner took place at one of her favorite restaurants; she had the gourmet mac & cheese, which I thought was basically an excuse to charge $15 for a seventy-nine cent item, and I had a salad that left me less than thrilled. We conversed easily, but after our meal I accidentally exposed my inner self.

To explain what happened next, I must offer up some background on who I am as a person: when around most animals, especially little woodland creatures, I lose control of most of my mental functions, which are questionable at best to begin with. I cannot fully explain why I find these mammals so endearing, and it is best to give an example of my mental retardation rather than to try to explain it any further. Though I am not proud of the action, I once tried to pet a bear. A *wild* bear. I was camping, and had been warned that the local black bears were used to humans and wandered into camp frequently. The park ranger told everyone sternly that should we come into contact with one, we should make loud noises to scare them off; under no circumstances was anyone to approach them. Naturally, one did come scrounging near my camp for scraps, and he was an adorable little black bear. Not a cub, which, given the protective nature of mother bears would have spelled immediate disaster, but a standard-size fluff-ball black bear. While most people in the camping area were curious, yet cautious, my first thought was to grab food and attempt to draw him close to me. Now, I say this in full awareness of what I was doing. Did I think the bear was tame, or would let me pet him? No. My mind was at war with itself; I was very calm, but had two internal voices speaking to me. On the one hand, my inner child was saying, "OMG, IT'S A BEAR! LOOK AT ITS LITTLE NUB-TAIL! I WANT TO GRAB HIS EARS AND GIVE HIS HEAD A BIG SCRUFF-SHAKE! WHO'S A BEAR? WHO'S A LITTLE BEAR WITH A LITTLE BEAR BLACK NOSE?" My quieter, more rational and therefore weaker responsible adult voice was calmly relaying the message: "You are a fucking moron. This thing will get near you, get startled, and rip your throat out. It is a bear, you assclown." Fortunately for my well-being, the bear, though somewhat interested in the idiot making kissy noises at him, eventually wandered off, leaving me to live another day. So, the point of the story is: if I lose my shit and attempt to hug bears, you can only imagine how I am when faced with non-threatening creatures. With that, I return to my first date with Lydia.

As it was a lovely summer evening, we decided to take a sunset walk along the Iowa River and burn off a few of the just-ingested calories our food had provided. Many other couples were doing the like, and all along the path little animals had crawled out from their homes. We watched squirrels skip across the path in front of us, ducks paddle lazily along the river's edge, and birds frolic in the red-orange sky. Everything was going swimmingly, when Lydia nudged me.

"Look at the rabbits!" she whispered, pointing at a large green shrub with three bunnies happily munching clover underneath it.

I could describe what I did, but think an outsider's perspective would serve best at this point and here turn things over to Lydia:

Nathan stopped walking, and I turned to see what happened. I was mortified to find he'd dropped my hand and was running toward the rabbit bush, although I'm not sure I would call what he was doing 'running,' per se. It was more of a gallop or a scamper, really, but with his arms thrown up loopily over his head. He was shouting, too. 'BUNNIES! BUNNIES! LOOK AT THE BUNNIES!'

I stood there dumbfounded, stunned, and profoundly embarrassed. What the hell was he doing? People were looking at us.

'Nathan!' I hissed. 'Stop it! Get back here!'

He didn't listen. The bunnies had started bounding away from him and he was giving chase, doing his best to zig as they zagged, and pounce as they bounced. I figured my only hope for saving my reputation was to pull the same trick my mother used when I'd embarrassed her. She'd simply walk away and pretend she didn't know me, so I did just that. A few seconds later I could hear him running up behind me, and felt him reach for my hand again. I was calming down a little, and underneath my still-fresh embarrassment, I was hiding a smile. A grown man who chased bunnies? Who was this guy?"

Like with the bear, though an internal logic might tell me it would be best to simply let the bunnies be, quietly enjoying their floppy ears and ever-wiggling noses from afar, it's all too much for me to process at times and I explode in excitement. Though I know it will never happen, I like to pretend that someday I might catch a bunny, and we will frisk through the meadow together, and be friends, and I will hug him and pet him and name him George. Yes, this from a man who once tested so well he was advanced several grades several times. If that isn't an indictment of our school system, I don't know what is.

Thankfully, Lydia was quite forgiving of my idiot's excursion, and our first date ended up extending from dusk into dawn. The next morning she rose to leave (very late) for work, and I went my merry way back on the road. As our first date had gone well, it was decided we would have a second, and possibly even a third. I was still touring, so Lydia made plans to spend a getaway weekend with me while I performed in a small Illinois town. If we were keeping in line with our hold-no-secrets approach to getting to know one another, this was a bold step. After telling her mother she had met someone, "a comedian," the response had been a cool, "That's nice, but what does he do for work?" The idea someone could make a living as a comedian hadn't really crossed Lydia's mind, but if she was wondering what kind of future provider I could be, an eye-opening insight into the world of entertainment was about to take place.

Our weekend trip had me working a club I'd been to many times before, each time as the middle comedian of the three-man show. I always did well there, and my ego told me it was my turn to move up, but I sadly had no fame to my name and wasn't going to be allowed the top slot. That weekend, the headliner, on a name recognition scale of zero to ten, was only a one, and that's on a good day. But as I was a zero, that made him more marketable than me. Unfortunately, he had better management than comedic skills and had been performing for fewer years than I had. In an embarrassing move for the club, I got bigger laughs and more positive audience responses than he did. Every night, while I was on stage, he sat at the bar getting drunk. By the time he grabbed the microphone the man was a slurring, incoherent mess; instead of performing focused bits of comedy, he would meander down verbal tangents. It was immediately proven he didn't have enough material to fill his contracted time, because around the thirty-minute mark the club would play several tracks off his CD of phone pranks over the house PA system. I thought I had seen unprofessionalism in my time, but was still stunned by the spectacle of it all. I was actually watching people who had turned over their hard earned money to see comedy, watch a man sit on stage, drunk, while his CD played over the sound system.

Lydia was somewhat aghast. She lived and worked in the corporate world, where if you worked hard and built your résumé, you were rewarded. Not so in comedy, where personality and press trump ability almost every time; whether or not you are funny is always less important than whether or not you've been on TV.

It doesn't mean anything to the narrative at hand, but I have yet to be re-booked at the club despite repeated attempts to play there, while I've seen the other comic's name on the calendar several times. Good times.

* * *

Lydia and I dated long distance for the better part of a year. My schedule allowed us to never be separated for more than several weeks at a time, and Lydia was able to make her way to the West Coast a couple times. Cell phones, instant messaging, and video chat kept us sane, but as we grew to enjoy one another's company more and more it was well understood carrying on a long distance relationship wouldn't work long term. Something had to give.

I had already grown tired of Los Angeles and its disheartening comedy scene; meanwhile Lydia had a job she (now) liked and was an Iowa girl at heart. She was uninterested in the grimy cement jungle of Hollywood, so it was ultimately decided I would uproot myself and live among the cornfields of the Midwest. I'd like to pretend there was struggle involved in the decision-making process, or that I wondered whether leaving Hollywood to pursue an artistic dream was wise in the slightest, but I didn't. I was really more interested in being personally happy than professionally successful, which, like my inability to play the social game in Los Angeles, probably helped stymie my growth there. Overall, I believed Iowa offered much greater opportunities.

I wasn't moving just to be closer to Lydia; we decided to go all out right away and move in together. I had never lived with a girlfriend before, and Lydia had never lived with a boyfriend, so the arrangement was going to be interesting, but hopefully not too trying. Unfortunately, one of the first situations I encountered was an examination of my own mortality. Growing old is something we rarely imagine happening while in our childhood or teenage years. As kids, we run around wildly, flail our arms like idiots, pick our nose and see adults as boring creatures that have no fun. By eighteen, we are invincible, standing on the hoods of cars tearing down the highway and drinking to blackout status at concerts, passing out in the port-a-potty, pants around our ankles for the duration of the show, waking only at the end of it as huge cannons blast the finale to "For Those About to Rock—BOOM!—We Salute You," and adults are our enemy.[1] But at some point in our mid-to-late twenties, we start slowing down, looking around and realizing that our best years are probably behind us and that we might want to do something with our lives. If this revelation doesn't strike, it's even more depressing. Anyone above twenty-five still hanging out in a college bar is sad in one of two ways: they're either pathetically wearing clothes like the kids of the day and failing miserably, or, possibly worse, still wearing their old outfits, five years out of style and a billion brain cells away from reality.

Being stuck in one phase of your life isn't limited to bars and acting how you did at twenty; you can get stuck in any age. For over fifteen years, my dad wore the same clothes repeatedly. It was as if he had gone shopping one day in his mid-thirties and bought everything he thought he would need for the rest of his existence. Dad would usually be wearing some awkward combination of a ten-year-old, K-Mart-style shirt tucked into Sears-brand not-quite-dress, not-quite-casual pants of the same age. This ensemble was worn without a belt, naturally. My father's lack of style was so humiliating my sister tried to pick his outfits before being seen in public with him. So it was to my chagrin that as my life took a turn for the better—in relocating to Iowa and in with Lydia—I found I had been living my own life of blissful incomprehension.

---

[1] OK, maybe the AC/DC experience was a unique to me, but when you're young and someone hands you a bottle of Absolut, and has one of their own, and says, "Let's race!" you do so. Because you're dumb.

My awakening started gently enough, by packing my entire apartment into one car, and then finding out I was to fit that entire car's contents into approximately 37% of one closet. Not one whole closet, which is what I had been led to understand I'd be receiving, but a fraction of a closet; the remaining 63% was filled with Lydia's belongings. Little did I know, the female definition of "emptying a closet" is "creating just enough space for you to keep a few trinkets, while allowing me to hold onto clothes I no longer fit into but just might once again someday in the future when I start going to the gym."

Luckily, as I unpacked all my belongings, Lydia was right there to help me organize. By "organize," I mean: Give every item of clothing the once over, making either a "someone-just-farted" face, or nonchalantly allowing me to continue to own it. For now.

Our exchanges during this sorting involved pouting, by me, and steadfast, schoolmarm discipline, by Lyds.

"But I like that shirt," I'd protest.

"Honey," the gentle scolding would begin, "not only is it old and out of style, it's worn and stretched out."

"It's Urban Outfitters," I'd whine.

"Yes, and they update their clothes several times a year, not several times a century."

Then I would forlornly drop it into the charity pile. This process was repeated until a large hefty bag of clothes I'd just carted all the way across the goddamn country was sitting by the front door.

Fortunately, unlike my dad, while I did lament my lost treasures—and not everything went, I still have some "fine, you can keep that if you promise not to wear it in public" gems I refused to let go of—I have to admit a guilty pleasure at having someone provide a clue for me when it comes to dressing. After the purge came the binge, meaning we did a little "Welcome to the Modern Age" shopping. Though it started with me shooting down nearly everything in existence, such as Polo shirts, whose collars I promised to wear popped up if forced to buy, eventually we found stylishly "fun" (her word) articles of clothing at a reasonable price.

Lyds was happy, and I was happy. She now had someone on her arm that looked normal until his mouth opened, and I knew I didn't have to go shopping for at least five years. Heh.

If moving in with someone that I'd known for less than a year and only dated long-distance sounded like a recipe for disaster, I'd agree. But somehow, Lydia and I gelled. There were a few minor bumps in the road, but nothing that ever seemed overly disastrous.

One difference in our personalities was discovered via the casual nature two people have to have when sharing close quarters. I don't really think of myself as a prude person, nor am I a germophobe. That said, when it comes to stepping out the shower and drying my body, I stop at the crack at the bottom of my back and reach for toilet paper. This t.p. is for a quick, final dab at my delicate, between-the-cheeks pucker. This action makes Lydia laugh, as she says, "You know it's fresh-clean from the shower you just took, right?" Such things do not matter to me, as maybe it's a psychological quirk, but I still don't appreciate the idea of sticking a toweled finger up in there, then using that same cottony spot to dry my face the next day.

On the subject of towels: I sometimes wonder if Lydia and I should take two of them to bed for our little liaisons. It would make more sense to clean up afterwards using a towel apiece; our current ritual involves duck-waddling to the bathroom, attached by a single piece of terrycloth and delicately trying to avoid spilling sputnik on the carpet. Our kitties, from what I've been able to tell, find this event quite confusing. Not the sex part, which they seem to watch with a casual disinterest, the question "Can I get fed soon?" painted across their faces, but the towel-attached shuffle afterwards. That they stare at with uncomprehending eyes. Lydia and I are aware we look quite silly, yet continue the act after each and every, well, act.

For the record, the kitties have their own set of ceremonies that I don't entirely understand. Every morning, Lydia showers before work, and, and especially so in winter, the kitties join her in the bathroom. They jump up onto the counter and enjoy a little steam-sauna to start the day. Upon completion of her cleaning, Lydia opens the curtain to see both staring at her naked body, each relaxed and hydrated. Meanwhile, neither joins me whenever I get around to showering. They could get the same little burst of moisture they seem to enjoy in the morning, but opt not to. Simon, however, always, always, always seems to come running when it's time for me to enjoy a relaxing constitutional. As I rest on the throne, I find a gray kitty rushing in to sit at my feet, stare up at me, and meow until I pet him. When I stand and flush, he then props his front two paws up on the toilet to peer down at the swirling water, his kitty curiosity asking, "Hey, what's going on in here?" Pandora's quirk seems to be that she finds me dirty somewhere around the 2 a.m. hour. About once a week I awake to hear a purring kitty atop the pillow by my head, at the same time feeling a sandpaper tongue running roughshod across my hair. I'd almost find it flattering, my being worthy of a kitty-bath, if not for the implied message, "You are one filthy motherfucker."

Another adjustment to communal living was in the department of sleeping arrangements. When living quarters combine, you go from having a nice, wide bed for your single whole self, to a space you have to share. Lydia likes to sprawl out, meaning I immediately became an invasive burden to her slumber. I often wake to find body parts littering my person.

At bedtime, I generally fall asleep while she reads whatever it is she's currently using to expand her mind: a book, Time or Fitness Magazine, Harlequin Romance Novels... What's strange is, before co-habitation, I usually had to be completely exhausted in order to sleep. If I wasn't, I'd just lay wherever I was, thoughts bouncing around my noggin. But something about lying in bed with Lyds makes me relaxed enough to drift off when I'm only nominally tired. I like that. A few months into our co-habitation, she asked, "Do you feel me rest my hand on you when I finally turn out the light?"

Surprised, I responded that I did not.

Lydia informed me that when she sets aside her book and settles in for bed, her first sleep position involved touching me in some way; a rested hand, an arm draped across me, or her head nuzzled into the back of my neck, depending on how I happened to be facing (usually turned away from her light).

Again, I was surprised. I'm usually a fairly light sleeper; for years the easiest way to wake me was to whisper my name. I don't know why, but I respond to a soft "Nathan" as well as an alarm clock. I found it strange that where a mere murmur usually woke me, manhandling did not. So a couple nights later, I lied. I rolled onto my side while she read, then gradually changed my breathing pattern. I deepened my breaths, slowed them to a most un-hurried pace, and feigned sleep. I'm not sure how long she read, but after the light went off, I felt a warm body nestle up behind me, throw an arm over my side, and let loose all tension from the day.

And I thought, "Goddamn."

And I mean that in the most amazing of ways.

Sleep and scent combine in ways we don't always realize, and Lydia's nuzzling ways provided new insight into how we were now relating to one another. When living with another, everything becomes as familiar to your senses as your eyes, sometimes even more so. During a week of performances at the Chicago Improv, I lodged at my friend and fellow comedian Joe Hamilton's apartment. After the Sunday show I drove home to Iowa and crawled into bed somewhere around two in the morning. Lydia immediately curled up to me, paused, then pushed back a little.

"You don't smell like you," she said unhappily.

I hadn't thought about it, but there is a certain security in the scent of your lover, a familiarity that you react to unconsciously, and positively. When I moved in, the condo smelled like Lydia; every time I returned to it her scent filled my nostrils and made me feel peace. Returning from Chicago, I smelled like Joe Hamilton's apartment and guest bedding. It being dark and Lydia being half asleep, she was relying on senses other than sight to relate to me, and the fact I "wasn't me" set off confusion in her.

Thankfully, the situation was rectified the next morning after a shower in which I washed the stench of other off me, and after which I tore off several sheets of toilet paper for my final starfish of drying.

Lydia laughed at me for it and reminded me she dries 100% of her body with her towel.

And she wonders why I do the laundry so often.

* * *

As any grade school child can tell you, there is a natural progression to relationships. After you are discovered in a tree, "k-i-s-s-i-n-g," first comes love, then comes... well, not marriage. The kids skipped a step.

Lydia's friends had us engaged well before I did; our second Christmas together they were all bundled together and whispering invented gossip into her ear, "He's going to pop the question! We just know it!" I could only imagine the chagrin they wore when this did not come to pass. "Oooh," they then justified, "Valentine's Day is coming up! He'll do it now!"

What her friends didn't know was that I was saving up for a ring, I just didn't want to get engaged in such a cliché manner. Popping the question on a holiday seemed too trite; I wanted my approach to come out of the blue.

Around Valentine's Day I dropped half the cash necessary to procure Lydia's dream gem, but didn't tell a single soul. Not because I didn't feel I could trust anyone, it generally never crossed my mind. I wasn't bursting to share my secret; I was approaching the next stage of my life, and was doing so contentedly.

Eventually, I shared the news with he who would be my Best Man, Brian Jones. I told Brian about the ring for two reasons: One, we had been on the phone the better part of an hour and out of things to discuss when he asked, "So, anything else going on?" I started out naturally enough, "Not that I can think of," when it popped right in there: "Oh, wait. I put money down on a ring." It wasn't an announcement, it was an afterthought.

The second reason I told Brian is: he lived almost a thousand miles away in New Orleans. Though he and I carried a friendship all the way back to junior high, we rarely saw one another and Lydia had never met him; who the hell would Brian be able to tell that the words could somehow end up in Lydia's ears?

Oh, fate, you fickle, funny fuck.

Two days after I told Brian of my impending bending of the knee, Lydia came home from work, excited: "I'm going to a conference in New Orleans! I'm going to meet your best friend!"

Really?

I mean, really?

The jewelry store had informed me up front it would take four weeks from the order date to have the ring crafted and the stone set, yet somehow Lydia got asked to attend a conference before it would be ready. Suddenly, the only person in the world who Lydia would never meet before I had the chance to surprise her was the one person she would be hanging out with.

Brian had already informed his wife Chris I was gearing up to propose, so when Lydia visited they treaded lightly over certain topics. One dinner conversation became fairly amusing when Lydia herself brought up the lack of an engagement ring on her left hand, but Brian and Chris held their tongues, and Lydia returned to Iowa as clueless as ever.

I said I wanted to pop the question in a surprising fashion, and easily decided the best manner of doing so: while she was sleeping. Lydia hates, hates, *hates* to wake up in the morning. And she hates to be woken up at any time. So, being the kind of fella that I am, a few days after her trip to New Orleans I woke up at 2:00 a.m. and silently stole out of the bedroom. I grabbed a handful of votive candles, fashioned them into a heart on the countertop and lit each one. I positioned the ring in the center of the flames, turned on the stereo, set the song *Open* by Peter Gabriel on a continuous loop, then returned to the bedroom to nudge away.

"Sweetie," I whispered. "Get up, you have to come see something."

Lydia resisted. She was expectedly groggy, but eventually cracked her sleep-caked eyes just wide enough to see me staring at her with a shit-eating grin.

Normally, such a smile and request meant I wanted to show her something one of the kitties was doing, but not this time.

Not this time.

If it seems somewhat dismissive that I didn't excitedly tell anyone about the imminent event, it's because I felt very few nerves; I had no "cold feet" moments.

If anything, I felt comfortable. There was no weight upon my shoulders, or worry in my eyes. In fact, it felt like the most natural thing I've ever done.

I've said it in the past, but it bears repeating: therapists, friends, family, and psychologists will all ask you the wrong question: "Have you ever been in love?"

Of course. Everyone has. Who cares?

What should be asked is: "Have you ever felt loved?"

When you can answer yes, your life will begin to take shape.

And I felt loved.

* * *

I was thirty-six years old the first time I saw my father smile. There are natural milestones in life; we celebrate certain ages due to advancements we make. "I'm sixteen, I can drive!" "I'm eighteen, I can vote!" "I'm twenty-one, I can drink! Well, legally, that is. I've been drinking since I was sixteen."

Thirty-six will be etched in my memory as the age my life finally started to make sense. I had the moment of awareness involving my father, I met Lydia, and somehow granted my mother absolution from sins she had never committed.

A few months after being exposed to my father's happiness, I was visiting my mother. Out of the blue, she started sobbing. I don't know what brought it on, but she sat at her kitchen table for several minutes, crying. Her eyes were puffy and bloodshot, and a thick molasses of mucus ran from her nose. Invented guilt sent her into this state of mind, and the words she spoke were so foreign I could barely comprehend them.

"I'm sorry," she choked. "I just want you to know I'm sorry. I did the best I could. Your father and I both did the best we could. We were young parents and did the best we could in raising you and Amanda. We just didn't know what we were doing, but we tried; we did the best we could. We just did the best we could."

I let out an uncomfortable giggle, a defense mechanism acting as the nervous response to a situation I was ill-prepared to witness and too emotionally immature to address. I'd long known I was an accident, a child born to two people not ready for the shotgun's pump, but for the life of me, at that moment, trying to imagine blaming either of my parents for either my existence or life, I was coming up blank. I grew up in a household filled with secrets and cold emotions, affairs and hidden anger, and we moved so often I didn't learn what maintained friendship was until well into my teenage years. But I didn't think any of that was done to punish me.

The self-help lobby of America has latched onto two tools to make people feel "better" about themselves: blame, and invented guilt. The former is for those who like to believe we are not responsible for our own actions, lives, and dealings with others. People like that point fingers, invent enemies, and then "forgive them" their wrongdoing. Invented guilt is a trickier bit of mischief and is for those who want to take the weight of the world upon their shoulders. Whether it be their responsibility or not, they believe their life fails to live up to the expectations of others, and thus usually feel the need to apologize for fanciful misbehaviors.

My mom, for the record, *loves* self-help books.

A multitude of these betterment books discuss forgiveness, the idea being "if you do not forgive, you will remain stuck in your 'Spiritual Journey.'" While I agree with the concept on certain levels, the problem comes when you are asked to forgive something the person created in their own mind, not deliberate action taken against you. The process becomes a cop out, a tool to first invent blame, then forgive a transgressionless action. Forgiveness, in such a situation, becomes almost an attack.

While I've felt exceedingly unhappy from time to time, even for years on end, and though I've even questioned whether or not any of the waking moments ever endured are worth it when added up against the day to day mundane of pain, I've never been so disconnected from reality as to blame others for my lot in life. In any situation, I am ultimately responsible for my own actions. I can be fucked by any relationship, be it business, romance, or otherwise. At the end of the day, however, I have to acknowledge my responsibility in the situation; how I ended up in the "fucked" position in the first place. Crying foul is like crying wolf; you can only get away with it for so long. I don't know that I've ever actually uttered the phrase "I forgive you" to anyone, because I've either not blamed them their actions, or the offense is one grievous enough not to be exonerated from.

Standing in front of my mother, her sobs weakening in strength and composure getting the best of her again, I may have smiled in slight amusement. Not out of tension or an inability to connect mind with mouth, but a smile of situational confusion, one arising from a moment that tickles the heart.

And I explained to Mom that I couldn't forgive her.

After all, I'd nothing to blame her for.

ACKNOWLEDGEMENTS, DISCLAIMER, AND EXPLANATION

Few creations make it to the finish line with input from only one source, and this book is no different. A team of people helped me; I owe them a debt of gratitude I doubt I'll be able to repay. In no real order, I would like to introduce you to:

- Lydia Fine, the Mrs.—she = <3, and probably deserves more reverence than I can offer given her tolerance of my quirks and belief in my abilities. If the writing in here is at all interesting, it's probably her doing.
- Kasey Befeler, the graphic design artist. I was an indecisive, pouty little child; she was very tolerant and made many changes to match my whims and moods.
- Kristine Bjork, the editor. I'm a sloppy writer; she tidied things up nicely and challenged me often, giving me notes like: "This is vague, this is redundant..." If you spot an error in here, it's because I did something stupid *after* she finished looking it over and no reflection on her skills.
- Greg Frieden, the photographer. Greg's camera captured the images on the cover, of the chessboard, the picture of me on chapter 13, and graphic nudes involving an Oak tree and me in very compromising positions (which were removed by censors after much protest by yours truly). Greg is an excellent picture-snapper and can be found at www.gregfrieden.com
- Ben Kieffer, the interviewer. Ben has invited me on his talk show multiple times, and I cannot thank him enough for his interest in my career and travels. Look up "The Exchange" on Iowa Public Radio. You won't be disappointed.
- My mom & pop, the interviewees. They sat with me and told their stories; I listened and wrote, doing the best I could to keep up.

And therein lay the disclaimer: as I am the author here, it is obviously written from my point of view. I believe I did my best to be both honest and fair, but there are several sides to every story. I didn't consult everyone in my past, which leaves open the door to the idea I misinterpreted certain actions and consequently painted certain individuals in a poor light. Such, as the kids say, is life. In many places I used false names to protect identities; in other sections, I purposefully refused to name a place or person. The last thing I wanted to do was use this little scribbling as a means of pointing fingers and whining about perceived injustices, so there seemed no point in being specific with any past frustrations.

The explaining I feel that needs done involves what's called "proper grammar." On occasion, I prefer the way something reads or sounds to the way something is "supposed to be." Case in point, there are certain places in this text where parenthetical asides add a bonus thought to whatever I am writing about. For some reason, I find that a period inside those lovely, curved brackets looks ugly. I therefore leave the sentence technically open ended, but aesthetically pleasing.

(To me, anyway)

(See what I just did there?)

All of the above aside, I'd really love to create a Kevin Smith-type endless list of thanks here, naming everyone in my life I owe kudos to, but that would be an entire book in itself. I have many, many friends who help and support me, and I will do my best to both thank them in person and return all favors. Until that time, then, hugs all around.

ABOUT THE AUTHOR

CPSIA information can be obtained at www.ICGtesting.com
Printed in the USA
LVOW101321181212

312238LV00007B/57/P